Blairsville Junior High School
Blairsville, Pennsylvania

	DATE DUE		
AP 26 '02			

The Complete
Peace Corps Guide

FOURTH EDITION

The Complete Peace Corps Guide

FOURTH EDITION

BY ROY HOOPES

Introductions by
JACK H. VAUGHN
Director of the Peace Corps
and

R. SARGENT SHRIVER
Former Director of the Peace Corps

THE DIAL PRESS, INC. 1968 NEW YORK

To Spencer and Sallie,
two 1980 Volunteers, without whom this book
would have been much easier.

This new edition is
also dedicated to a new
addition—Tommy.

COPYRIGHT © 1965, 1966, 1968 BY ROY HOOPES
MEMBER OF THE AUTHOR'S LEAGUE
ALL RIGHTS RESERVED
LIBRARY OF CONGRESS CATALOG CARD NUMBER: 65-23958
FIRST PRINTING, FOURTH EDITION
MANUFACTURED IN THE UNITED STATES OF AMERICA

Acknowledgments

THIS BOOK could not have been written without the cooperation extended me by the Peace Corps staff, and I am especially indebted to William Haddad, Associate Director of the Peace Corps, Edwin Bayley and Thomas Mathews, the former and present Peace Corps Director of Information, who were my guides during the hectic early days of the new agency. Several very busy Peace Corps staff members either took the time to discuss various aspects of the emerging Peace Corps or read the first draft of one of the chapters; hence, a special word of thanks to: Timothy Adams, Maury Broderick, Robert Bryan, Dr. Joseph G. Colmen, Ann Doyle, Jim Gibson, Nicholas Hobbs, Padraic Kennedy, Roger Kuhn, Wilson McCarthy, Joshua Miner, Charles Nelson, Bradley Patterson, Thomas Quimby, Derek Singer, Lee St. Lawrence, Harris Wofford, and of course, R. Sargent Shriver. In addition, Theodore Sorensen, Richard Goodwin, and Myer Feldman of the White House staff, Assistant Secretary of State Roger Tubby, and USIA Deputy Director Donald Wilson were kind enough to take time off from very busy schedules to discuss the question of the Peace Corps and the Presidential campaign of 1960, in which they all participated. I also wish to thank Andrew Rice, co-author of the Colorado State University pilot study on the Peace Corps, Kenneth Coffey, on the staff of Congressman Henry Reuss, Mary Clynes and the staff of the Democratic National Committee library, Richard Murphy, former Executive Secretary of the Young Democratic Clubs of America, Charles Manatt, present Executive Secretary, and Dr. Howard Maxwell Merriman of George Washington University for the research assistance they so kindly gave me in the preparation of this book. For the section on community development, I am indebted to *Colombia Community Development*—a survey report prepared by CARE—whose chapter on community development was contributed largely by Richard W. Poston, Research Professor at Southern Illinois University.

In the preparation of this revised edition, the staff of the Peace Corps has extended me every cooperation, which I greatly appreciate. I also wish to thank those who have directly or indirectly made a special contribution to this revised edition: Timothy Adams, Ann Anderson, Gerald Bush, Charles Caldwell, Dr. Joseph G. Colmen, Nathaniel Davis, Dr.

Joseph T. English, David Gelman, Dr. John Grobli, Philip Hardberger, Sally Horner, Robert Iverson, George Nicolau, Richard Nolan, David Pearson, James Walls, Warren Wiggins, Harris Wofford, and above all, the Peace Corps Volunteers, particularly those who have been quoted in the following pages.

Finally, I am especially grateful, once again, to my wife for her assistance in the typing and editing of the manuscript and proofreading of the galleys.

*   *   *

Additional assistance for this edition, for which I am indebted, was supplied by Markham Ball, Dr. Al Carp, Victor Chricton, Lorraine Farinha, Robert Hatch, Andrew Hays, Mary Juricak, Allen Kulakow, Tedson Meyers, Richard Nolan, Tom Page, Tom Plaut, Francis Quinn, Alexander Shakow, and, of course, Jack Vaughn.

Contents

New Introduction by Jack H. Vaughn ix

Introduction by R. Sargent Shriver xi

PART ONE: AN IDEA WHOSE TIME HAD COME

1. A Monument to JFK 3
2. Background 15
3. Origins 25
4. The Creation of the Peace Corps 35

PART TWO: UNDERSTANDING THE PEACE CORPS

5. Objectives 53
6. How the Peace Corps Functions 59
7. What the Peace Corps Does 66
8. The Peace Corps Around the World 77

PART THREE: THE PEACE CORPS VOLUNTEER

9. Does the Peace Corps Need You? 121
10. Joining the Peace Corps 131
11. Training 139
12. Life in the Peace Corps 148
13. The Returning Volunteer 176

PART FOUR: CONCLUSION

14. Challenge and Response 187
15. The Future 200

New Introduction

by JACK H. VAUGHN
Director of the Peace Corps, 1966—

YEARS HAVE PASSED since John F. Kennedy held a mirror to our spirit and dared us look.

For many Americans, the test of a "Peace Corps" was unnerving. It threatened exposure where many at home, and more abroad, believed us weak: not in our arms, but in our ideals; not in our courage, but in our character.

We have not failed.

Thousands of Peace Corps Volunteers have proved the wisdom of President Kennedy's challenge, and freedom's image has emerged with impressive clarity and promising vigor.

Like few of my countrymen, I have been privileged to work closely with the Volunteers, and to observe their achievements overseas. But like all of my countrymen, I must acknowledge that my thrill and pride of such achievements are at best vicarious.

The victory of the spirit which the first years of the Peace Corps comprise belongs to the Volunteers alone.

Twenty-five thousand Volunteers have served or are serving now in half the world's developing lands. Volunteers have brought over 325 different arts and skills to the people of those lands, and they have served those people in 60 different languages.

Yet, however diverse their station or their service, Peace Corps Volunteers have discovered that their worst enemies were everywhere the same: not ignorance, but indifference; not poverty, but apathy; not hunger, but despair.

Thus Volunteers have learned that above all their other arts, they have had to practice and master the art of the possible. For as Aristotle said, "They can, because they think they can."

They "think they can" because to complement their own qualities the Peace Corps has reposed in them greater confidence and broader discretion than ever before has been accorded a group of Americans serving overseas. Right from the outset, Sargent Shriver chose to make the Peace Corps no shallow, timid response to the challenge all Americans had been given.

As a result, today the Peace Corps is America's most selective service.

We have tried to choose our Volunteers with utmost care, yet they tend to choose themselves. A Volunteer's first trial occurs long before he enters training. It takes place at home, first within himself, when he examines the nature and extent of his own interest; and second, when he ventures the idea and finds apathy or resistance on the part of relatives and friends who simply could never understand, let alone undertake, the challenge.

For those who are at just such crossroads, future Volunteers and loved ones alike, we hope this book will offer insight into the Peace Corps. It is a thoroughly revised edition, and so are we.

I commend to your attention, especially, the chapter "Life in the Peace Corps," in which the author has captured the special flavor of Volunteer service overseas.

Moreover, those who ponder service now, or who merely seek to learn more of our work, may find it useful to consider here the fundamental purpose of the Peace Corps. The challenge to our spirit questioned America's fitness to lead the free world. Our Volunteers have responded with rare success. But we have taken time to ask ourselves, "Lead the free world where?"

And in the special service which the Peace Corps offers we have learned the answer: Toward lasting peace.

Peace in our time has been deadly, just as peace in most other times has been an illusion. People, half-starved, half-fed, and only half out of the eighteenth century—no matter the repose of armies—are simply not at peace.

Thus the challenge Volunteers are given merits the greatness of their service. The cause is pressing and will demand the best of us, far into the future.

Yet, as President Kennedy told us, "All this will not be finished in the first 100 days. Nor will it be finished in the first 1,000 days, nor in the life of this Administration, nor even perhaps in our lifetime on this planet. But let us begin."

Introduction

by R. SARGENT SHRIVER
Director of the Peace Corps, 1961–1966

THE QUESTION before our generation is whether America is qualified to lead the free world.

It is a question asked at every corner of freedom.

Why are they asking it? Why is there doubt? Because of the widespread belief that many Americans have gone soft and are no longer capable of sustained personal sacrifice for their country, for human rights, or any other ideal bigger than self-interest.

There is fear that we lack understanding of the world challenge, the vision without which freedom will perish.

There is also fear that this nation may lack the understanding heart which is so essential for the leadership the world requires.

One university president here in the United States said that we are beset by "spiritual flabbiness." I recently also heard it said that we are producing a strange new kind of human being: "a guy with a full belly, an empty mind, and a hollow heart."

Americans are not alone, however, in doubting the intellectual and spiritual fiber of modern America. I encountered these doubts all around the world. "Yours was the first revolution," I was told in India by Ashadevi, a vigorous woman associate of Mahatma Gandhi. "Do you think young Americans possess the spiritual values they must have to bring the spirit of that revolution to our country? Your Peace Corps must touch the idealism of America and bring that to us. Can you do it?"

The thousands of Americans who have volunteered for the Peace Corps provide one answer to the skeptics. These Volunteers have said "Yes, we can do the job." From the experience of three and a half years, I think they can.

We have never minimized the dangers and difficulties of service in the less-developed areas of the world. Each Volunteer approaches the overseas assignment with the full understanding of what to expect. The Volunteers know they will be exposed to diseases unknown in our country. They know their work may be routine and full of frustration. They know that although they won't live in a thatched hut with mud walls, their environment will certainly differ sharply from what they experienced here at home. The comforts of our plush society will not be duplicated overseas. Yet the Volunteers continue to come forward.

We expect a lot from the Volunteers. They have to speak the language of the host nation. They must know its customs and its traditions. They must study its history and problems and understand and sympathize with its aspirations.

Early in our search for qualified men and women we warned that the Volunteer must realize that he is going to make only a very little dent in the problems of the emerging nations. The individual contribution, measured in the whole spectrum of the world's difficulties, will probably cast only a sliver of light—and that sliver may go unseen.

After his years of hard work the Volunteer may change a few attitudes, but he probably won't be around to see the results. In the Peace Corps the potential for frustration is great.

The exciting thing about the Peace Corps is that we are finding the Americans who have the faith and the conviction to make the sacrifices necessary to serve under Peace Corps conditions and according to Peace Corps standards in various parts of the world, despite all these problems and difficulties.

They have been called the silent generation, these men and women who are volunteering to serve in the far-off corners of the world, as surveyors in Tanganyika, farm extension workers in Colombia, teachers in rural schools in the Philippines, and as community development workers in Chile. They are coming quietly to enlist for two-year terms of hard work in Africa, Asia, and Latin America. I believe they will meet the great tests they face abroad with calm humor and steady perseverance.

For inside the silence, contained by a tough shell of skepticism, is a core of idealism. The stirring words of Wilson and the radiant optimism of Roosevelt have been tempered by world wars and depressions and by the long winter of the cold war. But I am convinced that faith in democracy, the belief in a civilization based on the God-given dignity of the individual human being, the readiness to sacrifice to enable such a civilization to live and grow—these are the qualities the Peace Corps is tapping.

Men and women with these ideals are the ones we are seeking as Peace Corps Volunteers because they can succeed in doing the job skillfully, energetically, and with compassion.

It is our hope that this book, with its factual account of how we came into being and what we are doing, may help to direct the Volunteers with these qualities to our door.

PART ONE

An Idea Whose Time Had Come

1

A MONUMENT TO JFK

Neither money nor technical assistance, however, can be our only weapon against poverty. In the end the crucial effort is one of purpose, requiring not only the fuel of finance but the torch of idealism. And nothing carries the spirit of American idealism and expresses our hopes better and more effectively to the far corners of the earth than the Peace Corps.

> —PRESIDENT JOHN F. KENNEDY, in his last State of the Union Address, January 14, 1963.

WILLIAM WALTON, former President Kennedy's unofficial adviser on the arts, once interrupted President Kennedy to discuss one of the many Washington architectural projects in which the President was interested. When he apologized for bothering the President with something "less than global in content," the President replied, "That's all right. After all, this may be the only monument we'll leave."

Although many monuments have been erected in honor of the late President since his tragic death, certainly there is no more fitting memorial to him than the Peace Corps. As a thriving, bustling government agency, the Peace Corps stands as the manifestation of perhaps the most exciting and powerful idea harnessed by John F. Kennedy and his Administration. As will be seen in the following pages, the basic idea of a Peace Corps had ben kicking around for some time before it was mentioned by Senator Kennedy at the University of Michigan during the Presidential campaign of 1960. But it was John F. Kennedy who had the instinct and the vision to take an idea that had already captured the imagination of the intellectual and academic communities and pull it into the mainstream of American political action. Sargent Shriver, appointed by his brother-in-law, President Kennedy, to create and direct the Peace Corps, is fond of quoting the remark: "No army can withstand the force of an idea whose time has come." And from the first time Senator Kennedy mentioned the Peace Corps, it was obvious that the Peace Corps was an idea whose time had come.

Four years later, by the time John F. Kennedy was killed in Dallas on November 22, 1963, the Peace Corps was more than an idea: it was 5,937 Volunteers overseas in 46 countries, 1,215 more Volunteers in training for overseas assignments, 76,003 applications from Americans of all ages anxious to serve; and there were unfulfilled requests for Peace Corps Volunteers from 24 underdeveloped nations. And to many people abroad it was Kennedy's Peace Corps. Once, when a United States congressman was in Peru on an inspection tour of that country's Peace Corps operations, the leader of a *barriada* approached the congressman and asked if he would personally thank President Kennedy for sending the Volunteers. The congressman told the official that President Kennedy hadn't sent the Peace Corps all by himself— that Congress had appropriated the funds and authorized the project. The official asked the congressman to "thank Mr. Congress, also."

But after Kennedy's assassination, it was obvious that the people of underdeveloped nations had forgotten "Mr. Congress" and that they looked on the Peace Corps as John F. Kennedy's monument. "Our Volunteers in small Turkish villages told me how their students had come to class after the assassination weeping openly," Sargent Shriver told a National Press Club audience, describing the impact of the President's death in the Peace Corps countries. "In the countryside of Iran, one of our workers was approached on November 22 by a fellow worker who, with tears in his eyes, announced '*Our* President is dead.' In Nepal, villagers walked for more than five days to the place where our Volunteers were working, just to bring them the news. In other towns of the Near and Far East, people spontaneously assumed the garb of mourning. In several places local high schools searched for a flag, which they ordinarily did not use, just so they could fly it at half-mast."

Shriver said that when he arrived in Israel on the first leg of a journey around the world after the assassination, Prime Minister David Ben Gurion told him that the death of President Kennedy was the occasion of the "first worldwide mourning in the history of man." Shriver also noted that "everywhere, mayors and tribal chiefs, as well as kings and presidents, told us they had never seen such a universal outpouring of emotion, of grief and loss, at the death of a foreign leader." And he could not help but be impressed. "Why was it that Kennedy, by himself, one man, could penetrate into corners of the world more effectively than all our propaganda apparatus for twenty years?" Shriver asked a *New York Times* correspondent. "We all need to study what it was that he did or said and why our society was so incapable of perceiving that he was so effective."

Shriver also could not help but see the similarity between the worldwide effect of Kennedy's assassination and the impact of the Peace Corps on the people of every country in which Peace Corps Volunteers have served. As Shriver saw it, both impacts rested on the same foundation: John F. Kennedy was a man of ideas and ideals; the Peace Corps is committed to an ideal. President Kennedy was a man of peace; the Peace Corps is an instrument of peace. President Kennedy was a man of this generation; Peace Corps Volunteers are primarily men and women of this generation. President Kennedy, although an extremely wealthy man, was not content to sit back and idly enjoy the comforts that great affluence could provide; Peace Corps Volunteers, although citizens of the most affluent nation on earth, are not content to sit back and idly enjoy that affluence, but have given up opportunities to live in comfort because they find more meaning in service than in the pursuit of pleasure. President Kennedy cared—for the hungry, the dispossessed, the hated, and the fearful; the Peace Corps is an organization that cares—its Volunteers are overseas because they want to help.

Sargent Shriver's deep emotional attachment to his martyred brother-in-law and to the organization that he translated from an idea into an exciting American contribution to the twentieth century's revolution of rising expectations is understandable. He could be forgiven even if he *were* guilty of a too-emotional reaction in the aftermath of his brother-in-law's assassination and of stretching a point here and there to equate John F. Kennedy and the Peace Corps. But in all probability, he was not guilty of even this very human reaction. There is much validity in the similarities between the late President and his Administration's most successful and publicized creation. Certainly, the death of no American statesman, even that of Franklin Roosevelt, so stunned the world as the murder of John F. Kennedy. And it is becoming increasingly obvious that no American organization, governmental or private, has been received around the world as enthusiastically and affectionately as the organization that grew directly out of the Presidential campaign of 1960. As President Kennedy said in his last State of the Union address, ". . . . nothing carries the spirit of American idealism and expresses our hopes better and more effectively to the far corners of the earth than the Peace Corps."

In a somewhat sour appraisal of the Peace Corps, columnist Eric Sevareid once wrote that "there is nothing so irresistible as pure inten-

Blairsville Junior High School

tions backed by pure publicity." It is true that the Peace Corps has received its share of publicity, some of it of questionable purity, but there has never been any question about its intention. It is the pure intention of the Peace Corps that has most impressed the rest of the world. For instance, Peace Corps Volunteers in the Far East were awarded the Ramón Magsaysay Award, the first time a group of non-Asians had received the honor. In explaining its selection, the Magsaysay Board said:

> The problem of achieving peace amidst the tensions and dangers of a nuclear age occupies the mind of much of the human race, yet few within it discover a useful way to contribute. In reaffirming the essential community of interest of all ordinary people, regardless of creed or nationality, the Peace Corps Volunteers belong to that small but growing fraternity who by their individual efforts do make a difference.

The Peace Corps has also been awarded the Silver Medal of Arequipa—from that second largest city in Peru. In honor of Peace Corps Volunteers in Thailand, the Chulalongkorn University presented Sargent Shriver with an honorary degree. "Many of us who did not know about the United States," said the Foreign Minister of Thailand in presenting the award, "thought of this great nation as a wealthy nation, a powerful nation, endowed with great material strength and many powerful weapons. But how many of us knew that in the United States ideas and ideals are also powerful. This is the secret of your greatness, of your might, which is not imposing or crushing people, but is filled with hope of future good will and understanding. It is indeed striking that this important idea, the most powerful idea in recent times, should come from this mightiest nation on earth—the United States."

At every level of society abroad, Peace Corps Volunteers are making the same impression:

• In the midst of a ceremony dedicating a road linking a village in Sierra Leone with the outside world, a tribal chief said to Shriver: "Your Peace Corps has shown us a world we never knew existed. We had never seen a truck or people from the outside world who wanted to help us. We had heard of America, but now we know what it means."

• "Without the Peace Corps," said an official in one of the new African nations, "there would have been no secondary school system in West Cameroon."

• Eight months after the first volunteers arrived in St. Lucia, an editorial in the *Voice of St. Lucia* said:

> When the Peace Corps . . . first landed in St. Lucia, there was

skepticism behind the welcoming speeches. "Here they come," said one socially prominent St. Lucian woman, "straight from school to people who manage very nicely earning nothing—to teach them about refrigeration and 'The Star-Spangled Banner' . . . Today, America's Peace Corpsmen in St. Lucia have assimilated themselves into St. Lucian society with an enthusiasm that would have made the first missionaries quail in horror. They are on first-name terms . . . with thousands.

• A Tanganyikan editorial asked: "If they [Peace Corps Volunteers] are willing to offer their services for our benefit, why shouldn't our young men also go into the village and into the fields and volunteer for service in national projects?"

• According to the Director of the Pakistan Academy for Village Development, the Pakistanis who worked with Peace Corps Volunteers "were better men and better workmen as a result of their experience."

• "They are extraordinary people. . . . They do not consider themselves superior. I find I can mix with them in a way I never could before with white men or Asians," a Tanganyikan surveying assistant said after working in the field with Peace Corps Volunteers.

• A Turkish educator, discussing Peace Corps Volunteers with an American, said: "Rightly or wrongly, we think of ourselves as a people with a past filled with accomplishments but temporarily left far behind by many other nations. In our eagerness to catch up we have to accept material aid: economic aid, military aid, sometimes even food to eat. Our gratitude for such aid is diluted with a measure of shame that we have fallen into such a state that we must accept gifts and loans.

"What these people [the Volunteers] are doing is something infinitely more appreciated. It is aid acceptable without any sense of unfillable obligation. These people, of course, are giving something they alone can give. They are giving themselves. There is nothing like it in the world."

• "It will soon be six months since you arrived to help us in North Borneo. . . . I want you to know that I am delighted with the way in which you are tackling the assignment that has been given to you. I admire your absolute sincerity of purpose. . . . All this is beginning to show results and to spell a wonderful success."—A letter to Peace Corps Volunteers from North Borneo's Director of Education.

• An official of Somaliland commented: "When they [the Somali people] saw the Volunteers living in accommodations that were suitable but not luxurious, willing to share the type of life our people live . . . this was a revolutionary thing."

Perhaps nothing has caused as much open-eyed wonder and admiration abroad as the willingness of Peace Corps Volunteers to live in quarters similar to those lived in by local citizens engaged in comparable work. That Americans should do this is looked upon almost with disbelief by many foreigners—and, incidentally, it led to one of the Peace Corps's favorite anecdotes. As Shriver tells it, an anti-American Latin American businessman was being shown around a slum area in Peru by a local social worker when they arrived at one of the worst streets in the *barriada*. Dismal shanties were crowded together without any regard for human comfort or dignity, but in the middle of the block stood a newly painted home, complete with lace curtains in the window and a shingled roof.

"Who lives there?" the businessman asked.

"Our Peace Corps Volunteers," his escort said.

"Leave it to the gringos—they always grab the best for themselves," the businessman replied caustically.

"No, no, you don't understand," said the social worker. "When these Americans moved in their house looked like all the rest. But they fixed it up themselves—mainly to show their neighbors how to do it and prove that it could be done. In fact, if you look closely you will see that others on this street already have curtains in their windows. And some are even getting together to do painting."

Peace Corps officials, proud of the way in which their Volunteers have been received abroad, can go on providing examples of the kudos that have been bestowed upon the Volunteers as long as anyone will sit and listen. But the impressive thing is that they are genuine; the Peace Corps is easily the most spectacular success story to come out of Washington in recent years. The story has, in fact, been so incredible and so well publicized that it once prompted a Washington newspaperman to greet the Peace Corps Director on the program "Meet the Press" with this opening gambit: "Mr. Shriver, all we ever hear about the Peace Corps is what a howling success it is. What about some of your failures?"

Considering that the Peace Corps had political origins, that it was organized perhaps faster than any other government agency in recent years, and that it rushed hundreds of young college students from the world's most affluent society overseas to live and work in the most underdeveloped lands on the face of the earth, it is amazing that there have not been more failures. But to date, only a handful of derogatory incidents mar an otherwise glittering record, and even these have supplied precious little ammunition for the Peace Corps's diminishing critics. Even the Communists, who are pretty good at attacking the

United States, have had to be content to brand the Peace Corps as an arm of the CIA and a "very cunning trick by which Kennedy is carrying out aggression under the name of Peace." In fact, Jack Vaughn, the new Director of the Peace Corps, who replaced Sargent Shriver on March 1, 1966, is fond of telling this story of meeting a Guatemalan Communist in exile in Cuernavaca, Mexico. "He had the normal things to say about our institutions," says Vaughn, "our actions, our behavior, our policy—except the Peace Corps." About the Peace Corps the Guatemalan said:

> I've only met a couple of Volunteers. The first one I met was along a dusty road in the highland of Guatemala. It was a Sunday and I was driving along with my wife when we saw this obviously North American young man standing beside the road. He flagged us down and said in very polite Spanish, "Could you please take this letter to the Post Office?" He paid us for the stamp. He had no doubt that we as complete strangers and nationals from another country would deliver that letter. You know, we don't trust anybody, not even our colleagues. We stand in profound awe, we Communists, in profound awe of the Peace Corps.

Even more significant is the appraisal of Jiri Hybner and Valdmir Novak, two Czechoslovakian political scientists writing in *Mecinarodni Politica*:

> It must be admitted that the Peace Corps Volunteers have indeed established close contacts with local inhabitants in many countries. The overwhelming majority have succeeded in adjusting to the unfavorable climatic, material and other living conditions of the new surroundings. This has been the basis of their success. Their activities have produced concrete results in education, health services, construction of various installations, etc.
>
> The Peace Corps is an extraordinarily important tool for anti-communism. It achieves its goals not with subversive activities, but on the contrary—with most effective help in those sections of national economics, culture, education and welfare and in other branches of life where the developing countries feel the acute necessity of help.

Another measure of the Peace Corps's success is the reaction in the United States—in the Congress, among politicians, and in the press. Although the response was overwhelmingly favorable to the Peace Corps, there was some skepticism. Richard Nixon attacked it during the campaign of 1960, although he had the political instinct to remain silent during the early days of its creation, as did most Republicans— but not all. Former President Dwight D. Eisenhower, for instance, called it a "juvenile experiment" and Representative H. R. Gross (R-Iowa) described it as "this boondoggle known as the Peace Corps."

The Peace Corps also had its critics in the press. The *Wall Street Journal* opposed it as a "Children's Crusade"; the *Richmond News Leader* termed it a "cheap substitute for that true patriotism"; and the *Philadelphia Inquirer* called it a "staggering example of John F. Kennedy's loose thinking. . . ."

Most of the loose thinking in those early days, however, seems to have been done by the Peace Corps critics in the press who were usually guilty of condemning the Peace Corps for things it had no intention of doing. For instance, the *New York Daily News* was alarmed "because we're having visions of a horde of well-meaning youngsters sticking their snoots into people's private lives telling them how to bring up their children and what or what not to eat and drink. . . ." The *National Review* wondered "why American youth are so caught up in the enthusiasm for bringing electric dishwashers to the Angolese," and columnist Robert Ruark remarked, "You can train any dimwit to keep his rifle clean and march in step. Can you train a rabid Fabian fan to respect the religious position of the goat in a Kikuyu economy, or expect a crew-cut product of togetherness to understand that a Masai knows all he wants to know about milkless cattle?"

But such comments were not heard for long. Even Congress, thanks in part to a superb lobbying job by Sargent Shriver, was agreeable to giving the idea a chance. The Peace Corps bill was passed with the second largest majority of any Kennedy legislation presented to Congress in the first year. The continuing enthusiasm in Congress can be seen by the fact that it has regularly increased the Peace Corps budget without even groaning. In the second year, the Senate passed Peace Corps legislation without a dissenting vote, and the House voted 361-70 in favor, partly because of comments such as this one from Howard Smith, ultraconservative Chairman of the House Rules Committee: "I had considerable reservations about [the Peace Corps] when it came up last year and was not sold on it. I voted against it. I am happy to say that I think they have done a good job. I think they have made a good start. . . . I'm supporting the measure this year." Further testimony is evident in this comment by Representative Cornelius E. Gallagher (D-New Jersey) when Shriver and his staff were presenting their first annual report to Congress: "I think the highest compliment that perhaps can be paid to you is the fact that we asked you to come back here today and bring along some criticisms. Normally, we don't need a staff to dig up criticisms for us. . . . Expecting you people to give us some criticisms to criticize you back is the supreme compliment that any Congressional Committee can pay to you."

As the reports came back from overseas about how well the Volunteers were doing and how enthusiastically they were being received, the compliments poured in from all quarters: those who had supported the Peace Corps became even more generous in their praise; those who had been against it maintained a flattering silence; and some of its most violent critics openly admitted that they might have been wrong. For instance, Robert Ruark, coiner of such labels as the "Kiddie Korps" and whose critical comments have already been quoted, had this to say in September of 1963: "Wherever I've been in the world over the last six months—and my worst enemy can't accuse me of immobility—all I've heard is praise for the Peace Corps's solid, helpful work and generally fine projection of the best American image with the downtrods."

By the time that the Peace Corps's second annual report was presented to Congress, the reaction in the press had become an "embarrassment of riches." "As the Peace Corps enters its third year," Shriver said in his message to Congress, "Volunteers and the staff alike have the feeling that the Peace Corps stories most often repeated are too glamorous, too glowing, too pat. Few of these stories talk of the day-to-day problems, the frustrations, the harsh disappointments, and the serious occupational hazards—as one Volunteer put it, of 'dysentery and boredom.' In a sense, the most unsettling challenge the Volunteer faces is his publicity. A generous world press has drawn an unvarying image of Volunteers effortlessly spouting Pushtu, Swahili, or Tagalog, of Volunteers winning legions of friends while transforming economies. . . . To sum up: While the Peace Corps may not be as good as its reputation, it is almost as good as its intentions."

Shriver and his staff may have been worried by the favorable press, but their concern was nothing compared to that of the political opposition. Perhaps the most complimentary thing that could be said about the Peace Corps is the fact that it was not mentioned during the Presidential campaign of 1964. Long before '64, Barry Goldwater had ceased his cautious criticism of the Peace Corps and, despite the Peace Corps's close identification with John F. Kennedy (whose Administration created it), Lyndon Johnson (chairman of its National Advisory Council), and Hubert Humphrey (who introduced legislation for a Peace Corps early in 1960), Goldwater was unable to launch an attack on the Peace Corps during a desperate campaign in which almost every conceivable issue was exploited by the Republican candidates.

Although by 1964 the Peace Corps had become an American institution almost as sacrosanct as motherhood, there were, of course, still some dissenters. In Illinois the *Rockford Star* called it the "most over-rated, over-publicized and over-sold travel club in the world," and the *San Diego Union* thought that the "Peace Corps rests on the fundamental error that we are going to advance civilization and world peace by helping a handful of people on the edge of a sea of human want."

The reaction of the Peace Corps's more thoughtful critics will be considered in Chapter 14, but in assessing the validity of their views, it must be borne in mind that the Peace Corps was created not to eliminate worldwide poverty, but to provide an outlet for a whole generation of frustrated, idealistic young Americans who wanted to show that they *cared* about the poverty and lack of opportunity in the emerging nations.

From this viewpoint alone, and this is not to imply that it is the only measure of the Peace Corps, the experiment has been an unparalleled success. By mid-1967, 28,000 Americans of all ages had served in the Peace Corps in 58 nations. No Volunteers are sent to a country unless it specifically asks for them and virtually all of these nations have asked for additional Volunteers; 22 other countries are on the waiting list. Over 210,000 Americans have applied for service in the Peace Corps and applications have been coming in at a rate as high as 5,000 a month. Thousands of Volunteers are now returning, but increased recruitment plans call for 17,750 Volunteers to be overseas or in training by June 30, 1968. Less than 5 percent of the Volunteers come home before their two years are up and over half of these return for reasons beyond their control, such as illness or a death in the family.

The ease with which these young Americans have made the adjustment to lower living standards, different climates, and foreign lands and customs has been almost unbelievable. "The first law of Volunteers," says Shriver, "seems to be—the rougher it is the better they like it. Almost all the complaints we receive in Washington have a reverse twist—they complain things are 'too easy.' In Ethiopia, the Volunteers in Addis Ababa want to move out to the provinces; those in provincial towns want to move on into the wilderness." And he told a *Time* magazine reporter: "Two years ago, the skeptics and the cynics were convinced that modern Americans were too flabby in body, too flaccid in spirit, to meet the rigorous challenges of life in the underdeveloped world. Today we know from experience that the skeptics and the cynics and the doubters were wrong. They have changed the world's slogan from 'Yankee Go Home,' into a new cry, 'Send us more Peace Corps Volunteers.' "

In a 1963 cover story on Sargent Shriver, *Time* magazine decided that the Peace Corps "is the greatest single success the Kennedy Administration has produced." At the same time, the magazine said, it was "a loosely ruled, badly dressed, often complaining, yet highly motivated melting pot of individuals scattered through the jungles, slums and mountain peaks in some of the most backward countries of the world." And as the stories of the individual Volunteers' experiences and accomplishments began to filter back to a nation preoccupied with the problems of overabundance, it was becoming increasingly apparent that maybe the Peace Corps had helped discover a new American. Sargent Shriver, at least, thinks so: "The Peace Corps Volunteer is a new breed of American. He journeys to a foreign land to work within that nation's system; to speak a strange language; to live as nationals do and under their laws. Because of this he has been welcomed where others have been turned away. And he is admired. Because of this, the world is learning that Americans have not gone soft and really do care about people living in faraway places."

Another observer agrees. Morris Stein, a New York University psychologist who tested Peace Corps Volunteers in training for Colombia, says, "These kids represent something many of us thought had disappeared from America—the old frontier spirit. These kids are skilled, resourceful, nonmaterialistic, and definitely socially oriented. They love working with people and do so without sloppy sentiment. I think we're leading with our best in Colombia."

That Peace Corps Volunteers somehow represent a new breed of men has been sensed around the world. Three of Shriver's favorite anecdotes illustrate the point:

• In the Dominican Republic a group of people were writing "Yankee Go Home" on a wall while a Peace Corps Volunteer watched. When they finished, the Volunteer said, "I guess that means I'll have to go home."

"No, we mean Yankees," the demonstrators said, "not the Peace Corps."

• In Africa, a child seeing a Peace Corps Volunteer enter his village, turned to his mother and said, "Look, there's a white man."

"No," she answered, "he's not a white man. He's a Peace Corps Volunteer."

• In a remote area of Nepal, some Peace Corps Volunteers were introduced to the local citizens as "Westerners." After they had worked there for a few months, a delegation cautiously approached them and said, "You can't be Westerners. What are you?"

A Volunteer answered, "We are Peace Corps Volunteers."

"Oh," the Nepalese replied, "and where is the Peace Corps?"

The Peace Corps may not be a new country, but there seems to be general agreement in the underdeveloped nations that the Peace Corps Volunteers are different. As the largest newspaper in Tunisia said, when sixty-five Volunteers arrived in August of 1963: "The Peace Corps may be the first refutation of Khrushchev's claim that only socialism has created a new man."

Certainly twenty-three-year-old David Crozier of West Plains, Missouri, was a breed of American the Russians have a hard time explaining. Soon after beginning his volunteer work at Jardín, a *barrio* deep in the jungles of southern Colombia, young Crozier wrote his parents: "Should it come to it, I had rather give my life trying to help someone than to give my life looking down a gun barrel at them." In his rural community development program, Crozier encouraged village leaders to build an elementary school, and he was helping them to construct it. Other projects were to be started as soon as he returned from an Easter trip to Bahia Solano which he planned to take with another Volunteer, Lawrence Radley, of Chicago. On Easter Sunday, returning from their trip, both Crozier and Radley were killed.

President Kennedy was fond of quoting Oliver Wendell Holmes's remark that "it is required of a man that he should share the passion and action of his time at peril of being judged not to have lived." Thirty Peace Corps Volunteers have been killed overseas and, like the President who created the Peace Corps, they risked their lives to share the action and passion of their time. Thousands of other Americans are sharing the same action and passion of our time in dozens of emerging nations around the world. And until that distant day when the last Volunteer returns from the last country to throw off the oppressive yoke of poverty, hardship, and disease, the Peace Corps will stand as a living monument to John F. Kennedy and a generation of Americans that cared.

2

BACKGROUND

Put peace men in power; educate the editors and statesmen to responsibility. . . . Seize every pretext, however small, for arbitration methods, multiply the precedents; foster rival excitements, and invent new outlets for heroic energy; and from one generation to another the chances are the irritation will grow less acute and states of strain less dangerous among nations.

—WILLIAM JAMES, in an address
at a Universal Peace Congress banquet
in Boston, 1904.

ALMOST IMMEDIATELY AFTER John Kennedy injected his proposal for a Peace Corps into the Presidential campaign of 1960, people began stepping forward to point out that the idea behind it was not exactly new, that it had existed in various forms for a long time. In fact, dozens of organizations were soon "discovered" by the press as Peace Corps prototypes. For instance, while the Boston *Globe* headlined the fact that BOSTON COLLEGE PIONEERED THE PEACE CORPS and Drew Pearson credited the president of the Jerrold Electronics Corporation with implanting the idea in candidate Kennedy's head, Washington *News* columnist Tom Kelly reported the discovery of "our first Peace Corpsmen"—Bernie Ervon and Jim McKinley, two young men who had just finished six months in Jordan with the International Farm Youth Exchange. Many religious groups and private organizations had, in fact, long been active in sending volunteers abroad on very much the same type of missions to be undertaken by the Corps. Nor were these precedents confined to the United States; numerous prototypes existed in other countries. When the United Nations voted on a motion to have the Economic and Social Council consider a Peace Corps, French Delegate Maurice Viaud said he thought sending young volunteers out into underdeveloped countries was a fine idea—France had been doing it for years.

The idea of young people voluntarily helping others less fortunate than themselves is as old as the human race. As Congressman Henry S. Reuss pointed out on the floor of the House of Representatives, one example dates back at least fifteen hundred years, when St. Benedict led missions of young men from the affluent society of Rome out to work in the underdeveloped areas of northern Europe. In more recent times the efforts of missionary groups to channel the ideals and energy of youth into improving mankind offer an even closer parallel, and many nonreligious organizations have also been active in sending volunteers into underdeveloped countries. In fact, Senator Kennedy's campaign proposal declared in essence that, if he were elected, the force of the United States government would be put behind a kind of program that had been successfully carried out for several years by numerous private organizations.

There are two main roots to the Peace Corps idea. One can be traced back to the work of Christian missionaries, with emphasis upon selfless sacrifice to help the less fortunate and thus to win converts. The other derives from the suggestion of American philosopher William James that to conscript a "peace army" of young men to "go to war against nature" would not only be of great help to the less fortunate of the world but would at the same time be very enlightening and inspiring to those who took part.

James first mentioned his idea in 1904, during an address to the Universal Peace Congress in Boston. He despaired of eliminating war, he said, because "the plain truth is that people want war." He felt it was a waste of time to talk of universal peace and disarmament; "preventive medicine," not a "radical cure," was what was needed. He assumed that war and armies would always exist, but practical machinery should be created to redirect the instinct to war: "we should invent new outlets for heroic energy."

Later, in *The Moral Equivalent of War,* a pamphlet published by the Association of International Conciliation in 1910, James elaborated on his idea. "The war against war is going to be no holiday excursion or campaign party," he wrote. "The miltary feelings are too deeply grounded to abdicate their place among our ideals until better substitutes are offered."

James's substitute was to be an army conscripted for war against poverty, ignorance, and disease. "There is nothing to make one indignant in the mere fact that life is hard, that men should toil and suffer pain," he observed:

The planetary conditions once for all are such, and we can stand it. But that so many, by mere accidents of birth and opportunity, should have a life of *nothing else* but toil and pain and hardness and inferiority imposed upon them—*this* is capable of arousing indignation in reflective minds. If now—and this is my idea—there were, instead of military conscription, a conscription of the whole youthful population to form a certain number of years a part of the army enlisted against *Nature,* the injustices would tend to be evened out, and numerous goods to the commonwealth would follow. The military ideals of hardihood and discipline would be wrought into the growing fibre of the people; no one would remain blind, as the luxurious classes now are blind, to man's relations to the globe he lives on and to the permanently sour and hard foundations of his higher life.

There was to be nothing voluntary about James's peace army; the aim was not only that the energies of youth would be enlisted against Nature, but also, as James put it, "that our gilded youth would be drafted off . . . to get the childishness knocked out of them, to come back into society with healthier sympathies and soberer ideas."

James's proposal was never tried, the idea of conscription for other than national defense being especially repugnant to Americans, but from time to time the government has sponsored programs that contained aspects of James's peace army. In fact, one such program came into being even before James's Peace Congress address. In 1901, following the Spanish-American War, American soldiers in the Philippines were asked to stay on to teach English, and many of them did so. Later the same year the Philippines' teaching program was transferred to a civilian authority, and a volunteer program was organized in the United States to furnish young English teachers. Twelve thousand young American men and women volunteered for the program, of whom about six hundred were chosen to go in the first contingent. They arrived in the Philippines on the Army transport U.S.S. *Thomas,* and as a result acquired a lasting name—the Thomasites. They were all college graduates, but most of them had little if any teaching experience.

The program lasted until 1933. It is a tribute to the dedication and service of the Thomasites that—although they were first sent out to help convert a former Spanish colony against its wishes into an American colony—they are today fondly remembered in the Islands. Many present leaders in the Philippines remember the Thomasites and recall getting their first intellectual encouragement from those young American teachers. They lived in the provinces, often in the small one-room schoolhouses in which they taught. They endured the same hardships the local people did.

Because the United States government was directly involved, the Philippines teaching project is the closest precedent to the Peace Corps of today. It is significant that the first Peace Corps project for Asia called for three hundred teachers to be sent to the Philippines.

Perhaps the first government programs that can be traced directly to William James's proposals are the youth organizations launched during the Administrations of President Franklin Roosevelt. There was, of course, no conscription involved. However, the main purpose was to channel the energies of young people into constructive work—one of James's principal concerns.

The work of the Civilian Conservation Corps, established in 1933, is probably the best remembered. The CCC resembled James's peace army in one important respect: paramilitary discipline. Its members wore uniforms and lived in the field in camps containing, on the average, about two hundred young men. It was administered jointly by the Departments of War, Interior, and Agriculture. The work done by the CCC in national parks—roads, firebreaks, clearings, stone retaining walls, buildings, picnic facilities, and the like—is still evident; it has been estimated that this work put the national-park program ahead about fifty years. The CCC also did a considerable amount of work on federal irrigation projects, making it possible for the government later to meet wartime demands for increased farm production.

The National Youth Administration, established in 1935, employed an even larger number of people and came closer to embodying the ideals of the present Peace Corps. The NYA consisted mostly of out-of-school young people who could find no employment. Unlike the CCC, the members of the NYA did not live in camps or wear distinctive uniforms. "Working in small units," as the Editorial Research Report, *Government Youth Corps*, describes the operation of the NYA, "often of no more than 15 or 20, N.Y.A. youths performed a kind of domestic Point Four service at a time when economic conditions in some parts of the United States differed little from those in under-developed countries today. N.Y.A. enrolled boys and girls in jobs that ranged from clearing swamps to assisting in hospitals."

President Harry Truman was also interested in a peace army of the sort recommended by James. The congressmen who drafted the Universal Military Training bill, which was shelved after much acrimonious debate in 1951, were instructed by President Truman to study the possibility of conscripting young American men and women for both military and civilian service. The idea of conscription for other than military purposes still did not find widespread favor. The conservative

Chicago *Tribune* was not alone in suggesting that "this device was actually a method of subjecting youth to the political discipline of the state."

If William James first publicly formulated the idea of an official, government-sponsored program of youth service, the precedents of almost a century and a half of work by American missionaries is probably even more important as a source of plans and methods for the present Peace Corps. Since 1809 American religious organizations have been sending missions abroad to work in underdeveloped areas. And missionaries have traditionally done many things other than build churches and preach the Gospel. They have built schools and taught trades, built hospitals and educated doctors and nurses. They have trained local leaders in administration, developed social welfare programs, and shown farmers how to increase the yield of their crops. It is significant that the first American missionary group to Hawaii, which sailed from New England on the *Thadeus* on October 24, 1819, included two teachers, one doctor, one printer, and one farmer. Their instructions could easily apply to almost any modern community redevelopment program: "to aim at nothing short of covering those Islands with fruitful fields and pleasant dwellings and schools and churches; of raising up the whole people to an elevated state of Christian civilization."

Through the years, missionary programs have put more and more emphasis on material, as well as spiritual, well-being. "The missionary function has changed over the years," says Mrs. William F. Pruitt, recently returned after spending fifteen years as a Presbyterian missionary in the Congo. "We realized long ago that a handful of missionaries could not evangelize or educate Africa, that our efforts must be multiplied by training Africans. And more and more our program is a training one."

At the time the Peace Corps was created, the Protestant and Catholic churches combined had 33,000 missionaries overseas; in Africa, there was one missionary to each 3,503 inhabitants. Many missionary programs were very similar to those later undertaken by the Peace Corps. The Methodist Board of Missions, for instance, sends some 125 young people each year to spend about three years overseas; their training—which stresses language and practical skills—is similar to the training program of the Peace Corps.

Similarly, the American Friends Service Committee has, since 1917, been sending young volunteers abroad to work in war relief, refugee resettlement, and community development projects of all kinds.

However, the organization most often described as the real proto-

type of the Peace Corps is the International Voluntary Services. IVS
was formed in 1953, to some extent as an effort to reorganize and
give more specific direction to all American missionary programs. It
is governed by a board composed of both Catholic and Protestant representatives. It is, however, essentially a nonreligious as well as non-
denominational operation: the volunteers who go abroad make no
attempt to proselytize foreign citizens.

According to the late Dr. N. S. Noffsinger, former IVS director,
and Peace Corps consultant, IVS grew out of a concern that our foreign-
aid program was not succeeding because the International Cooperation
Administration, being a government agency, was forced to operate on a
government-to-government basis. Many people in underdeveloped
countries lived in villages seldom reached by American representatives.
The men who founded IVS were aware that something had to be done
at the grass roots, but the problem was: who could be sent? The
answer, they decided, was to send young Americans just out of college,
but many of these were facing at least two years' service in the Army.
In 1953 the founders of IVS went to General Lewis B. Hershey, Director
of Selective Service, to see what could be done about obtaining a draft
deferment for IVS volunteers. General Hershey was sympathetic but had
no authority to give blanket deferment. He did suggest, however, that
if IVS would supply Selective Service with a list of IVS volunteers, plus
a description of their abilities and majors, the list would be passed
on to the local draft boards. In eight years, two hundred IVS volunteers
were sent overseas and not one was drafted during or after his tour of
duty. So that IVS would not outbid the Army for talented people, it was
decided to give volunteers the same pay they would get in the Army,
$80 a month.

IVS started work primarily in rural areas; at first, in fact, IVS would
take only boys who had been raised on a farm or who had agricultural-
college training. The requirement is not quite so rigid today, but IVS
still insists that its volunteers have some background in the programs
undertaken, in the fields of agriculture, poultry and animal husbandry,
youth clubs, resettlement, crop and horticultural experimentation and
propagation, sanitation, home economics, public health, applied mechanics, road building, well drilling, education, carpentry, low-cost
housing, and so on. IVS accepts unmarried recent B.S. and M.S. graduates who are in good physical and mental health. Married members are
accepted only if there are no minor dependents and both husband
and wife are acceptable as team members.

IVS volunteers are offered a two-year contract. During this period they are guaranteed all necessary expenses, including transportation to and from the assigned projects, housing, subsistence, clothing allowance, medical care, insurance, and an annual thirty-day vacation. The projects themselves were at first financed by private foundations, although in recent years most have been financed under contract with the ICA. IVS volunteers always work under the general guidance of American technicians overseas; their primary objective is to establish goodwill and understanding through being good neighbors and showing local people how to use more effectively the assistance they get from various foreign-aid programs.

Before the Peace Corps had sent its first Volunteer overseas, the IVS had sent teams to Egypt, Jordan, Iraq, Vietnam, Laos, Nepal, Cambodia, Ghana, and Liberia. They cleared jungles, experimented with crops, resettled refugees, dug wells, installed power generators, developed poultry-raising projects, and taught peasants how to maintain machinery. Although these young "ugly Americans" received very little publicity, their impact was strong. For instance, in 1956 two young IVS volunteers were operating a 33-acre experimental farm in Egypt. When the Suez war broke out, they were evacuated. After the truce, one of the first communiqués received from the Egyptian government was a request to "get those two men back here and give us ten more just like them." Their fame had spread up and down the Nile.

Just as IVS was in many ways the logical culmination of the work of American missionary groups, the formation of numerous nonreligious organizations to send volunteers abroad was a logical outgrowth of the increased interest on the part of universities and foundations in the underdeveloped areas of the world. Since World War II, and especially since the launching of the Marshall Plan, dozens of private organizations have been formed for the purpose of bringing America closer to the people of foreign countries—especially the underdeveloped ones.

One of the earliest plans for sending young Americans abroad to work in underdeveloped countries was the International Farm Youth Exchange program of the National 4-H Clubs, started in 1948 and still in operation. IFYE has sent hundreds of young Americans abroad to work on farms in those countries.

Another plan was originated by Doug Kelly, a former president of Students for Democratic Action. In 1951, with the financial assistance of the Foundation for World Government, Kelly formed the International Development Placement Association, a recruiting center and employment agency for American students who wanted to work in the underdeveloped countries at local wages. Although a small organization with limited funds, the IDPA did valuable pioneer work in recruiting workers and demonstrated the role such an organization could play. In 1954, lack of funds forced IDPA to disband, but the eighteen pioneer "peace corpsmen" who went abroad under this program helped prove that young, educated Americans working at the community level in the underdeveloped countries could make a unique contribution not only to our foreign-aid program but also to the cause of better understanding.

A more recent, and very successful, attempt to bring about a closer understanding between American students and the people of underdeveloped countries was the widely publicized Operations Crossroads Africa. In 1954 Dr. James H. Robinson, a Negro pastor and director of New York's Morningside Community Center, became aware of the urgent needs of African villagers during a tour of Africa. He came back to the States determined to promote the idea of a college program that would enable students to spend their summers in Africa working on specific community projects, while also getting to know more about the Africans—and vice versa. "Everyone thought the idea was crazy," as Dr. Robinson put it, until he got to Occidental College in Los Angeles. There, he was able to generate enough enthusiasm to get a pilot program launched, and in 1958 he and ten American students spent the summer in Africa.

By the summer of 1961 Operations Crossroads Africa had organized its third full-scale program. The 1961 project involved about two hundred students who spent two months in fifteen African countries. The students themselves had to put up about $900 each, which covered half the cost of going to Africa. The other half was raised by Operations Crossroads. Both Negro and white students participated.

Many universities organized their own programs for sending students to underdeveloped countries to work—either in the summer, during their junior year, or during their graduate work. For instance, Williams College, which has long had a program in which the student spends his junior year in Europe, planned a similar program for Africa. Several colleges, including Harvard, Columbia, MIT, and Williams, had been cooperating with Nigeria in their efforts to obtain teachers for their secondary schools. Harvard alone was deluged with 350 applications for the 28 teaching posts it had agreed to fill. The University of California at Los Angeles had a summer program called "Project India," which sent a dozen or so students to India each summer to work on specific projects.

As a matter of fact, organizations pioneering in one phase or another of the kind of work the Peace Corps does seemed almost endless—CARE, Foster Parents, the Near East Foundation, Experiment in International Living, the American Korean Foundation, and many others. One of the best known, primarily because of the work of the late Dr. Tom Dooley, was MEDICO, an organization which raised money to send medical teams to establish hospitals and clinics in underdeveloped areas. And in 1960, the Association of American Medical Colleges, in cooperation with a Philadelphia pharmaceutical company (Smith, Kline & French), organized their own MEDICO program—a plan to send twenty to thirty junior and senior medical students to hospitals in under-developed countries to work for ten to twelve weeks.

One of the most exciting of these pioneering medical ventures is Project Hope, originated by Dr. William B. Walsh and sponsored by the People-to-People Foundation. In 1960, the Foundation sent a hospital ship—the former naval hospital ship U.S.S. *Consolation*—to Indonesia, where it went from port to port in an effort to assist the Indonesian government in fighting disease and training local medical personnel. Since then, the ship has participated in many similar missions.

The Peace Corps is not solely an American idea. Several other countries—including the Netherlands, Switzerland, and West Germany —had organizations similar to private voluntary agencies in this country. In Italy Danilo Dolci formed an organization which brings young people from England, Holland, and Scandinavia to work in poverty-stricken Sicily. Australia has developed an organization called *Pegawai* (the Indonesian word for "government servant") which sends young university graduates out to live and work in Indonesia. It is essentially a voluntary technical-assistance program and has been operating since 1952. And many countries have overseas work-camp programs, under which young people volunteer to go abroad for varying periods of time to work in groups, often at unskilled labor. According to UNESCO, more than 300,000 volunteers from 41 countries were active in such work-camp programs at the time the Peace Corps was created.

The foreign organization that comes closest to embodying the Peace Corps idea was Britain's Voluntary Service Overseas, a program similar to that of the International Voluntary Service, though without IVS's religious sponsorship. It was started in 1959 by Alec Dickson, a former UNESCO social worker who felt he saw a way to tap the energy, drive, and idealism of young Englishmen. VSO takes volunteers from age eighteen to twenty-four and sends them out to various underdeveloped countries within the Commonwealth. They are "apprenticed to a nation," as one British newspaper put it; 120 of them served their apprenticeship in 1961. The impact of service abroad is described in this letter home from one VSO volunteer in Southern Cameroon:

This seems to me to have been one of the important things I have gained—to see my life and ideas in England in a new perspective; to find certain ideas which I had always taken for granted actually questioned and defied. . . . Deeper than this, on these expeditions, I began to realize the value of human relationships of mutual trust and faith, as I had never done before. So many of my relationships with older people had been on the basis of irony and cynicism that to find this was not even understood, let alone common, was at first very jarring. And to think that I might have been working in an office!

3

ORIGINS

Too often we seem to emphasize military alliances with corrupt or reactionary leaders; furnishing military hardware which all too frequently is turned on the people of the country we are presumably helping; grandiose and massive projects; hordes of American officials living aloof in the country's capital. Would we not be farther along if we relied more heavily on a group of some thousands of young Americans willing to help with an irrigation project, digging a village well, or setting up a rural school?

> —REPRESENTATIVE HENRY S. REUSS,
> in *Commonweal.*

BECAUSE THE GENERAL IDEA of a "peace corps" has existed for so long, it is difficult to pinpoint exactly when the first proposal was made that the government organize an army of young people to serve in underdeveloped countries.

Ten years ago, David Lilienthal, former chairman of the Tennessee Valley Authority, was one of the most prominent advocates of a universal public-service plan in which every educated person would be expected to set aside a number of years for service in some branch of the federal government both at home and abroad, although he made no specific recommendation about the underdeveloped areas of the world. As early as 1949, some young World Federalists advanced the idea for a peace force to be called Community Development Projects. And in the summer of 1951 a convention of Students for Democratic Action endorsed an idea to recruit members for worldwide community development work. About the same time, New York Congressman Jacob Javits was proposing that the United States recruit a million young Americans for an "army of peace" which would work abroad improving standards of living. And just before he died in 1952, Senator Brian McMahon of Connecticut urged that the government send young American volunteers into the underdeveloped countries as "full-time missionaries of democracy"—a peacetime army, as he called it, carrying "not arms, but hoes and healing medicines and faith in our liberty."

In 1950, the Public Affairs Institute published a pamphlet by Dewey Anderson and Stephen Raushenbush recommending 250 "work centers" to be established in underdeveloped countries over a six-year period. Each center would be staffed by ten technicians, plus twenty native assistants who would in time take over. And in October 1953, President A. Ray Olpin of the University of Utah, returning from a trip around the world, reported to the State Department that the government should

> . . . call a sizable number of young men on missions to Japan or other foreign countries for a two or three year period with no remuneration other than living expenses. It would be understood that these men were not career people and that after these few years of service the individuals would be expected to return to their homes. . . . In order to make certain that a quota of representatives of Americans of this kind could be available, it might be well to have the program coordinated with the Selective Service or Reserve Training programs. . . . They could live with the people in foreign lands, study their language and traditions and customs, teach the people American customs and language, serve as teachers in the schools, could even work alongside foreign peoples in certain forms of employment.

Another early proposal came from North Carolina industrialist Heinz W. Rollmann in his book, *World Construction.* One of the steps in his program for popular participation in international affairs was: "Congress will have to establish a Peace Army consisting of at least three million men and women." Rollmann's army was to be composed of skilled technicians who would travel to all parts of the world, teaching their knowledge and skills to the people of underprivileged countries.

Of all the advocates of a government-sponsored youth service corps, the one who played the most important role was probably Democratic Representative Henry S. Reuss of Wisconsin. Congressman Reuss tells how, while on a visit to Cambodia in 1957, he was driving along a magnificent highway built with American funds. "This road cost thirty million dollars to build," said his guide.

"Who uses it?" Reuss asked.

The guide pointed to a barefoot Cambodian leading his water buffalo along the road's shoulder. The road itself was empty as far as the eye could see. Reuss asked himself, "How else might we have spent that money to serve more people?"

The answer was suggested later on his trip. "In the jungles of Cambodia," he later wrote in the *Progressive,* "I saw a team of four young

American school teachers who were going from village to village setting up the elementary schools that the French had neglected to provide in a hundred years of colonialism. The villagers and the young Americans loved each other, and I could only regret that there were four, rather than 40, or 400, Americans working on the project."

The four young Americans, who were working for UNESCO, made a lasting impression on Congressman Reuss. When he returned to the United States he decided to see what could be done to humanize our foreign-aid program and to restore some of the idealism which once animated the Marshall Plan. The method he decided on was the creation of what he called a Point Four Youth Corps. He first proposed the idea in a lecture at Cornell University in 1958. He called for "Americans, neither busybodies nor misfits, who have some degree of expertness . . . young people who are willing to serve their country for a few years in far-off places, at a soldier's pay . . . in the greatest adventure of the age." Reuss says the response was electric, and he continued to discuss the idea and to promote a Point Four Youth Corps for a year and a half. By the end of 1959, Congressman Reuss had prepared legislation, which he submitted to the House early in 1960, calling for a study of his proposal. At the same time, Senator Richard Neuberger of Oregon submitted similar legislation in the Senate. As a result, the Mutual Security Act of 1960 made available $10,000 for a study of a Point Four Youth Corps. The study was eventually assigned to the University of Colorado Research Foundation and put under the general direction of Dr. Maurice Albertson. The Albertson report was completed in May 1961, although a preliminary draft had been turned in to the President in February. Much of the concrete planning of the present Peace Corps was based on it.

The support by Congressman Reuss for a youth corps was important for a number of reasons. His proposal specifically tied the idea to the United States foreign-aid program and specified that the corps should be organized and administered by the United States government. His recommendations were picked up by the Organization of Young Democratic Clubs, which began promoting the idea extensively on the nation's campuses as one reason why young people should vote Democratic. The National Student Association also became active in promoting the idea; the activities of the NSA and the Young Democrats were, to a very considerable extent, responsible for the "spontaneous" enthusiasm which greeted candidate Kennedy's proposal during the Presidential campaign of 1960.

Reuss's enthusiasm also led to a specific plan for a Peace Corps submitted to the Senate by Senator Hubert Humphrey on June 15, 1960.

When Senator Humphrey introduced his bill a few weeks before the Democratic National Convention of 1960, he mentioned the earlier legislation sponsored by Congressman Reuss and Senator Neuberger and applauded "their vision and statesmanship . . . My bill differs from theirs," he said, "in that, instead of asking for a study of the Peace Corps, it asks for the Peace Corps itself. There is sufficient evidence now in hand to justify moving directly to the formation of such a corps now, rather than waiting for a study to be made."

Humphrey's bill drew heavily on the precedent of the International Voluntary Service, which he described as the "organization which has the experience most directly relevant to the proposed Peace Corps." The Peace Corps Humphrey proposed had many parallels with the program as it was finally instituted. It was to be a separate agency, working with the State Department, the U.S. Information Agency, and the International Cooperation Administration. A maximum of five hundred volunteers were to be enlisted the first year; thereafter the Corps would be increased gradually until the fourth year, at which time it was anticipated that the maximum strength of five thousand would be achieved. The term of enlistment was to be three years, with the first year devoted primarily to training. Volunteers selected would not be less than twenty-one and a half years of age and should possess a specific skill. Humphrey's Peace Corps would undertake a variety of projects, ranging from community development work to teaching, and no Peace Corps team would go into any country unless invited. The principal difference from the Peace Corps as it has now evolved is that under Humphrey's plan the selected volunteers would have received draft exemption.

Senator Humphrey pointed out one of the most important by-products of a Peace Corps: graduates from the Corps would form a large pool of experienced young men, trained in some of the more remote languages and possessing knowledge of the emerging areas, from which our Foreign Service, ICA, and USIA could draw. "There is a great body of idealistic and talented men in this country," Senator Humphrey concluded, ". . . The Peace Corps would tap those vital resources. There is nothing which will build greater people-to-people and government-to-government relationships than to have fine young American men helping the people of the emerging countries to help themselves. They will not only act as instructors but also will show that they are not afraid to dirty their hands in their common endeavors."

Senator Humphrey's proposal, which was submitted to the Senate not long before adjournment, was made more to awaken congressional and public interest than in any hope of quick passage. "I realize that the introduction of the bill is very late in the session," he admitted frankly. "I wanted the bill to be printed and appropriately referred to so that it could be the subject of discussion and the subject of intensive study in the coming months." But shortly thereafter the subject was projected into the public consciousness to a far greater extent than even Senator Humphrey could have expected: it became involved in the Presidential campaign.

Although the platforms of both political parties stated in general terms an aim to help improve living conditions in underdeveloped countries, neither proposed anything that could be construed as a specific intent to channel the energies of our young men and women into a technical-assistance program. Nor is there evidence that at the outset of the campaign either candidate included the idea of a youth corps in his arsenal of issues. However, candidate Kennedy was made conscious of the Peace Corps concepts as early as February 1960, when he was asked a question about the Reuss proposals on a television panel show.* He later discussed the idea with his staff, and one Kennedy staffer remembers discussing the idea with Senator Kennedy as early as the Wisconsin primary, when a Wisconsin newspaper poll showed favorable public response to the idea. C. L. Sulzberger of the *New York Times* also reports that during the summer of 1960 he discussed with Senator Kennedy a plan of his own for conscripting qualified technicians to serve abroad for twelve to eighteen months. And by September 1960, both Congressman Reuss and Professor Samuel Hayes of the University of Michigan were asked by the Kennedy campaign staff to submit "position papers" on an international youth service program, and both responded.

At the working level of the Democratic Party, the idea of a youth corps came up quite often during the campaign, mainly because of a long-standing interest on the part of the Young Democrats. They had, in fact, specifically mentioned a youth corps in some of the campaign literature. And whenever Richard Murphy, national director of the Young Democrats, or Charles Manatt, College Program director, spoke at any of the colleges during the campaign, they always listed the intent to establish a youth service corps as one of four reasons why young people should be in favor of the Democrats.

---

* *College News Conference,* February 21, 1960.

The first mention by Senator Kennedy of a Peace Corps during the campaign came, in fact, under the auspices of the Young Democrats. It appeared on October 5, 1960, in a special "Message of Senator John F. Kennedy to the Nation's New Voters." Kennedy proposed a specific program for youth, including

> . . . a proposition originally offered by my Democratic colleagues, Senator Humphrey and Representative Reuss, that some appropriate way be found to take advantage of the skills, the talents, the devotion and the idealism which is inherent in America's young people; and to utilize the services, of those properly trained, on the new frontiers of the under-developed world—which are in fact the new frontiers of humanity—to aid in building dams, teaching schools, operating hospitals, establishing irrigation projects, and to generally help other people to help themselves.
>
> Should I be selected to provide the Presidential leadership of our nation for the next four years, I would explore thoroughly the possibility of utilizing the services of the very best of our trained and qualified young people to give from three to five years of their lives to the cause of world peace by forming themselves into a Youth Peace Corps, going to the places that really need them and doing the sort of jobs that need to be done.

At least two papers, the *Washington Star* and the *Baltimore Sun,* gave the October 5 statement prominent attention. The story in the *Star* was headlined, PEACE CORPS FOR YOUTH SUGGESTED BY KENNEDY; the October 6 *Sun* headlined it YOUTH PEACE CORPS IS AIM OF KENNEDY. United Press International carried a ten-paragraph story written primarily around the Peace Corps proposal. The Young Democrats followed this up by sending copies of the statement to every college newspaper, college YD club, and Students-for-Kennedy group. The enthusiasm aroused was astonishing. According to Richard Murphy, although the Peace Corps proposal had always been greeted enthusi-astically on the campuses whenever he had mentioned it, it was usually only a "local" response, but the mail response to Kennedy's injection of the idea into the campaign began immediately after the October 5 statement and increased steadily not only through the campaign but into 1961.

The first time Kennedy himself publicly mentioned the idea of youth service was shortly thereafter, early in the morning of October 14. The campaign party had just flown to Michigan from New York, where candidates Kennedy and Nixon had engaged in their third television debate. It was a brisk night, and as the motorcade made its way from the airport to Ann Arbor, where the Senator was to say a few words at the University of Michigan, it became evident that a large crowd of students had waited up to see and hear him. At the university, the caravan was greeted by a crowd estimated at ten thousand.

Kennedy finally made his way to the steps of the Student Union Building where he made an extemporaneous speech that was not too easy to hear, because the Senator's voice was hoarse and the students were very noisy. "How many of you are willing," asked the Senator, "to spend ten years in Africa or Latin America or Asia working for the U.S. and working for freedom? How many of you [who] are going to be doctors are willing to spend your days in Ghana; technicians or engineers, how many of you are willing to work in the foreign service, and spend your lives traveling around the world? On your willingness to do that, not merely to serve one or two years in the service, but on your willingness to contribute part of your life to this country, I think, will depend the answer whether we as a free society can compete. I think we can, and I think Americans are willing to contribute, but the effort must be far greater than we have made in the past."

Four days later, Chester Bowles also visited the University of Michigan, where he urged the expansion of the United Nations International Civil Service. It was his hope that this would provide opportunities for young people to serve overseas helping the governments of the emerging nations meet their needs for skilled personnel. Inspired by these two talks, a group of University of Michigan graduate students formed a nonpartisan student organization called Americans Committed to World Responsibility, and sent messages to the camps of both Presidential candidates asking them to support the idea of a youth corps. A large number of students became active in this organization, and later a delegation went to talk with Senator Kennedy about the Peace Corps. The mail also continued to pour into the Democratic National Committee, and for the next couple of weeks the Kennedy camp became increasingly aware that their candidate had become identified with an idea which had widespread appeal among the nation's youth.

On November 2, 1960, in the Cow Palace in San Francisco, the future President made a formal campaign promise. "We are going to have to have the best Americans we can get to speak for our country abroad," Senator Kennedy said. "All of us have admired what Dr. Tom Dooley has done in Laos. And others have been discouraged at the examples that we read of the ugly American. And I think that the United States is going to have to do much better in this area if we are going to defend freedom and peace in the 1960s. For the fact of the matter is that out of Moscow and Peking and Czechoslovakia and East Germany are hundreds of men and women; scientists, physicists, teachers, engineers, doctors, nurses, studying in those institutes, prepared to spend their lives abroad in the service of world communism. A friend of mine visiting the Soviet Union last summer met a young Russian couple studying Swahili and African customs at the Moscow Institute of Languages. They were not language teachers. He was a sanitation engineer and she was a nurse, and they were being prepared to live their lives in Africa as missionaries for world communism.

"This can only be countered," he went on to say, "by the skill and dedication of Americans who are willing to spend their lives serving the cause of freedom."

The response to the San Francisco speech was immediate. The newspapers gave the idea extensive coverage and press aides who traveled with Kennedy report that from November 2 on, the Peace Corps proposal was the subject of repeated inquiries by reporters covering the campaign and by other people.

The Peace Corps was now a definite part of the Kennedy program to get America moving again; as such it could not be ignored by the Nixon camp. There were numerous rumors floating around that Nixon had been giving some thought to proposing a youth service corps, and it is entirely possible that Richard Nixon did consider the Peace Corps a "campaign promise." However, as with all such proposals for specific action, Nixon was in a difficult position. Having been the number two man in an administration which had been in office for eight years, and much having been made of the extent to which Vice-President Nixon had participated in the affairs of the Eisenhower Administration, he could not very well propose an idea which had been in the wind for so long without the question being asked, "If you think it is such a good idea, why haven't you already done it?" In addition, as Nixon was no doubt aware, the Kennedy campaign camp could have made mincemeat of the proposal if he had made it, pointing out a long Democratic interest in the subject that included specific legislation already submitted to Congress by Democratic Senator Hubert Humphrey.

As a matter of fact, President Eisenhower himself, in the first Republican response to the Peace Corps proposal, was to use this "we-thought-of-it-first" technique of rebuttal, with little ground for the claim. On November 4, President Eisenhower gave his answer to the Peace Corps idea in an address at the Public Square in Cleveland, Ohio. "There is something almost amazing," said the President in a highly partisan speech based on a White House staff paper, "about the way some politicians can twist things. Here is an example: Within the last few days I heard of a plan for forming a great corps of 'workers for peace.' The time given to this project—for which the Federal Government would of course pay—would be a substitute for a tour of duty in the uniformed service. This is apparently intended as one of the new ideas that will help produce the New Frontier. Strangely enough, this brand new plan is amazingly similar to a proposal made in 1954 in a book by Heinz Rollmann, who is not a member of the party whose spokesman made the recent announcement. Mr. Rollmann, the original author, is the Republican candidate for Congress from the Twelfth District of North Carolina. It makes us wonder how many other proposals are not original and not new—merely immature."*

Candidate Nixon also opposed this Democratic program, as might have been expected. In doing so, he made one important contribution to the present form of the program, albeit a negative one. He concentrated his attack on the single most controversial point of the earlier proposals, draft exemption, and effectively destroyed this possibility:

> Here in California a few days ago Senator Kennedy proposed the establishment of a so-called peace corps. In doing so he was appealing to one of the higher aspirations of our Nation—that of serving not ourselves alone, but also the peoples of other nations.
> But the plan he proposed for achieving this objective is superficial and obviously concocted solely for campaign purposes. If put into effect it would be harmful both to the Selective Service and to those so ably representing the U.S. abroad.
> The proposal he makes is to say in effect to young men who are eligible for the draft, "if you will volunteer for a peace corps, you can evade your obligations under the Selective Service and Training Act."
> . . . Insofar as serving the peoples of other nations is concerned, he proposes to send as America's representatives to other nations young men whom he calls volunteers but who, in truth, in many instances would be trying to escape the draft. Instead of sending to these nations young men and women who are genuinely eager to dedicate their lives to the service of others, Mr. Kennedy would cater to draft evasion.

The last mention of the Peace Corps in the campaign came on election eve when a very tired Senator Kennedy discussed it briefly in answer to a question on a television program: "I have suggested having

* On November 5, the Washington *Star* had this to say about President Eisenhower's reference to Heinz Rollmann: "Mr. Rollmann is the Republican candidate for Congress in North Carolina's 12th District this year. A wealthy Waynesville, N.C., shoe manufacturer, and German immigrant, Mr. Rollmann was a Democrat when he wrote the book in 1954. He ran for the Democratic nomination for Congress in his district in 1958 but was defeated. He announced early in 1959 that he was changing parties." It can also be noted that Congressional candidate Rollmann was again defeated in 1960.

a peace corps of young men and women," he said, "who will be willing
to spend two or three years of their lives as teachers and nurses, working
in different countries which are backward and which are just beginning
to develop, spreading the cause of freedom."

4

THE CREATION OF THE PEACE CORPS

This is a great historic occasion, a reaffirmation of America's warm heart, bright conscience and dedication to the Bill of Rights and the rights of man around the world.

—SUPREME COURT JUSTICE WILLIAM O. DOUGLAS,
at the swearing-in of Sargent Shriver,
Director of the Peace Corps.

As THE EXCITEMENT of the 1960 Presidential campaign began to subside, it became evident that at least one campaign issue was not to be forgotten. The Peace Corps continued to generate enthusiasm. Mail from young and not-so-young people volunteering to serve poured into the White House and the Democratic National Committee. In fact, according to the President's press secretary, Pierre Salinger, President-elect Kennedy received more mail on the Peace Corps than on any other subject he raised during the campaign. It is not surprising, then, that included in the many studies ordered by President-elect Kennedy in the period between his election and inauguration was one on an international youth service to be prepared by Dr. Max Millikan, director of the Center for International Studies at MIT.

Furthermore, numerous groups interested in the Peace Corps organized conferences to discuss the practical application of their long-cherished dream—and usually sent the White House their recommendations. The most demonstrable enthusiasm continued to come from the campuses.

In addition to rapidly expanding university programs designed to send young students to work abroad, students themselves had already shown an impressive willingness to take the initiative in organizing and supporting technical-assistance programs for underdeveloped countries. Active support from student groups for such programs was evident as early as 1949. However, the movement really gained momentum after

Congressman Reuss and Senator Humphrey began speaking on the subject in 1958 and 1959. Both the Young Democratic Clubs and the National Student Association became interested in the idea and, when Congressman Reuss submitted his Peace Corps legislation in January 1960, the NSA began its own study. In March 1960, 270 Antioch College students sent a petition to the Senate Foreign Relations Committee favoring the idea; in August, Professor Walt W. Rostow told one conference that hundreds of MIT and Harvard students were anxious to serve overseas in underdeveloped countries. And, as noted earlier, in October, after Senator Kennedy made his first brief public reference to the idea at Ann Arbor, a group of graduate students at the University of Michigan formed an organization called Americans Committed to World Responsibility to study and support the Peace Corps.

Student enthusiasm continued after the campaign. On November 11 and 12, 1960, a conference of more than a hundred student and business leaders met at Princeton University to discuss the formation of a Peace Corps. At Ohio State University a Peace Corps Council was formed. Over the Thanksgiving holidays, several students of eastern colleges held a meeting at the United Nations at which they drafted a resolution in support of a national youth service program to send qualified American youth to work in the newly emerging nations. During the Christmas holidays, twenty students representing fifteen eastern colleges gathered at New York University to discuss the controversial aspects of the Peace Corps and offer their own ideas and endorsement. The Associated Students Council of Eastern Washington College of Education passed a resolution endorsing the Peace Corps idea; at the University of Michigan more than 750 students signed petitions supporting an expansion of the U.N. Civil Service and the U.S. Foreign Service to include an overseas program for young graduates; 500 Amherst College students signed a letter to President Kennedy endorsing the Peace Corps; at Harvard, immediate action was proposed on a pilot project to send dozens of young Harvard graduates out to teach in the secondary schools of Nigeria. In April 1961, the National Student Association and American University in Washington, D.C., organized a National Conference on Youth Service Abroad attended by more than 400 young Americans representing 256 colleges and 30 youth organizations.

The most important factor leading to Senator Kennedy's decision to propose the Peace Corps was the tremendous response—especially from college students—which greeted his first references to the subject. The continuing response after the campaign was equally important in the White House's decision to act immediately in the spring of 1961 to establish a Peace Corps. Further impetus was supplied by numerous nonstudent groups which demonstrated their support. For instance, on December 18, 1960, the Institute of International Education sent President-elect Kennedy a study on the organization of a Peace Corps prepared by its Committee on Educational Interchange Policy. On December 20, a major conference on the Point Four Youth Corps, organized by Congressman Reuss, was held in Washington, D.C. More than fifty representatives of groups which had long been interested in a Peace Corps—including a representative of President-elect Kennedy— attended the conference, the main purpose of which was to discuss the many problems to be faced. The Public Affairs Institute published *An International Peace Corps* by Professor Hayes of the University of Michigan, an expansion of the "position paper" he had prepared during the campaign. In addition, many labor leaders were supporting a plan to recruit a hundred thousand idealistic youths immediately for peaceful service abroad.

In January 1961, the President received the report he had requested from Dr. Millikan; the following month he was given the preliminary report of the study made by the Colorado State University Research Foundation, authorized by Congressman Reuss's legislation. Both studies endorsed an organization for youth service abroad, although neither recommended the formation of a completely independent government agency similar to the present Peace Corps.

The combined activities of these many individuals and groups made it evident that the enthusiasm surrounding the Peace Corps was not merely the result of campaign fever. A Gallup poll released in January, moreover, showed that 71 percent of the American people favored the idea of a Peace Corps and only 18 percent opposed it.

President Kennedy decided to appoint his brother-in-law, R. Sargent Shriver, to study the feasibility of organizing a Peace Corps immediately. He also made a further personal commitment to the idea in his State of the Union Message:

> An even more valuable national asset is our reservoir of dedicated men and women—not only on our college campuses, but in every age group—who have indicated their desire to contribute their skills, their efforts and a part of their lives to the fight for world order. We can mobilize this talent through the formation of a National Peace Corps, enlisting the services of all those with the desire and capacity to help foreign lands meet their urgent needs for trained personnel.

On February 28, 1961, Shriver submitted his report to the President. He referred specifically to the Millikan report, the study of Professor

Hayes, the reports of the Institute of International Education and National Student Association, the proposals of Congressman Reuss and Senator Humphrey, the report of Dr. Albertson of the Colorado State University Research Foundation, and the suggestions of his own task force—which included White House assistant Harris Wofford and representatives from private organizations and the International Cooperation Administration. His conclusion was that the "Peace Corps can either begin in very low gear, with only preparatory work undertaken now and when Congress finally appropriates special funds for it—or it can be launched now and in earnest by executive action, with sufficient funds made available from existing Mutual Security Appropriations to permit a number of substantial projects to start this summer." Shriver recommended, however, that the "Peace Corps should be launched soon so that the opportunity to recruit the most qualified people from this year's graduating classes will not be lost. Nor should we lose the opportunity to use this summer for training on university campuses."

Two days later, March 1, 1961, President Kennedy issued an Executive Order (10924) establishing the Peace Corps as a new agency within the Department of State. On the same day, he sent a message to Congress stating that he had established a Peace Corps on a temporary basis and recommending that Congress create a permanent Peace Corps —"a pool of trained American men and women sent overseas by the U.S. Government or through private organizations and institutions to help foreign countries meet their urgent needs for skilled manpower." On March 4 the President announced that he was appointing Sargent Shriver as Director of the Corps. On March 30, the President announced the appointment of a National Advisory Council for the Peace Corps.

On May 31, 1961, President Kennedy sent to Congress the Administration's bill "to provide for a Peace Corps to help the peoples of interested countries and areas in meeting their needs for skilled manpower." The following day the proposed Peace Corps Act was introduced as Senate Bill 2000 by Senator Hubert Humphrey of Minnesota, with the co-sponsoring of several other Senators. It was introduced in the House by Representative Thomas E. Morgan of Pennsylvania, Chairman of the House Foreign Affairs Committee. Several identical bills also were introduced in the House, including one by Representative Reuss. The final legislation providing for a permanent Peace Corps was signed by the President on September 22, 1961.

However, the Peace Corps was actually off and running from the first day of March, 1961, when the President's Executive Order brought it into being. Within a week, there was a whirlwind of activity in the offices of Washington's newest agency, colorfully described in the March 10, 1961, issue of *Time*: "Telephones jingled, the switchboard blinked, and drifts of incoming mail accumulated on the desks. Workmen pushed official furniture around the corridors. The scene, in a suite of offices in Washington's International Cooperation Administration Building, was chaotic. Earlier in the week, President Kennedy had announced the formation of his Peace Corps of volunteer workers in underdeveloped countries, and the half-organized headquarters was engulfed with requests for information and applications from would-be recruits. In other parts of the capital, the story was the same: Congressmen reported a deluge of mail; the White House was hard pressed to answer 5,000 letters. The Peace Corps had captured the public imagination as had no other single act of the Kennedy Administration."

Up to now, the latent enthusiasm for the Peace Corps idea which had existed among the nation's youth was enough to sustain the new organization's momentum. But if in the unlikely event that the enthusiasm for the Peace Corps should begin to dwindle, there was little danger that the lull would last for long. One of the most adroit moves President Kennedy made in his early days in office was the appointment of his brother-in-law to launch the Peace Corps; Sargent Shriver and the hustling young staff of New Frontiersmen he brought to Washington had no intention of letting the early excitement sparked by the Peace Corps become stifled in bureaucratic Washington.

Robert Sargent Shriver was born in Westminster, Maryland, in 1915, graduated from Yale (*cum laude*) in 1938, and received his law degree from Yale in 1941. In 1940, with World War II on the horizon, he had also enlisted in the V-7 Naval Reserve program. Shriver was commissioned ensign in 1941 and served aboard submarines and a battleship in the Atlantic and the Pacific until 1945, leaving active duty as a lieutenant commander.

"I just couldn't see myself settling down to a lawyer's life again," says Shriver. "At Yale, I'd been active on the college paper, I'd been a stringer for *Time* and I'd always had my finger in the journalistic pie. So I turned to journalism after the war." Shriver, working at *Newsweek* as an assistant editor in 1946, met the father of a girl he had met at a dinner party the year before. The girl was Eunice Kennedy; her father was Joseph P. Kennedy. He had a son who was preparing to run for Congress in Massachusetts; his name was John F. Kennedy.

Joseph Kennedy was looking for a writer to edit the letters of his eldest son, Joseph, Jr., who had been killed on a wartime mission in

Europe. Shriver did the job. He so impressed Mr. Kennedy that he was taken into the Kennedy firm. One of his first assignments was to survey the Merchandise Mart in Chicago, a huge commercial building which Mr. Kennedy had purchased. Shriver became its assistant manager and has made Chicago his home ever since. He and Eunice Kennedy were married in 1953.

Shriver became active in various civic projects in Chicago, including many in education. He was a member of the Chicago Board of Education from 1955 until 1960 and has served as a trustee of numerous universities, including De Paul, the University of Chicago, and Loyola. His offices included those of national chairman of the Yale Alumni Board and vice-president of the Chicago Council on Foreign Relations. He has long been interested in student exchange; in fact, while still an undergraduate, in 1937, 1938, and 1939, he led student groups to Europe under the Experiment in International Living program. In 1937 he delivered a series of speeches in which he advocated teaching Americans more about other cultures and nations. The following year, after a trip to the Far East, he gave another series in which he proposed "that we send American businessmen, American labor leaders and American political leaders to the Far East. . . . Young business executives, young labor leaders, and young politicians working together," he said, "would astound many people."

When his brother-in-law decided to run for President, Shriver, along with all the other Kennedys, pitched in. During the campaign he worked primarily in the area of civil rights; immediately after the election he became the new Administration's number one talent scout. The President offered him his choice of four jobs: in Health, Education and Welfare; Defense; Commerce; and on the White House staff. When a *New York Post* reporter asked him how he wound up as Director of the Peace Corps, Shriver laughed and said, "That's something you'll have to ask the President. But I think it's because I was known to him as someone who organized things that had never been organized before." Later, he became fond of saying that the President had made him Director of the Peace Corps because if it failed "it would be easier to fire a relative than a friend." Although the rumor circulated regularly that Shriver was going to quit to run for political office, there had never been any talk of his being fired—by either his brother-in-law or President Johnson. However, on March 1, 1966, five years after the creation of the Peace Corps, Shriver resigned to become the full-time Director of President Johnson's War on Poverty program. For nearly a year before resigning, Shriver had been handling both jobs, an arrangement that brought increasing criticism from Capitol Hill. He was replaced as Director of the Peace Corps by Jack H. Vaughn, former Assistant Secretary of State for Inter-American Affairs and U.S. Ambassador to Panama (see Chapter 15).

Shriver is a tall, handsome man who rarely walks; he jogs along on the balls of his feet as if at any moment he might take off in full sprint. He is "an innately buoyant personality," Charles Bartlett wrote of him in the *Washington Star,* "and one of the qualifications he brings to his role is a talent for lively salesmanship. But he is tempering these talents —to avoid being type-cast on the Washington stage as one of those fuzzy-minded do-gooders. . . . "

Shriver brought to his job a flair for sparking others into action— a persuasiveness that enabled him to charm the most reluctant college professor or government specialist into coming to work for him. As a result, he was able to put together in a very short time what he did not hesitate to describe as the best staff in Washington. One old ICA hand, firmly opposed to the Peace Corps both in principle and in practice, grudgingly agreed: "It'll work OK," he said shortly after Shriver had assembled his staff; that "bunch they got over there can make anything work."

Shriver's boys, as the young men he assembled to launch the Peace Corps were often called, were versatile, enthusiastic, and energetic. Although they had widely varying backgrounds, they had one thing in common—the right combination of idealism and pragmatism that it takes to get anything truly worthwhile accomplished in Washington. Included in this group of early Peace Corps staffers were Bill D. Moyers, who was described as the ablest assistant Senator Lyndon Johnson had ever had and who, at the tender age of 27, was appointed Director of the Peace Corps's Public Affairs division; Warren Wiggins, a deputy director of the International Cooperation Administration, who first heard from Shriver via a telegram at 3 o'clock in the morning after Shriver had finished reading Wiggins' paper, "The Towering Task," in which he presented his views for operating a Peace Corps; Franklin Williams, an NAACP lawyer and regional director; William Haddad, a prize-winning *New York Post* reporter and former campaign worker for Senator Estes Kefauver and John F. Kennedy; Lee St. Lawrence, a young ICA employee who received the ICA Meritorious Service Award for negotiating an economic program with the late Patrice Lumumba; Harris Wofford, author of *India Afire,* former University of Notre Dame law professor, and Washington lawyer who specialized in civil rights and had had considerable practical experience in community development work abroad; Padraic Kennedy, a Ph.D. candidate on a Woodrow Wilson fellowship at the University of Wisconsin who had also been Senator Kennedy's (no relation) campaign director in Madison; Derek Singer, who had worked with AID and CARE; Dr. Nicholas Hobbs, a psychologist who had served on the faculties at Columbia, Harvard, University of Pennsylvania, and Louisiana State University; Lawrence Dennis, a one-time editorial writer for the *Des Moines Register and Tribune* and vice-president for Academic Affairs at Penn State; Edwin Bayley, a reporter for the *Milwaukee Journal* and executive assistant to Wisconsin Governor Gaylord Nelson; and others with equally unusual backgrounds. "Simple addition would reveal that the Peace Corps administrators in Washington have lived abroad for a total of four centuries," Shriver once wrote in a pamphlet of thumbnail biographies of the Peace Corps staff.

It was a diversified collection of individualists, Democrats, foreign affairs experts, lawyers, and Ph.D.'s, and, of course, the driving force behind it was Shriver. As Ed Bayley said, "Shriver . . . runs the Peace Corps as if it were in the last stage of a political campaign. Everything has to be done instantly! His directives, even those addressed to the senior officials in the older, slower, established agencies, carry deadlines." One evening a management consultant said to some of Shriver's assistants, "You guys had a good day today. You broke fourteen laws. But keep it up," he added, "we're making progress." Another Peace Corps staff member reported that a friend of his in government could explain how they got things done. "You people are so new to government," he said, "that you haven't learned how to do things wrong yet."

It was fortunate that the young staff had the instinct for doing things right, because hardly a day went by without the new organization facing a fresh problem. Even its name was controversial. During the campaign, Kennedy usually used the name "Peace Corps" when discussing the idea for a youth service organization, but there were those who argued that the Russians had corrupted the word "Peace" and that "Corps" sounded too warlike. Shriver dismissed the arguments and stuck with Peace Corps.

A more serious problem was the attempt by many of Kennedy's advisers to have the Peace Corps incorporated in the AID program. This issue came to a head while Shriver was abroad, and he met it by instructing his lieutenants to talk with Vice-President Johnson who had told Shriver that in his experience new government agencies always worked better if established independently. With Johnson's help, the Peace Corps was kept independent of any existing government agency.

The importance of Johnson's role in keeping the Peace Corps free of existing agencies has always been acknowledged by Shriver. "In a very real sense," he says, "Lyndon Johnson is a founding father of the Peace Corps. The organization charts would have looked better if we had become a box in a single foreign-aid agency. But the thrust of the new idea would have been lost. The new wine needed a new bottle."

The question of the draft was another sticky problem. Nixon's attack on the Peace Corps during the campaign as a spawner of draft dodgers had resolved the question of draft exemption because it was not difficult to imagine a similar attack when the Peace Corps bill went to Congress for approval. However, there was still the question of draft deferment, and in his report to the President, Dr. Millikan concluded that ". . . It would be desirable therefore for authority to be provided for deferment of individuals in the service on much the same basis as deferments are granted to students in the United States taking graduate training."

Immediately after the establishment of the Peace Corps, members of its staff met with General Lewis Hershey, Director of the Selective Service. It was agreed that since a Peace Corps Volunteer would be engaged in work in the national interest, he could therefore be granted a deferment while engaged in such work. At the same time, it was agreed that Peace Corps service would not prevent a Volunteer from qualifying for further deferment.

As General Hershey pointed out, "Men who serve overseas for two or three years with the Peace Corps are not likely to be drafted." Mainly, it was felt that Peace Corps Volunteers would be too old by the time they came back from service overseas—probably nearing twenty-six, the age at which draft boards lose interest in a potential draftee. The fact was that since the draft boards were reaping the benefit of the rise in male births which began in 1942, returning Volunteers probably would not be needed, except for national emergencies when all available men would be called up. Furthermore, it was generally assumed that a Peace Corps Volunteer would continue after his return to engage in work considered vital to the national health, safety, or interest, which has thus far proved to be the case.

In actual practice, very few of the volunteers serving in the many private agencies doing the kind of work envisaged by the Peace Corps had been faced with summons from their draft boards after returning from service abroad. No former member of the International Voluntary Services, for instance, has ever been drafted. In the case of Peace Corps returnees, the Corps has tried to guide Volunteers into occupations considered essential to the national interest and thus to continue their deferment; of the first 8,707 ex-Volunteers, only 131 have gone into the service.

As for charges of draft-dodging, as Shriver wrote in the March 17, 1961, issue of *Life,* "I want to warn anyone who sees the Peace Corps as an alternative to the draft that life may well be easier at Fort Dix or at a post in Germany than it will be with us. The military life may not only be more glamorous, but it could be safer."

Another problem, in a sense, was the selection of that all important *first* project. Shriver's men knew that a worldwide spotlight was already on the Peace Corps and that their first overseas project would be the subject of special attention. Hence, they were aware that they had to come up with a mission that could be easily understood, not only by potential Peace Corps Volunteers, but by their families, the American public, the rest of the world, and—not to be overlooked—the Congress of the United States and the press. There was also general agreement that the first project should be in Africa. After careful consideration it was decided that Tanganyika had all the ingredients needed for a Peace Corps project that everyone could comprehend. The story of how this first project developed illustrates the careful planning that went into the creation of the Peace Corps.

Tanganyika, before it combined with the Republic of Zanzibar to form the new state of Tanzania, was the largest of all former British African dependencies, covering 362,688 square miles, 20,000 of which are lakes. It was the second African state since World War II to gain independence, having moved steadily toward its freedom, first as a British Mandate, later as a U.N. Trust Territory. The dominant political figure in Tanganyika was the thirty-eight-year-old Julius Nyerere, leader of the Tanganyikan National Union (T.A.N.U.) and one of the most respected men in Africa. (In fact, the great respect of African political leaders for Nyerere's judgment and wisdom played an important part in Peace Corps interest in Tanganyika. It was felt that if Nyerere showed he had faith in the program it would go a long way toward dispelling the suspicions other African leaders had.)

Topographically, Tanganyika is one of the more spectacular African countries. Within its boundaries are Mount Kilimanjaro, which rises 19,340 feet above sea level and has a permanent ice cap, and Lake Tanganyika, the world's second deepest lake. The largest town and seaport is the capital, Dar-es-Salaam.

Tanganyika lies in the tropics and has three main climatic zones: a hot and humid coastal zone, a hot and dry central plateau, and semi-temperate regions on the slopes of the mountains. The country has large numbers of wild animals, including elephant, hippopotamus, rhinoceros, and giraffe. There are also many species of monkeys and at least one thousand species of birds—from the ostrich to the tiny sunbird.

The country's nine million Africans are divided into approximately 120 tribes, some numbering as few as a thousand members, while the largest, the Sukuma, has a membership of over a million. The languages spoken in Tanganyika are almost as numerous as the tribes. Although the majority of Tanganyikans speak Bantu, there are many variations, and tribes speaking different Bantu dialects may be unintelligible to one another. Swahili, the language of the coastal people, is understood in parts of the country and serves as a *lingua franca*. Bantu in origin, Swahili is enriched by words from Arabic, English, Persian, Hindustani, and Portuguese.

The bulk of the people who live in the coastal cities are Moslem, and Moslems also live in a number of the older inland cities, especially those on the routes of the caravans of the last century. Christianity has been making an increasing number of converts during the last fifty years and is now predominant among the people of several districts.

Tanganyika was a country of experiment and innovation, and the explanation most often given for its steady political progress is the harmony which exists there among Africans, Asians, and Europeans. One has only to visit Dar-es-Salaam to see members of all three groups mixing freely and on good terms. However, Tanganyika had pronounced economic and social problems. The coastline, like that of most of East Africa, has a long history of contact with the outside world, but very few, if any, of the outsiders who touched on the coastline ventured very far inland. For fifty years the problem in Tanganyika was not unlike the problem in most of Africa—opening up the continent to the outside world. Today, the problem is one of opening up Tanganyika, or Tanzania, to its own people.

Although industry had not yet developed in Tanganyika, considerable progress had been made in recent years in the growing of important crops—sisal, cotton, and coffee, among others. (Diamonds, discovered in Tanganyika in 1940, now bring the country $12.6 million a year.) However, only 9 percent of the land was cultivated, partly because of the absence of a year-round water supply but mostly because of the lack of roads. The problem in Tanganyika is that there are no feeder roads running into the interior, and it is thus impossible for the farmers to bring their produce to the markets through the dense rainforests. A three-year development plan was drawn up for Tanganyika; it included the construction of feeder roads to enable the small farmer to bring his produce to the main market centers. However, construction of these roads could not go forward until critical surveys were made. The Tanganyikan government had made requests to the ICA, but the latter was unable to furnish the kind of technical assistance required. The request was uncovered early in 1961 by a Peace Corps staffer, Lee St. Lawrence, who was in search of a project with the necessary prerequisites for that all-important first mission.

The Corps sent St. Lawrence to Dar-es-Salaam to explore the project with the government. His first stop was the Colonial Office in London. The British, who were the administrators of the Territory and whose information concerning the Peace Corps derived largely from inaccurate newspaper accounts, were concerned about the possible placement of unqualified or overzealous Americans in Tanganyika. They were equally concerned that the United States intended to fill positions at a lower rate of pay than that of British overseas civil servants.

St. Lawrence's discussions with the Colonial Office lasted three or four days. He assured the British that Peace Corps Volunteers would be qualified personnel, placed in a supernumerary status and paid from United States funds administered by the government of Tanganyika, and working under the immediate direction of the government of Tanganyika. As a result he was given approval to make his visit.

St. Lawrence's discussions with Prime Minister Nyerere and other members of his cabinet went very well. After St. Lawrence explained the Peace Corps program and told them that the Corps would have available the kind of technicians Tanganyika needed to complete its feeder-road system, they immediately became enthusiastic. The extent of Nyerere's confidence in the Peace Corps may be surmised by the considerable contribution the government of Tanganyika has made to the project.

As a result of these talks, the Tanganyikan government sent to the Peace Corps office in Washington a request for twenty to thirty young American surveyors and engineers for the road program. In all, twenty surveyors, six geologists, and four civil engineers were to be supplied by the Peace Corps.

The first Tanganyikan project was to be composed of three parts: feeder-road surveys; engineering on main territorial roads; and geological-survey mapping. The Peace Corps Volunteers were to carry out their work in districts designated by the office of the District Engineer, and the Volunteers were to train young Tanganyikans in their skills.

The chief assignment of the civil engineers was to supervise the maintenance, grading, and surfacing of main arteries. They were also to oversee the construction of bridges and feeder roads, and the installation of culverts. The four geologists were responsible for geological surveys in areas selected by the Tanganyikan government. The Volunteers were to conduct field work in the dry season (May to December) and for limited periods in limited areas in the rainy season. When field work was unfeasible, they would give courses in the techniques of surveying and engineering.

The Volunteers were assigned to the government of Tanganyika for a two-year period. They came under the administration of the Ministries of Communications and of Commerce and Industry and received technical direction from the provincial engineering headquarters to which they were assigned. In contact at all times with their headquarters, they were to be visited from time to time by the District Engineer or Deputy Chief of the Geological Division. The United States government would grant funds to be used to pay Volunteers' allowances through the normal government of Tanganyika channels. Logistic support—such as transportation, tentage, mosquito nets, etc.—was to be supplied by the District Engineers.

The Peace Corps Volunteers in Tanganyika were not, as had often been maintained, to live at the same level as native road laborers, but at the same level as Tanganyikans with comparable education and skills. The ticks, flies, poor food, and crowded conditions would not permit them to maintain the stamina and health necessary to get their work done. This applied to Tanganyikan technicians as well as Americans. Peace Corps Volunteers in Tanganyika were based in the provincial capitals, but would live in tents while in the field.

Other projects were organized with similar care, and soon the Peace Corps was preparing programs for Colombia, Chile, and the Philippines. To find and determine the interest abroad, Sargent Shriver decided to make a tour of Africa and Asia. With staff members Harris Wofford, Franklin Williams, and Edwin Bayley, he set off in May for an eight-country tour. Everywhere he went he was greeted with enthusiasm for the new agency. As a result, he returned with a briefcase full of requests for Volunteers and the realization that instead of sending over 300 to 500 Volunteers in the first projects it would be necessary to put at least 1,000 in the field if the initial projects were to have their full impact.

There was still, however, the question of whether Americans would respond in enough numbers to satisfy the demand for Volunteers. In the spring, 400,000 questionnaires were sent out to post offices, colleges and universities, and to the more than 25,000 people who had written requesting information. "It is a remarkable document," said *Richmond Times-Dispatch* columnist Charles McDowell with irony. "Obviously the Peace Corps is still too new to know how to make up a proper government form. This thing is written in simple English. It is easy to understand. The questions are specific and sensible, and there is room for the information requested. The Peace Corps doesn't even know enough to ask that this one be submitted in quadruplicate, or at least triplicate. One copy will do for this naive crowd.

"Imagine trying to save the world with a form that is easier to fill out than an application for a Christmas vacation job at the local post office."

Despite the enthusiasm for the Peace Corps, its officials were frankly disappointed at the number of people who showed up for the first tests. One reason, they felt, was the lack of available information and hard facts about the Peace Corps. There was very little concrete information to give out: "We could only talk about the over-all picture," said the chief recruiting officer, Thomas Quimby. Later, as the Tanganyika, Colombia, Chile, and Philippines programs began to take shape, they could talk about specific projects. In addition, Peace Corps officials were finding that the caliber of those who did apply was very high, hence they were able to revise their estimate that only 10 percent of the 12,000 applicants would qualify for selection. This meant that it would be possible to start with fewer and still end up with the desired number for a specific project. And, on July 13 and 14, 1961, when more than 2,500 applicants appeared to take the second Peace Corps exams, Dr. Nicholas Hobbs, chief selection officer, said, "We are over the hump for this year."

Finally, there was the biggest problem of all—steering the Peace Corps legislation through Congress. The President had created the Peace Corps by Executive Order, but if it was to have any hope of permanency it had to be approved by Congress. Beginning in March, Shriver launched a five-month campaign of selling his pet project on Capitol Hill. Whenever he was not traveling in the developing countries telling their leaders "that the Peace Corps was in business," as he put it, he could be seen on Capitol Hill having breakfast or lunch, or button-holing congressmen in the corridors telling them how much it would mean to the nation to put the Peace Corps in business permanently. "The Peace Corps has three great constituencies," said Shriver, "the American people, the people of the host countries, and Congress. That's why I travel around the United States, I travel overseas, and I travel on Capitol Hill."

Although Congress has since adopted the Peace Corps as one of its favorite government agencies, winning approval for it in the early days was not an easy task and it probably could not have been accomplished without Shriver's "travels." Congresswoman Frances Bolton, for instance, was fond of saying that the whole idea gave her the "shivers." And Senator Bourke Hickenlooper summed up the feelings of many of his Republican colleagues when he asked Shriver at a committee hearing, "How are you going to revolutionize the world with the altruistic claims and statements that are breathlessly made about the Peace Corps?"

Shriver's reply was typical of his approach to Capitol Hill: "Well, Senator, I know of no member of my staff who has ever claimed that we were going to revolutionize the world, nor do we think we are going to change the world overnight or over a generation."

Shriver's performance on Capitol Hill was so impressive that President Kennedy once introduced him with a grin as "the most effective lobbyist on the Washington scene." When the Peace Corps legislation passed in September, it went through with the second highest majority of any nondefense legislation submitted by President Kennedy.

And none too soon—because Peace Corps Volunteers were already overseas. "The first Peace Corps Volunteers to set foot on foreign soil," says Sargent Shriver, describing this historic moment in the September 1964 issue of the *National Geographic,* "stepped off a plane in Accra on a hot and dusty day in August of 1961. These young American men and women were destined to teach in the secondary schools of Ghana, which had gained its independence only four years earlier.

"This should have been an anxious moment for me—but frankly, I had been too impressed by the caliber of Volunteers in training to believe they would let us down. They didn't.

"A number of high Ghanaian officials, including Minister of Education A. J. Dowuona Hammond, waited at the Accra airport with U.S. Ambassador Francis H. Russell. The fifty-one Americans who emerged from the plane were not loud and flippant, chewing gum and taking pictures of everything and everybody, as some might have expected. They behaved in a quiet, unassuming manner, and the only loud thing they did was to sing a song in Twi, the commonest of Ghana's languages."

The Peace Corps was now a reality. Today, as it bathes in the warm, friendly waters of success, it is difficult to recall that at one time the Peace Corps was an orphan on the New Frontier—an unwanted child that few people gave much of a chance for survival. "I do not think it is altogether fair to say that I handed Sarge a lemon from which he made lemonade," President Kennedy once said in an informal talk to the Peace Corps staff. "But I do think that he and other members of your staff were handed one of the most sensitive and difficult assignments which any administrative group in Washington has been given almost in this century."

Perhaps more than any other single act in recent years, the Peace Corps has altered the image of America as seen abroad. But despite all this, as a recent Peace Corps report to Congress says, "A surprising number of misconceptions about it persist."

The following chapters are intended to clear up these misconceptions.

PART TWO

Understanding the Peace Corps

5

OBJECTIVES

The purpose of the Peace Corps is to permit America to participate directly, personally and effectively in this struggle for human dignity. A world community is struggling to be born. America must be present at that birth, helping to make it successful.

—SARGENT SHRIVER, Director of the Peace Corps,
in an address at Notre Dame University,
June 4, 1961.

IN THE COLD, PRECISE LANGUAGE of the Peace Corps Act, the objectives of the Peace Corps are "to promote world peace and friendship through a Peace Corps which shall make available to interested countries and areas men and women of the United States qualified for service abroad and willing to serve, under conditions of hardship if necessary, to help the peoples of such countries and areas in meeting their needs for trained manpower, and to help promote a better understanding of the American people on the part of peoples served and a better understanding of other peoples on the part of the American people."

Officially, then, the objectives are threefold: (1) to provide interested countries with qualified Volunteers to help these nations meet their needs for trained manpower; (2) to help other people understand America better; and (3) to help Americans understand the other peoples of the world better.

The Peace Corps is a uniquely American response to suffering and human hardship, especially in those parts of the world where, in Eric Sevareid's words, "history has not happened." The Marshall Plan has been called the most generous single act of any nation in history, but it was intended primarily to rebuild a war-torn Europe and it involved mostly money. The people of the underdeveloped world certainly need financial assistance, but they also need people—technically trained people. More than that, they need a helping hand: like anyone struggling against overwhelming hardships, they need to know they have friends, people they can count on to pitch in and help.

The Peace Corps was created, in part, to show the underprivileged people of the world that Americans have not forgotten what it is like to struggle against nature, and that we want to help. Whether we can send enough Americans to have a significant impact on the economic lot of the countries where they will serve makes no difference. The point is that thousands of young Americans are willing to help and are willing to make sacrifices to do so; the principal purpose of the Peace Corps is to provide the organization through which this desire can be channeled. For the Peace Corps says to the world as no private agency or technical-assistance organization could say it, that the American people themselves want to help the people of the emerging nations fight the poverty, disease, and ignorance which are the greatest obstacles to progress.

Of course the Peace Corps has a multitude of additional goals: to help Americans communicate with and understand millions of people who have little in common with us; to help identify America with the revolution of rising expectations taking place in the world; and to help their fellow Americans learn more about the twentieth century and their fellow men, without which they will be unable to understand the onrushing course of history.

There are no quick and easy ways for a nation or a people to win the friendship or admiration or respect of the people of other nations. This can only be done—when it can be done at all—over a long period of time, and it can be undone far more quickly. At the end of World War II, the United States had managed to win the friendship and respect of a large proportion of the world's people. This was a remarkable achievement, all the more so because it was generally not consciously pursued—for the most part it just happened, as does the development of friendship and respect between individuals. After the war, however, the international climate began to change. The respect and admiration for Americans around the world seemed to dissipate, despite the adoption by the United States of one of the most generous aid programs in man's history—the Marshall Plan. Although it was highly successful, the rest of the world, especially the newly emerging nations, were preoccupied with their own problems and did not pay much attention. Since then, when the United States has tried to apply the same techniques in efforts to solve problems facing underdeveloped countries, the program has not always met with the same success.

Point Four, as this technical-assistance program came to be known, is believed by many to have been unsuccessful. "I am convinced from my

own experience with the upper echelons of foreign-aid administrators,"
wrote Thomas Loeber in *Foreign Aid, Our Tragic Experiment,* published
in 1961, "that those who direct it no longer believe in it. They give every
indication of believing that it has failed." At the time the Peace Corps
was conceived, President Kennedy apparently agreed: "Existing foreign
aid programs and concepts," said Mr. Kennedy in a message to Congress
on the foreign-aid program (March 22, 1961), "are largely unsatis-
factory and unsuited for our needs and for the needs of the underdeveloped world as it enters the sixties."

Despite widespread reservations about foreign aid, however, no
better alternative has ever been suggested. As the President said in the
same message, "The economic collapse of those free but less-developed
nations which now stand poised between sustained growth and economic
chaos would be disastrous." The President also said that "There exists,
in the 1960s, an historic opportunity for a major economic assistance
effort by the free industrialized nations to move more than half the
people of the less-developed nations into self-sustained economic growth,
while the rest move substantially closer to the day when they, too, will
no longer have to depend on outside assistance." The Peace Corps is
one phase of the effort to revitalize our foreign-aid program. "The Peace
Corps is your *punta de lanza*—the point of your lance," was the way
Bolivia's Minister of National Economy put it to Sargent Shriver, describing the Peace Corps's relation to the Alliance for Progress.

Perhaps the most persistent complaint heard about the foreign-aid
program was that we were "winning the governments, but losing the
people." Although there is some question as to how well we have been
winning governments, until the Peace Corps came along there was little
debate about our success at losing the people. The hotly debated book
The Ugly American gave wider circulation to already growing doubts
about our aid efforts. As Thomas Loeber, who speaks Arabic and
Indonesian and since 1944 has traveled in twenty-seven countries, says:

> Let the self-styled "realists" [those who defend our aid program]
> get out into the rice fields, among the mud huts, the mosques, the
> pagodas, the tea plantations, and down the endless crooked streets of
> these lands. Let them go out and learn what the crowded masses there
> in the obscuring darkness of distant lands feel about America. . . .
> These are the men and women our diplomats never meet, who fre-
> quently are not represented by their own governments. Theirs are the
> voices we never hear until it is too late. They are often the ignorant
> and illiterate people of the world, but they know something we educated
> Americans apparently do not know. . . . They know that in the ultimate
> contest for men's hearts and emotions we are losing.

A major Peace Corps objective has been to send young, technically trained Americans out into these rice fields and down these crooked streets, where it is hoped they will once again reunite America and the aspirations of common men everywhere. The question is often asked: What purpose can be achieved by sending young, inexperienced college graduates out to underdeveloped areas? The answer is that the critical need in the underdeveloped countries today is *not* always for experienced technical advisers. These can be obtained through the United Nations, through ICA, or from several Western nations which send out skilled technicians to work in development programs. What is needed is "middle manpower"—young, trained men who are "assistants" in the real sense of the word. As Dr. Max Millikan stressed in his report to the President on an international youth service corps:

> Many of the underdeveloped countries engaged in active programs of modernizing their political, social, and economic life confront over the next two or three decades serious shortages of educated and trained people to carry out programs of education, improvement of health, reform of agriculture, promotion of industry, improvement of government administration, expansion of technical training, development of programs of social welfare and community development, and the like. Most of these countries are developing plans for the training of suitable numbers of their citizens to fulfill these functions, but because training and education are inherently slow processes with long lead times the flow of indigenous personnel will be grossly inadequate in the early years.

In many developing nations, through community development programs, progress has been made in the past decade toward gearing their societies to the requirements of economic and social development. The question that remains to be answered is whether the pace of development will be adequate to satisfy the peoples' aspirations, or whether they will be tempted by outside forces offering what appear to be quick and easy ways to social and economic improvement. "Since the gap between rich countries and the poor," writes C. P. Snow in *The Two Cultures and the Scientific Revolution,* "can be removed, it will be. If we are shortsighted, inept, incapable of either good will or enlightened self-interest, then it may be removed to the accompaniment of war and starvation; but removed it will be. The questions are, how, and by whom." The Peace Corps feels it can have some impact on how this gap is removed and who removes it.

Last but not least of the many objectives of the Peace Corps is that of broadening the understanding of a whole new generation of Americans —a generation soon to inherit the burdens of world leadership. From the thousands of returning Volunteers will come better teachers, broadened foreign service officers, more understanding government officials, more enlightened neighbors, and better citizens of any community in which they settle. To help us understand the world better and to help others understand us better are obvious objectives of the Peace Corps. Less obvious has been the Peace Corps's contribution to understanding ourselves. "We were in danger," says Sargent Shriver, "of losing our way among the television sets, the supermarkets, and the material abundance of a rich society. Our debt of gratitude to the developing and emerging nations of the world is that they have reminded us of our own traditions and given us a treasured opportunity to sacrifice and work once more for those principles which created our own nation. By letting us participate in their struggles, they have given us a chance to find ourselves." This was not one of the original Peace Corps objectives, but its significance cannot be overlooked.

Finally, there are certain things which the Peace Corps is *not* trying to achieve. As Sargent Shriver has said, the Peace Corps does not intend to send people abroad who think they are carrying the "white man's burden." The Peace Corps makes no effort to propagandize others.

It was suggested—for instance, by the late George Sokolsky in a "debate" with Shriver in the *Saturday Review*—that young Americans must first decide what it is they are trying to present abroad. "What we need to find," said Sokolsky, "is an ideal that will enrich life and make it possible for a person to look toward Washington as a Moslem does toward Mecca—as the place whence cometh peace and contentment and hope for the future."

Shriver disagreed, and his answer to Sokolsky provides an effective summing up of the Peace Corps's ultimate mission:

> Certainly it is not the purpose of the Peace Corps to unite Washington with Mecca, or Jerusalem, or Rome, or Geneva, or Canterbury, or Salt Lake City. Our purpose, in line with our national policy, is to help individual people succeed in their personal development, to help people everywhere strive toward human dignity and physical health and political self-government. Our purpose is peace—not salesmanship.
>
> If Peace Corps volunteers ever did seek to persuade other people to "look toward Washington as a Moslem does toward Mecca," they would be laughed out of any country I have ever visited. If they even secretly harbored this hope, it would corrupt their approach to their mission.
>
> Their mission is not to convert, but to communicate—and if they must communicate a spiritual idea, let it be with the object of getting all men everywhere to look up to "Heaven" rather than to Washington. For no matter whether a man be Jew, Buddhist, Moslem, Hindu, Communist or Christian, he has been born of woman like every other

man alive; he needs food, shelter, and spiritual comfort like every other
man alive. . . . The new generation . . . is beginning to realize that
whereas political nationalism and economic aggressiveness may divide
men, the most important of all experiences unite them—birth, marriage,
death, destiny.

6

HOW THE PEACE CORPS FUNCTIONS

The Peace Corps has built a bridge between the developed world and the underdeveloped world.

—MINISTER OF EDUCATION, Sierra Leone.

THE PEACE CORPS HEADQUARTERS is in the twelve-story Maiatico Building at the corner of Connecticut Avenue and H Street—a block north of the White House. The organization plan on the following page outlines its bureaucratic structure. Overseas, each country's operation is under the supervision of a Peace Corps Representative, who acts primarily as the liaison man between the Volunteers and the host government. He must also watch over the health of the Volunteers and keep in constant touch with the local American Embassy so that he is always aware of the diplomatic situation between the United States and the host country. He usually has one or more assistants, including a doctor, nurse, and numerous Volunteer leaders—Volunteers who act as team leaders in the field.

The first, and most important, thing to bear in mind about Peace Corps projects is the fact that no project is undertaken unless it is specifically requested by the host country. Such requests may come through the AID office in the host country, through universities or private agencies engaged in overseas-assistance programs, the American Embassy in the host country, or they may be made directly to a Peace Corps official by personal contact. The Peace Corps only has a limited number of Volunteers to place in relation to the number of requests for Volunteers, hence careful consideration must be given to every project requested. To guide its staff, the Peace Corps has worked up a detailed directive outlining the criteria governing the selection of a project. "It is to be emphasized," the directive says, "that each of these criteria should be considered in the light of promoting mutual understanding and friendship as well as of the job assignment to be done. In this connection, it should also be remembered that through the Peace Corps this country can gain as well as give. Peace Corps projects will have value for the long-term interests of the United States, its citizens, and its institutions through participation and through association."

Here are the criteria which govern the selection of a Peace Corps project:

1. *Need and Interest.* The project must make a contribution to the economic, social, cultural, or political development of the host country, and the government of that country must have requested the project.

2. *Relationship to United States Foreign Policy.* The project must not be inconsistent with United States foreign policy. However, in order to make the maximum contribution to the foreign policy effort, the project should maintain the unique role and separate identity of the Peace Corps.

3. *Type of Work.* The project must require primarily "workers" or "doers," as distinct from advisers or consultants, with skills not sufficiently available in the host country.

4. *Personnel Policies.* The project must provide for the maintenance, supervision, and remuneration of Volunteers in accordance with applicable Peace Corps Volunteer personnel policies.

5. *Health and Medical Care.* The project must provide living and working conditions which will contribute to the maintenance of health; assignment locations must permit accessibility to medical care facilities throughout the year.

In addition, a number of more flexible criteria exist as guides in program development and in determining relative priorities for choosing among competing project proposals. They should not be viewed as absolute requirements.

6. *Cohesiveness.* The Peace Corps should avoid projects which utilize a few Volunteers in each of a number of unrelated activities. A project should consist of a minimum of ten Volunteers working toward a single, central, and well-defined objective, though diverse skills may be required to carry out the project. Unity and cohesiveness may be achieved in terms of homogeneity of Volunteer jobs, singleness of goal, or unity of geographical location, such as the use of various related skills toward various ends in a single community. Project cohesiveness is important in terms of the economy and efficiency of recruitment, selection, training, and administration.

7. *Impact.* Peace Corps projects should have a visible and definable impact upon the development of the host country or upon an activity being undertaken to foster that development. Such a criterion contributes

to the demonstrable effectiveness of the Peace Corps and to increasing a country's initiative toward self-help and toward training its own citizens in the jobs performed by Volunteers.

8. *Magnitude.*   For economy of training and administration, initial country programs should consist of a minimum of thirty to forty Volunteers although they may be working in two or more projects.

9. *Skill Requirements and Flexibility.*   Projects should not require particularly highly skilled or specialized Volunteers. In addition, flexibility in the number of Volunteers who can be effectively utilized in each general category should be encouraged. In formulating and negotiating programs, minimum and maximum requirements should be obtained whenever possible.

10. *Host-Country Contributions and Participation.*   The Peace Corps should undertake projects which involve maximum contact between the Volunteers and the people and society of the country served. Thus, contributions by the host-country government and institutions to the project should be encouraged, and host-country nations should participate in the work and/or be trained to take over eventually the jobs of the Peace Corps Volunteers.

11. *Self-Help.*   Peace Corps programs should be undertaken in countries in which the needs for social and economic development are recognized and where the country is demonstrating those efforts which its own development requires. In addition, the Peace Corps should serve in dependent areas only if the projects requested by the government have the support of the indigenous leadership.

12. *Effect on Local Employment.*   The use of Peace Corps Volunteers should not result in the loss of employment or employment opportunities for host-country nationals.

13. *Feasibility.*   Selection of projects should take into consideration the Volunteer skills most likely to be available and operational feasibility in terms of adequate working, living, and health conditions for Volunteers.

14. *Capital Contributions.*   Projects should not involve costs to the Peace Corps for items needed in specific job assignments (i.e., tools, equipment, and other materials, but not logistic support items) of more than $1,000 per Volunteer.

15. *Type of Administration.*   The policy of the Peace Corps is to give preference to the administration of projects by private agencies and universities. In cases in which a suitable and qualified university, voluntary agency, or other institution is interested, available, and acceptable to the host-country, projects should be undertaken in cooperation with such private institutions.

As indicated by the above paragraph, the Peace Corps not only encourages the development of projects in cooperation with private organizations, but recommends that preference be given to such projects. Organizations such as the 4-H Clubs, the National Grange, and Heifer Project, Inc., have joined with the Peace Corps in administering projects, and on a practical administrative level the partnerships have, for the most part, been mutually beneficial. The Peace Corps has found that it has learned much from working with such organizations, many of which had been sending volunteers overseas for years before the Peace Corps was created. At the same time, the Peace Corps has helped to stimulate the private organizations. For example, Heifer Project, which was established to furnish livestock and poultry to upgrade and enlarge herds and flocks overseas, has been able to expand its program greatly through joint projects involving Peace Corps agricultural workers. The National Grange never had an overseas program until it joined forces with the Peace Corps. Now the Grange is extremely active in the development of overseas projects.

Some agencies have established Peace Corps desks at their own expense to provide information about the Peace Corps to their membership and to represent their membership in dealing with the Peace Corps. Notable among these are the Catholic Relief Services, the National Council of Churches, and the National Education Association. Material support of many kinds has also been directed to the field through private organizations. CARE, for example, has contributed more than $200,000 worth of equipment to projects developed in cooperation with the Peace Corps, and Heifer Project has made available more than $100,000 worth of livestock.

At first there was some confusion and controversy over the working relationship between the Peace Corps and private agencies, especially those of religious sponsorship. On the one hand, a Catholic bishop charged that the Peace Corps had demonstrated an aloof and hostile attitude toward religious and private organizations; at the same time, a Protestant denomination and the American Jewish Congress protested to the Peace Corps against the signing of contracts with any religious groups at all.

The Peace Corps has stated repeatedly that a project which meets Peace Corps criteria will *not* be barred from receiving support providing that it does not further any religious, sectarian, or commercial cause, or release funds for such proposals. Sargent Shriver stated flatly at Senate hearings in 1961 that "the Peace Corps is not going to provide funds to enable religious organizations to organize groups or to conduct church services or to proselytize or recruit persons for religious services or preach on behalf of religious institutions."

Shriver also said that the Peace Corps would *not* support a group which confined its recruitment to a specific religion. The Peace Corps insists on what it calls "open recruitment" and that question has come up not only in regard to religious groups but also with regard to some projects developed in cooperation with universities. "We say," Shriver testified, "that every American has a right to participate in a Peace Corps program, provided he has got the qualifications, and that religious qualifications, or having gone to a specific university, are not relevant to the selection."

The question was also raised as to whether the use by religious organizations of Peace Corps funds was not a violation of the constitutional requirement on the separation of church and state. Justice Department lawyers ruled there would be no violation of the Constitution in the Peace Corps's developing an overseas project in cooperation with a religious organization. The final decision, in the view of the Peace Corps, is up to the churches: Do they want to work with the Peace Corps under the Peace Corps's ground rules? "There are some of these religious groups," Shriver once said, "that come in here and say, 'We don't want to have anything to do with the Peace Corps unless we can select our own people and they are all of our own religion.' Well, that's just too bad. This is the taxpayers' money and they have got to be protected."

Participation by private voluntary agencies may take several forms. For instance, the agency may take the initiative in requesting the assignment of Volunteers to any of its existing projects. An agency with extensive experience may also develop new projects and submit requests for Peace Corps Volunteers to help man them. Or the Peace Corps may wish to use the services of private agencies to implement certain phases —recruitment, selection, training, field operation and administration, evaluation, or research—of Peace Corps-originated projects. In such cases, the Peace Corps approaches selected organizations interested in and capable of providing these services.

Listed below are the private and international organizations which thus far have joined with the Peace Corps in administering overseas projects:

Agri Research
Credit Union National Association
Korean International Corporation
American Association for Physical Health, Education, and Recreation
Development and Resources Corporation

Co-operative League of the United States of America
CARE, Incorporated
Laubach Literacy Fund
CUNA International
Food Agriculture Organization of the United Nations
Experiment in International Living
Future Farmers of America and New Farmers of America
Heifer Project
YWCA
YMCA
National 4-H Foundation
National Farmer's Union
National Grange
Near East Foundation
American Institute of Architecture
International Voluntary Services
Leo Daly and Sons
Agricultural Technical Assistance Foundation
United Auto Workers
Westinghouse Corporation

For the most part, the nation's universities and colleges have been extremely cooperative in working with the Peace Corps. All universities have cooperated in recruiting Volunteers, and faculty members at many universities have assisted the Peace Corps, often without compensation, in a variety of ways. Dozens of universities have administered training programs for the Peace Corps, which will be discussed further in Chapter 11. Finally, several universities have taken over the actual development and administration of projects in Asia, Africa, and Latin America.

The Peace Corps is a semiautonomous agency of the Department of State, with a status similar to AID's. In practice, the relationship works in the following way: The Peace Corps obtains the approval of the Under Secretary for Economic Affairs and the clearance of the interested regional bureau in the Department of State and AID before any new project is authorized, and again before it is finally approved. In addition, the Peace Corps staff endeavors to maintain the closest possible contact with interested offices of the State Department and AID, as well as with interested offices in the USIA.

The operation of a Peace Corps project overseas is subject to coordination and supervision by the chief of the United States diplomatic mission in each country or area. The general policy is to utilize wherever feasible the services and facilities of existing embassies, although in some cases, because of the size and complexity of a project or for political reasons, it is necessary, with the approval of the Secretary of State, to station a Peace Corps mission abroad.

Peace Corps Representatives abroad are in direct charge of the Peace Corps program and exercise such authority as is agreeable to the host country. Peace Corps Representatives are subject to the general direction of the United States Ambassador in the host country. Where a Peace Corps Representative is not present, the chief of the United States diplomatic mission in the area, in consultation with the Peace Corps headquarters in Washington, acts for the Peace Corps.

7

WHAT THE PEACE CORPS DOES

There is nothing complicated about what the Peace Corps is trying to accomplish. The Volunteer is a catalyst for self-help projects that will produce something of value that was not there before he arrived. It is that simple.

—SARGENT SHRIVER,
National Geographic
September, 1964.

THE QUESTION perhaps most often asked about tne Peace Corps is, "Just what does it do?" Because of misinformation about the Peace Corps circulated in the early days before specific projects were developed, many people had the idea that the Peace Corps was going to send young people abroad to dig ditches in Africa and Asia or plow fields in Latin America. This, however, is *not* the kind of program the United States would underwrite, for the simple reason that unskilled labor is one thing that most of the underdeveloped countries do not need; they have it in abundance. There is, however, a staggering need for young, *skilled* Volunteers in the underdeveloped nations of the world. In the words of the Millikan report, "Many of the underdeveloped countries engaged in active programs of modernizing their political, social and economic life confront over the next two or three decades serious shortages of educated and trained people to carry out the programs of education, improvement of health, reform of agriculture, promotion of industry, improvements of government administration, expansion of technical training, development of programs of social welfare and community development, and the like."

The question often arises as to just what Peaçe Corps Volunteers do that is different from work that was already being done. Essentially, the main difference between a Peace Corps Volunteer and a technician is that the Peace Corpsman is a doer, rather than an adviser. He works side by side with the people he is helping rather than advise local officials responsible for getting the job done. Many educated and trained young people in underdeveloped countries have not wanted to work on the village level. As a result, there are often two extremes among workers in these areas: trained technicians on the one hand and unskilled laborers on the other—with no one in between capable of taking knowledge from the technicians to the people. This is the area in which the Peace Corps is making the biggest contribution, by going out among the people and helping them to learn by actually working on projects with them.

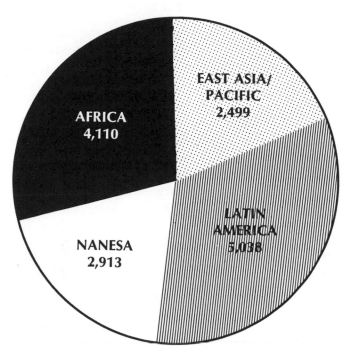

WHERE THEY ARE is depicted in pie chart above which includes Volunteers overseas and trainees preparing for specific regional programs. Latin America and Africa have historically had largest concentrations of Peace Corps Volunteers.

This concept of the doer, as opposed to the adviser or teacher, is the distinguishing feature of the Peace Corps. In the case of teaching, for instance, whereas Point Four technical advisers are sent out to teach others who, in turn, teach on the local level, for the most part the Peace Corps Volunteers actually do the teaching. In most cases, technical advisers cannot provide the same kind of service as the Peace Corps because advisers' responsibilities are usually national or regional and their assignments are to give advice and demonstrations, not to teach. The Peace Corps Volunteer works at the local level, translating advice into action and achievement. The Peace Corpsman, however, also is a technician himself rather than an unskilled laborer. In other words, he stands halfway between the technician and the main body of laborers; he is a "technician helper," middle-level manpower.

Today Peace Corps Volunteers are engaged primarily in four kinds of work: community development, education, agricultural extension, and public health.

COMMUNITY DEVELOPMENT

The term community development is relatively new, but although modern techniques are thought to have begun with Gandhi, the process has taken place since ancient times. However, as the term is used today, it is based fundamentally on the recognition of the community as an organic whole.

"Of course," as Dr. Richard W. Poston says in a study on community development problems in Colombia, "the concept and structure of the community has not always been the same. It has ranged from the tribal entity to the ancient city-state to the subsidiary unit of kingdoms and administrative units of empires, to the early medieval commune and the sometimes nearly forgotten village of the modern nation-state. These different types of communities were substantially different organisms. But what we think of as community is ideally demonstrable and traceable through the democratic city-state of ancient Greece, the communal life of the early church to the self-sufficient settlements of the New World. In modern times the community, as an instrument of producing collective well-being among groups of people, has been deeply overshadowed by the nation-state. But with the emergence of a new concept of community development it is evident that older ideals of civic health have not faded.

"Indeed, many a centralized modern nation-state, with insecurity at its local levels of power, has failed in its basic job of assisting the development of local life. Modern community development, in effect, is an evolution of simple basic techniques to fill that void."

Community development is based on the simple idea that the best way to improve the conditions of life in any environment is to devise a program that the people themselves can carry forward by their own efforts, after participating with others in its initiation. Despite the simplicity of its objectives, community development work is of the utmost importance. But it is not always easy to organize. "Plainly this kind of work," writes Andrew Shonfield in *The Attack on World Poverty,* "by its very nature, involves an element of quasi-revolutionary activity in the village, since its overriding aim is to force the pace by bringing in untraditional and more productive methods of agriculture—and that in turn almost inevitably involves social change, disrupting first of all the old patterns of behaviour and respect towards the landlord, the trader, the money lender. . . . The idea is, after all, to find a voluntary answer to the problems which the communists solved by forced collectivization of farms, backed up in China by further military regimentation of the peasants. There could hardly be anything more ambitious than the attempt to set up a free working alternative to the juggernaut."

The Peace Corps views community development as simply "teaching Democracy on a community level." How does a Peace Corps Volunteer abroad teach democracy on a community level? The Peace Corps says no one method is foolproof but experience has provided solid guidelines:

"First, the Volunteer is a stranger," a special Peace Corps brochure on community development says. "He must get to know the people— gain their confidence. He must seek out the local leaders, learn the needs of the community. This may (and often does) take months. Different routes are used in getting to know the people: some Volunteers just talk and visit. Most Volunteers, though, find that they are more effective if they become active in community affairs. For instance, playing a trumpet in the town band, organizing a 4-H club, teaching English classes, starting a baseball team.

"Patience, initiative and ingenuity are key qualities a Volunteer must develop. Patience because the work is slow and often frustrating. Initiative and ingenuity because he has only a few months to gain the confidence of the community, lead the citizens into an awareness of their needs, and guide them toward a solution.

"The second phase of the community development worker's job begins after he has acquired the confidence of the community. It is then time to organize a community meeting and talk about what needs to be done. At this stage, the villagers must decide for themselves if and how they are going to deal with their community's problems.

"The Volunteer can only offer encouragement, not give orders. During the first meeting, the lack of democratic training is demonstrated. Everyone talks at once, speakers are kidded, pestered, and hooted. People walk in and out of the meeting at will. No one listens. In short —bedlam.

"Very seldom is anything tangible accomplished at the first community development meeting. Volunteers compare it to the first day of school: it's mostly noise. The first meeting will meet its objective if it arouses the people to want to meet again.

"There will be subsequent meetings. Many will be fruitless. But some won't be. Gradually the Volunteer will lead the people into discovering their problems and finding solutions.

"A Volunteer in community development remembers that one day he will no longer be there and the community will have to find the answers to their own problems. His job is to teach them how this can be done. Included in this is helping the community to petition their local government for needed materials.

"Once the problem is defined, and the community has agreed on what needs to be done, community development enters into its third and final stage. This is the doing stage.

"Like an iceberg, most of community development lies beneath the surface. Only the last stage shows. It is here that the schoolhouse is built, a chicken cooperative formed, a cleanup program initiated, a road cleared.

"During the doing stage, the Volunteer acts as a general supervisor at times, and often as a common laborer. At all times he acts as a member of the community. His purpose, in working or supervising, is the same: to develop local leaders. The Volunteer can see things getting done at last in this stage. The progress is reflected in visible improvements."

If successful, the community development program achieves three objectives:

(1) Basic education of the people in working together to define their own goals and solving the problems necessary to achieve these goals.

(2) Getting the government to respond to community needs.

(3) Material improvement in terms of specific technological advancement and economic growth.

EDUCATION

Today, more than half the Peace Corps Volunteers sent abroad are teachers. In fact, one of President Kennedy's early advisers thought that the Peace Corps should be devoted entirely to teaching. Despite the increasing importance of community development, Harris Wofford, Associate Director of the Peace Corps, still considers teaching as the Peace Corps's most important function. It is estimated that the more than 4,000 teachers in the field teach not less than 800,000 students during their two years overseas. In Thailand, Peace Corps Volunteers are instructing 90 percent of all Thai students and 70 percent of the secondary students.

In British Honduras in a schoolroom that once served as a grand dining room, there hangs a sign which reads: *Upon the education of its people the fate of this country depends.* This is true in every developing nation, and today the need for school teachers is easily the greatest need of the developing nations. For instance:

• Only 14,000 Nigerian students attend elementary school, although more than 2 million are eligible.

• Of all Ecuadorian children who enter school, only 13 percent go beyond the primary level.

• The teacher shortage is so desperate in Sierra Leone that apprentice teachers often start instructing when they are only fourteen years old. These teachers have only finished the eighth grade themselves.

Peace Corps Volunteers are teaching in more than forty countries— in nursery, elementary, junior and senior high schools, even in colleges and universities. The desperate need for teachers abroad is indicated by the fact that every country that has played host to Peace Corps teachers has doubled or tripled its original request. The developing nations also need roads, improved farm techniques, and better sanitation, but as Carol Byrnes, a Peace Corps teacher in the Philippines says, "The important thing we are doing here is not something that can be measured with a camera. People in other projects can photograph a bridge they've designed, a road they've helped build or a latrine they have constructed. But who can photograph the mind of a child?"

The shortage of supplies and equipment soon tests a Peace Corps teacher's ability to improvise. Using ingenuity and materials at hand to fashion teaching aids, Volunteers have sent villagers scouting for native fauna to furnish menageries for teaching biology; taught English using airline posters as a visual text; persuaded churches, civic groups, and friends back home to donate thousands of books for understocked school libraries; constructed blackboards from Masonite and black paint.

Teaching duties abroad can easily turn into sixteen-hour-a-day assignments. In their spare time, various Volunteers have participated in extracurricular projects such as leveling the cricket field and building fences to keep out wandering goats and donkeys; organizing a marching band and securing donations of the necessary musical instruments; organizing and aiding students in the construction of a kitchen and dining room for the school; collecting native art and relics to furnish a museum; initiating and teaching classes in swimming, lifesaving, all sorts of sports.

Summer vacations are not wasted, either. In some countries school vacation periods can total as much as four months during the year. Volunteers have organized complex cooperative projects involving other Volunteers, local people, and numerous host country agencies during these vacation periods. At first the host countries had been counting on Volunteers only as teachers. Now, many host country agencies plan extensive vacation projects making use of the energy and organizational talents of the Volunteers. Such projects include census-taking, inoculation campaigns, summer workshops in education and language, and community action projects. Many summer projects have grown into year-round activities.

For example, seven Peace Corps teachers stationed in Dessie, Ethiopia, planning a summer project, learned that the Selassie Leprosarium in Dessie needed a school for its 300 patients. A local teacher, a local maintenance crew, and some twenty patients were enlisted. In a month and a half they had built a school structure, tin over a eucalyptus frame, consisting of five standard-size classrooms and a half-size classroom. Only the doors and windows remained to be installed and this the Volunteers did in a month by working after regular school hours. The Selassie Leprosarium now has a school for 150 students.

In Nigeria eight Volunteers and three Nigerian teachers from the Technical College in Ibadan ran a highly successful three-week camp for 65 fifth-graders on a borrowed school compound in Ibadan. They enlisted a local woman's organization as cosponsor and organized an advisory committee of neighborhood parents and community leaders. At the request of the Ministry of Community Development, the Volunteers wrote a thirty-three-page manual on the organization and operation of a day camp, and then decided to build a resident vacation camp where teachers and community leaders would be taught day camp administration.

As Mike Edwards, a former Peace Corps information officer, has pointed out, the Peace Corps, in a sense, is all teachers. "All of its Volunteers," says Edwards, "—the engineers, the nurses, the social workers, the agricultural extensionists, the machinery mechanics, the community developers, the nutritionists—are both doers in that they furnish manpower, and teachers in that they show how."

Most of the Peace Corps teachers are in their mid-twenties, although a great many senior citizens are now included in the ranks. The Peace Corps has often been accused of "raiding" the stable of much-needed American teachers, but the Peace Corps says that only a fourth of the Volunteers who teach abroad were teaching at home. Most begin work with a bachelor's degree, a Peace Corps training course, and a desire to do this kind of work.

AGRICULTURAL EXTENSION

In a world of rapid progress in science and technology, a centuries-old problem still plagues millions of people around the world: How to get enough to eat. One-half of the world's population is undernourished or malnourished. Peace Corps Volunteers are helping provide solutions to the problem by applying American agricultural knowledge and experience to farming practices in Africa, Asia, and Latin America. More than 80 percent of all Volunteers now overseas, regardless of their job specialties, are assigned to small villages or rural areas. Ten percent of the total number is working specifically in agriculture.

These agricultural Volunteers range in experience from the high-school graduates who grew up on a farm to soil scientists with doctor's degrees. They are working in soil conservation, land reclamation, animal husbandry, irrigation, forestry—all the skills that have boosted America's agricultural production to unrivaled heights. Projects now underway or planned call particularly for persons trained in agronomy, horticulture (vegetables and fruits), animal and dairy husbandry, poultry, vocational agriculture (teaching), agricultural engineering, foresters, forest technicians, forest rangers, irrigation, soil conservation, and home economists.

In some agricultural projects, Volunteers teach modern farm management to farmers who have already abandoned traditional patterns and are well on their way into the twentieth century. In the Cochabamba Valley of Bolivia, for instance, Volunteers work with the government milk plant to improve the health and production of the nation's only dairy herds. The Volunteers use modern methods of testing and inoculation and promote the acceptance of the latest dairy management techniques from forage raising to milking. Besides this work, which affects almost the entire commercial milk supply in the country, the Volunteers have organized 4-H type clubs among the farmers' children to plant the seed for further improvement in farm life in the valley.

Agricultural extension Volunteers have also been able to bring improvements to farming in areas untouched by modern methods. Indians in the highlands of Guatemala, on small pieces of poor land, are now raising broiler chickens with good results under the direction of agriculture extension Volunteers. On land where only corn has been raised for centuries, the same Volunteers are running experiments in wheat raising. They have also promoted development of family gardens, and the first use of fertilizer by seventy farmers.

In Niger, two Volunteers participated in the founding of a new kind of agricultural training institution, guided and financed by USAID. The Volunteers and forty students started a Young Farmers Training Center on a site of undeveloped bush. They cleared land, dug wells, built buildings, and planted and harvested crops in a single year. The successful results led to the planning of a second school and several more to come in the future.

Throughout the world, Peace Corps Volunteers are encouraging farmers to experiment with new crops, new methods of farming and of marketing. As in other areas of development, the key to success lies in triggering an organized and widespread effort with prospects of joining other streams of progress in the nation.

The broad field of cooperatives has proved to be a fertile area for Peace Corps Volunteers seeking ways to promote economic development. These undertakings are particularly appropriate because they tend to proliferate and because they serve as schools of practical democracy. Perhaps the most successful Volunteer efforts have been directed toward organizing small farmers into growing, marketing, and purchasing units. Some examples:

• Peace Corps Volunteers in Chile formed a vegetable-growing and -marketing cooperative which not only provided the farmers with greatly increased cash income, but introduced them to certified seeds, chemical fertilizers, weed killers, and pest control sprays.

• Villagers in Brazil now market pottery that was formerly produced only for local use. A Volunteer helped them improve their kilns, showed them the use of glazes, and helped to organize the marketing co-op.

• In the Dominican Republic, chicken is becoming a more attainable luxury food, thanks to poultry producers' cooperatives employing modern chicken-raising methods taught by Volunteers. The efforts of a single Volunteer and his young farmers clubs have also made chickens a common item in the diet of many families in St. Lucia.

However, chicken raising can be a problem, as one Volunteer, reporting from Africa, reveals: "It doesn't do any good to tell these people that they have to pen their chickens and feed them something better than they can get by scratching for themselves," he wrote home. "Their chickens have been running loose since the dawn of history. I didn't try to tell them anything; I just went ahead and started raising chickens my own way. But now I have a new problem—they won't believe my chickens and theirs are the same species. They want me to sell them some of my fat kind."

GROWTH OF AND CHANGE IN THE PEACE CORPS, 1962–1967

Continued growth marked the sixth year of the Peace Corps. By June 30, 1967 there were 11,912 Volunteers overseas in 50 nations, and another 3,056 in training (408 of whom were not yet assigned to specific regions) — a total of 14,968 men and women.

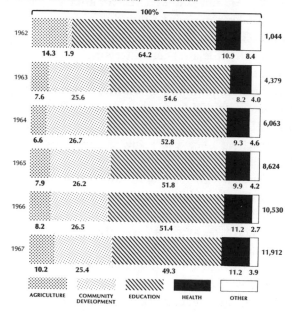

WHAT THEY'RE DOING by job assignment is charted above Education still occupies nearly half of all Volunteers, but major buildup continues in agriculture and public health projects.

PUBLIC HEALTH

In many areas of the world, the will to undertake the struggle for self-improvement is frequently sapped by sheer physical debility. In much of Africa there is one physician for nearly 80,000 people. In some Asian countries there are fewer nurses than in just one of our large hospitals. In parts of South America, 300 children out of every 1,000 born alive die in their first year. In most of the world there is a colossal waste of humanity—millions of lives are lost to diseases we consider conquered. Public health campaigns are desperately needed to salvage vast reservoirs of energy needed for development.

Over 1,000 Volunteers are assigned to Peace Corps public health groups. They include Volunteer doctors, nurses, nursing teachers, medical technicians, and sanitation specialists. One such specialized project is a medical team in Togo, originally requested to staff a provincial hospital. The Volunteers extended the project to a preventive health

program for the northern region of the country, and today they staff
the hospital and run fifteen satellite clinics established under the program.
In Malawi, Peace Corps Volunteers tested 16,000 villagers for tuberculosis. Nearly 400 were found to be infected; after six months all but one
of the 400 were taking medicine regularly.

Sooner or later, nearly all Volunteers overseas become involved in
health work, whether it is a matter of treating a snakebite or explaining
the hazards of drinking contaminated water to a class. Volunteer school
teachers often institute programs of medical examinations, inoculations,
and health training for their students.

In Gbarnga, Liberia, for example, Volunteers Dave and Carol Smith,
in addition to teaching a heavy schedule of secondary school classes, are
conducting a full-scale health study among their 160 students. Dave,
who teaches science, does stool, blood, and urine analysis on a systematic
basis for all the students, while Carol keeps charts on what the students
have eaten at meals each day, along with records of their illnesses. Carol,
in addition, conducts a nutrition and hygiene course. Together the
Smiths enlisted the help of the school nurse, a local public health nurse,
the school principal, and an AID doctor in setting up a coordinated
program to cut down the incidence of roundworm and schistosomiasis
which widely afflict the students. Dave persuaded Firestone officials in
Liberia to donate medicines, vaccines, malaria suppressants, and iron
and mineral tablets, and the Smiths then spent part of their summer
vacation in 1963 writing a comprehensive report on their study. He
spent the other half of his summer vacation breaking in a Liberian
apprentice in X-ray technique at the Gbarnga hospital.

Community action projects in the Peace Corps are often designed
to meet certain basic health considerations: pure water supplies, latrine
building campaigns, and village medical dispensaries.

The Peace Corps training program for all Volunteer groups now
includes, along with instructions for maintaining personal health, an
introduction to public health so that all Volunteers are better prepared
to teach health and sanitation wherever they work.

Although most Peace Corps projects fall into one of the four main
categories above, projects are by no means limited to these fields. There
are, for instance, specific projects devoted to physical education, geology,
engineering, construction, business administration, law, library work,
home economics, to mention some of the more specialized assignments.
In fact, the only way to really comprehend the breadth of Peace Corps
tasks abroad is to study the various projects. The following chapter
aims at giving just such a survey.

8

THE PEACE CORPS AROUND THE WORLD

These young men and women are true ambassadors—with their youth and vigor, their friendliness and kindness, their sense of mission, their conception of service to the community, their dedication to the work in hand, their feeling for justice and their tolerance—they embody characteristics to which your nation, Mr. President, owes much of its greatness.

—PRIME MINISTER BANDA of Malawi,
to President Kennedy.

BRIEFLY OUTLINED in the following pages are descriptions of all the Peace Corps projects which are either in existence or being planned for the next two years. The listing is broken down by area—Africa, Latin America, etc.—and according to the nature of the project—education, community development, etc. The projects described here not only offer an excellent thumb-nail account of what the Peace Corps is doing around the world, but also serve as an excellent guide to projects which will be available to Volunteers during the next two years. The Peace Corps is, in a sense, an international employment agency. Its clients are foreign governments who have requested volunteers with specific skills and backgrounds and this section serves as a guide to the "jobs" available to would-be volunteers. If you are interested in serving in a particular country or on a particular continent, you can go through the following pages, pick out your country, then find a project for which you consider yourself qualified. When you submit your application, indicate that you are interested in that project—i.e., Nigeria 112, or Brazil 302, etc.

These projects are, of course, subject to change—they can be dropped or altered and new ones can be added. But they offer the best information available, as this book goes to press, on what the Peace Corps is doing around the world and what opportunities are available to you if you are considering applying for the Peace Corps.

78

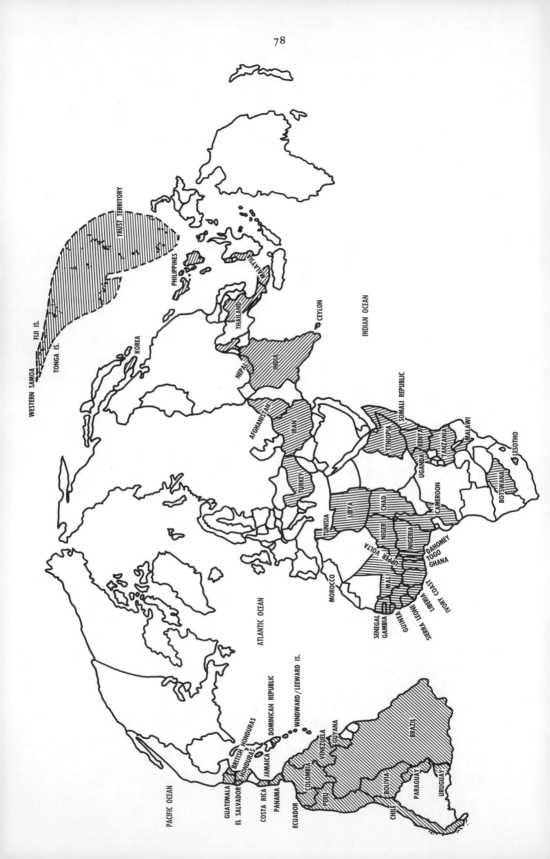

Even a hasty scanning of the following pages shows why former President Alberto Lleras Camargo of Colombia said of the first Peace Corps project in his country: "We can think of no finer way in which the United States could prove to the humble people of this and other lands that the primary purpose of its international aid program is to build a better life in all of the free world's villages and neighborhoods."

AFRICA

EDUCATION

101. BOTSWANA The former Bechuanaland first asked for Volunteers in 1966. They are now engaged in teacher training and secondary and upper primary education, as well as in local community development affairs. *Training projects are scheduled for spring 1968 and for 1969.* BA degree required. Language aptitude essential for learning Tswana.

102. CAMEROON Volunteers have been requested to serve as secondary teachers in the English-speaking and French-speaking areas of Cameroon. They will teach English as a foreign language, history, geography, math and science. Volunteers will be encouraged to prepare the students to pass the European examinations which determine academic advancement in Cameroon as well as to relate the materials studied as much as possible to African problems. Volunteers will be housed either in villages situated near the secondary school of assignment, or on the school compounds, where they will be isolated from rural Africa, and will have to make that much greater an attempt to relate the intellectual content of their teaching to the Africa that their students know and to which the vast majority of their students will return. The Volunteer teachers will be expected to put an enormous amount of effort into extracurricular efforts—sports, drama, sewing, cooking, art, music, activity clubs, school newspapers, school gardens, chicken-raising projects—and to involve the students in recognizing and helping to meet the needs of their nearby communities.

103. CHAD and GABON The Ministers of Education have requested Volunteers to teach English as a foreign language in rural secondary schools of Chad and Gabon. Volunteers will be expected to approach their teaching assignment with the goal of orienting the students' interests to the African scene, and of involving the student in identifying and helping to meet the needs of the local community. The Volunteers will be living in villages or towns near their schools of assignment.

104. ETHIOPIA Peace Corps Volunteers are teaching in secondary schools in more than 70 towns and villages in Ethiopia. Instruction is given in all the academic subjects plus vocational arts, commercial arts, educational television, music, art, and home economics. Although instruction is in English, Volunteers study Amharic, the first official language of the Empire. In addition to regular classroom responsibilities, Volunteers participate in various extracurricular and community activities. During the summer vacation period, Volunteer teachers are required to work for five-six weeks on a project of some social and/or economic benefit to the community. Volunteer teachers also serve on the faculty of the Haile Selassie I University teaching English and business administration, and on the faculties of the Teacher Training Institutes, preparing Ethiopian elementary school teachers.

105. GHANA In an educational system closely modeled after the British, Volunteers will teach English, geography, science and mathematics at the secondary level. Volunteers will teach about 25 hours a week and participate in other school and community activities. Although the official language in Ghana is English, Volunteers will learn in training to speak Twi, one of Ghana's major tongues.

106. KENYA Liberal arts graduates in math, science, English, geography and history are needed to teach in Kenya's British-patterned secondary school system. Volunteers, who will receive training in Swahili, may also be asked to teach subjects outside their major fields and to participate in adult education and community development programs.

107. LIBERIA Volunteers will teach in Liberia's elementary school system and participate in adult education and community development programs.

108. LIBERIA Bolstering Liberia's system of education, Volunteers will teach math, science, industrial arts, English, business education, French, shop, agriculture, physical education, music and art at the secondary level, and political science and history at the university level. Volunteers will teach about 25 hours a week and engage in outside activities such as adult education and community development.

109. LESOTHO The newly independent Kingdom—formerly the British High Commission Territory of Basutoland—has asked the Peace Corps to help staff its junior and senior secondary schools and teacher training colleges and aid its upgrading program for primary teachers. Volunteers will teach mathematics, science, English and social studies, and will participate in the full range of extracurricular and community activities. The language of instruction in Lesotho is English but Volunteers will learn to speak Sesotho, the language of the Basotho people.

110. MALAWI Teachers of English, history, math and science are needed to teach in the secondary schools, which follow a basic British syllabus. A few Volunteers teach in the teacher training colleges for primary school teachers, demonstrating improved teaching techniques and how to better relate course content to Malawian conditions, and helping to assimilate problem-solving attitudes and techniques into the primary school system. *This program usually trains each year in the fall.*

111. NIGER The Ministry of Education has requested Volunteers to work with its expanding adult literacy and education programs. Serving as regional agents with Nigerian counterparts, Volunteers will advise local literacy instructors, demonstrate teaching methods, inspect literacy centers, produce vernacular newspapers, provide logistical support to literacy instructors and encourage villages to start literacy programs. A Volunteer artist will develop visual teaching aids.

Nurses in the public health program will teach at the nursing school in the capital city of Naimey. Volunteers assigned to social centers and rural dispensaries will work in public health education, social work, home improvement and prenatal and baby care.

112. NIGERIA Teaching full time in teacher training colleges and demonstration primary schools or working on a tutorial basis with teachers already in service, Volunteers will help to improve the caliber of primary school instruction by uplifting the qualifications of the primary teachers. Volunteers will teach English as a second language, general science, teacher methodology, history and geography. Volunteers will live in villages, so involvement in local activities will be a natural and necessary part of the job. Training will be given in three Nigerian vernaculars—Igbo, Hausa and Efik. A bachelor's degree is required. *Fall 1968 and 1969 training.*

113. NIGERIA Volunteers will teach math, chemistry, biology, physics, general science, geography, history, physical education and English in new or understaffed secondary schools. Extracurricular activities in schools and surrounding communities, according to Volunteer skills and interests, will be considered part of the job. Instruction in the main Nigerian vernacular languages—Igbo, Hausa, Yoruba, Efik and Bini —will enable Volunteers to participate more fully in the life of their students and their communities. A bachelor's degree is required. *Training begins summer 1968 and 1969.*

114. SENEGAL Volunteers teach English in secondary schools in Senegal, with an eye to instituting modern aural-oral methods of language instruction.

115. SIERRA LEONE Volunteers will be assigned to secondary chools throughout this former British territory which relies heavily on the Peace Corps for qualified teachers. Volunteers will be expected to extend themselves beyond the classroom into literacy classes, libraries, school vegetable gardens and other community and agricultural activities according to the interest and skills of the Volunteer. A degree in the subject to be taught is required.

Elementary schools throughout the country also need teachers to cover a broad curriculum. Volunteers usually will be assigned to upper primary grades where instruction is in English. However, Volunteers will be trained in one of the two major indigenous languages. Elementary teachers will be expected to pursue the same activities beyond the classroom as secondary teachers.

116. SOMALIA Volunteers will teach basic math, science and English mainly in elementary schools in the southern region where English is increasingly being used as the medium of instruction. A few Volunteers are teaching these same subjects in secondary schools in the northern region. All Volunteers are involved in additional activities such as preparation of teaching aids, sports instruction, scouting and teaching of child care. *Training is usually each spring.*

117. TANZANIA Liberal arts and math/science graduates are needed to fill teaching positions in Tanzania's secondary school system. Because most are boarding schools, Volunteers will live on the school grounds and take an active role in school and community. *Beginning with training in fall 1968,* Volunteers will receive instruction in Swahili.

118. TANZANIA In an effort to interest young Tanzanians in and prepare them for careers requiring commercial skills, Volunteers will teach these and related subjects (such as typing and bookkeeping) at secondary schools, educational extension centers, technical schools and at the teacher training colleges in Dar-es-Salaam.

119. UGANDA Volunteers are to teach English, history, math and science in secondary schools using a British-oriented syllabus. Volunteers, who will receive training in the Luganda language, may also be asked to teach subjects outside their major fields and to participate in adult education and community development programs.

HEALTH

130. CAMEROON The Ministry of Health has requested Volunteers to assist in the development of a new program of health education in rural areas. Volunteers will be asigned singly to village dispensaries where they will work with Cameroonian male-nurses and itinerant health workers in instituting a health education program in five or six surrounding villages.

The Volunteers will establish and conduct well-baby clinics at the dispensaries; they also will perform home-visits and follow-up visits to the mothers of ill children. They will demonstrate improved food for infants and develop locally available dietary supplements. Volunteers will explain and demonstrate water purification measures and other environmental sanitation programs; they will organize immunization programs, school health programs, and they will organize the dissemination of visual aids, movies and other techniques of health education.

131. CHAD The Ministry of Health has requested the Peace Corps to provide Volunteer nurses, laboratory technicians and liberal arts majors to serve in a program of training and retraining for broadening the scope of paramedical personnel in Chad. In a land where there is such a crucial need for more medical services, what resources do exist must be made maximally effective. To this end, some Volunteers will be assigned to the school of nursing in Fort Lamy and some will be assigned to regional medical centers where they will work with Chadian practical nurses and nurse's aids as they carry the entire medical burden for people in the surrounding area. They will also attempt to teach sterile methods and proper diagnostic technique and other modern medical practices to these personnel.

Another group of Volunteers will work through the schools and with the teachers and students of the primary and secondary schools. They will organize medical check-ups, health records, immunization programs, will help install sanitary measures, and will prepare health-related teaching and curricular materials in a school health program.

132. ETHIOPIA In a wide-ranging health program, Volunteer nurses work with Ethiopian counterparts in organizing and operating elementary and advanced training schools for Ethiopian dressers and nurses. Medical technologists and pharmacists add to this program by training Ethiopians in their respective fields.

133. GABON Volunteers will be assigned to mobile teams working out of regional medical centers on immunization programs, nutrition programs, and health education programs. Other Volunteers will be assigned in villages where they will work at the village dispensary on a program of infant nutrition, child-care education, and environmental sanitation. Other Volunteers, in the effort of making protein-rich foods immediately available to the Gabonese rural village population, will work with teams of Gabonese agricultural personnel in a pond construction and tilapia fish breeding project designed to provide fast-growing sources of protein to villages locted in the isolated interior of Gabon.

134. LESOTHO The Lesotho government has asked the Peace Corps to help start a program of maternal child welfare comprising health/nutrition education of mothers and supplemental feeding of pre-school-age children. The program will be operated out of government and privately run district health clinics, and will involve consultation at the clinics as well as follow-up home visits in the villages. Volunteers will be trained in nutrition, sanitation and health education, food preparation and will learn the Sesotho language.

135. MALAWI Volunteers work with expanding public health and environmental health programs, concentrating on the prevention and treatment of tuberculosis. Volunteers are active in health education, community development projects and home and dispensary treatment. They help to develop an administrative structure to support and continue health education activities and train African co-workers who will eventually take over all phases of the program. *The next training program will be in the summer of 1968.*

136. NIGER The Minister of Health has requested Volunteer doctors and nurses to direct public health and curative medical care in one of Niger's seven medical districts. Volunteer women living in small outlying villages of the district will work in health education, emphasizing sanitation, nutrition and child care.

137. TANZANIA Volunteers will initiate a pilot public health project in an isolated area of Tanzania. The goal is to identify and control the incidence of tuberculosis, to immunize the population against several of the more prevalent diseases and to engage in health education activities. *Training will begin spring 1968.*

138. TOGO Volunteer teams of three, working with three Togolese co-workers, have launched village health development projects in several locations. They combine a variety of activities from giving inoculations and making health surveys to lecturing and demonstrating sound health practices.

139. UPPER VOLTA Volunteers, arrived for the first time in Upper Volta in the fall of 1967, will gear their efforts to improving the health of children ages one through five, the population group most vulnerable to debilitating and fatal diseases. They will concentrate efforts on urging mothers to improve nutrition and sanitary conditions for their youngsters.

COMMUNITY DEVELOPMENT/
LAND SETTLEMENT

150. BOTSWANA Volunteers will stimulate and assist self-help projects in local communities. They are to furnish technical and organizational advice to local foremen, as well as participate in simple rural and urban construction projects, including housing, dam and road construction, bush clearance and soil and water conservation. Some Volunteers will work with cottage-type local industries or serve as extension officers with the Cooperatives Department, working to establish thrift and loan societies and cattle-marketing cooperatives. *Training probably will begin in spring 1968 and in 1969.*

151. DAHOMEY Volunteers will work in model villages, set up under the joint efforts of Israel, U.S. AID, and the Dahomey government, where young farmers are trained in modern agricultural methods. These will be the first Peace Corps Volunteers in Dahomey.

152. ETHIOPIA Volunteers are to teach courses in community development—including sociology, literacy, health, construction, administration, handicrafts and home economics. They will either teach at the Awasa Training Center or will work in associated community centers in urban areas which are devoted to strengthening local institutions and eliminating social problems.

153. KENYA In the former "White Highlands"—fertile farmland once held by Europeans in the Rift Valley, now under government ownership—Kenya has asked for Volunteers to serve as assistant settlement officers to help with the resettlement of African families on the land and the organization and management of the cooperatives that will eventually administer the settlement schemes. A part of the task will be to foster a sense of "community" among people who have come from several areas and who previously knew only tribal or familial bonds. Several Volunteers will supervise and help with the installation of water systems on the settlement schemes.

154. LESOTHO The Lesotho government has asked the Peace Corps to aid its program of village development and self-help. Volunteers, working under the Ministry of Local Government and Community Development, will be assigned to work with district community development officers to assist villagers in constructing village water supplies, small conservation dams, markets, rural schools, clinics, recreational facilities, and roads. The teams will also help in promoting cooperatives, in organizing community social action groups and in training local community leaders. All Volunteers will learn the Sesotho language.

155. SENEGAL Volunteers will work with Animation Rurale, a government agency dedicated to motivating villagers to improve their own living conditions. They will work in a number of model pilot villages. Their aim will be to help people improve gardens, plant fruit trees, and build wells and latrines.

156. SIERRA LEONE Volunteers will work particularly in the field of agriculture-based community development as extension agents with individual farmers. Domestic and social development of women and children will be equally emphasized. In addition there is some small scale self-help construction which furthers the goals of community development. Volunteers with farm backgrounds and/or agricultural degrees are particularly valuable to this program.

157. UPPER VOLTA Volunteers, arriving for the first time in Upper Volta in the fall of 1967, will work in a program of well-digging and agricultural extension in southeastern Upper Volta. The well-diggers divide their time between well construction in the dry season and a variety of agricultural extension and self-help projects in the growing season, including organizing cooperatives, promoting construction efforts and teaching animal traction. The rest of the Volunteers will cover a range of activities designed to improve village life, from giving advice on staple, cash and subsistence crops to encouraging the construction of animal enclosures, bush stores, schoolhouses, and other village buildings.

WATER RESOURCES

160. CHAD Volunteers will be assigned in rural villages of Chad initiating well-drilling programs and generating participation in water resources projects generally. In the water-parched land on the thin edge of the desert, water becomes the determining factor in health, agriculture, and transportation. Volunteers will undertake a well-drilling program in the rural areas on a self-help basis. They will help design and implement irrigation systems using wells or rivers or the waters of Lake Chad. They will design and implement such irrigation as windmills, water sluices and other such installations. Volunteers will also be called upon to study terrain for well-drilling purposes and to determine water purity tests. The Volunteers will work with teams of Chadian technicians and in cooperation with villagers throughout Chad.

AGRICULTURE/HOME ECONOMICS

165. CAMEROON The Ministry of Agriculture in Cameroon is interested in increasing the quantity and quality of its extension services throughout this vast and fertile nation. Volunteers have been requested to help train Cameroonian extension agents and to develop small agricultural extension projects in various parts of the country. Most Volunteers will be involved in initiating and encouraging self-help efforts in poultry raising, cattle raising, vegetable gardening, crop diversification, improved seed schemes, animal-drawn farming, as well as sponsoring farm youth clubs and 4-H types of activity. Volunteers will be housed in small villages where they will provide follow-through on a local level of extension projects undertaken by the Cameroonian extension service personnel.

166. CHAD Volunteers have been working in small villages along the shores of Lake Chad attempting to introduce improved organizational techniques, developing cooperatives for the purchase of improved seed, establishing demonstration vegetable gardens to encourage crop diversification and to encourage diet supplementation, introducing principles of traction by teaching farmers how to train oxen and to use animal-drawn farming equipment. The Volunteers live in small, isolated villages several days distant from the major town. They are under the general supervision of a French development company, SEMABLE, whose purpose is to increase wheat production in the fertile polders of Lake Chad.

167. IVORY COAST Volunteers will teach adult Ivoirienne women literacy, basic health and child care, nutrition and home arts. In outlying areas, Volunteers will visit five villages on a rotating basis, emphasizing health education while working with a minimum of equipment.

168. NIGERIA Working throughout the country, Volunteers will stimulate self-help activities in the towns and provinces to which they are assigned. In the northern area, these activities include livestock management, forestry and the development of basic amenities such as water supplies; in the east, rural construction, surveying, poultry, and cash crop organizing; in the west, agricultural extension and Young Farmers' Clubs and rubber and cocoa plantations. Volunteers will be trained in the Nigerian languages—Hausa, Igbo, Efik, Yoruba and Bini—spoken in the villages where they will reside. A rural background or an agricultural degree would be helpful but not essential. A bachelor's degree is required only in specific skill areas such as surveying. *Training begins spring and summer 1968 and 1969.*

CONSTRUCTION

170. GABON Volunteers will be assigned to small Gabonese villages where they will help the community organize construction projects to build schools, teachers' houses, dispensaries and community centers. Volunteers will generate local enthusiasm for the projects, will help organize the logistics and supply of construction sites, will draw and interpret plans and assist in the layout and construction of the buildings. The Government of Gabon is interested in stabilizing the relatively mobile population of Gabon. Village improvement projects are crucial to the success of the rural efforts undertaken by the Government. An important side effect of the project will be to have trained Gabonese villagers construct durable buildings from locally available materials while utilizing local skills.

171. IVORY COAST In conjunction with the AID housing program, Volunteers will assist in construction, designing and planning new housing and in establishing the credit cooperative necessary for its financing. This program will be part of the effort to improve the quality of the rural life to help stem the rural exodus.

172. SOMALIA Volunteers working in mobile construction teams build one to four classroom schools and additions to existing schools, using local labor and, where possible, local materials. They are responsible for organizing the project, making arrangements with the community, supervising and handling all technical aspects of actual construction and advising the villagers on other self-help construction possibilities in the community. *The next training program will probably be in summer 1968.*

SMALL BUSINESS

175. IVORY COAST Through small business development centers under the Ministry of Plan, Volunteers will teach potential businessmen both in and outside the capital city marketing techniques, advertising, cost and market analysis, loan procedures, accounting and bookkeeping. In addition, Volunteers will make extensive follow-up visits to ensure that proper business procedures are being followed. They will also do market research-feasibility studies for proposed new businesses.

176. NIGERIA Volunteers will help increase the number of small Nigerian businesses by educating village entrepreneurs regarding loan opportunities, management and credit. They will also act as liaison men between local initiative and ministerial credit. Training will be given in two Nigerian vernaculars—Hausa and Bini—enabling the Volunteers to participate more fully in the affairs of their clients and communities. A business administration degree is required. *Spring 1968 and 1969 training.*

VOCATIONAL EDUCATION

180. GAMBIA The first Gambia Volunteers arrived in the fall, 1967. In schools, they will be teaching the much-needed skills of mechanics, carpentry, and construction.

181. IVORY COAST Volunteers are teaching carpentry, auto-mechanics and masonry in rural vocational secondary schools which were built by U.S. AID. This program is under the Ministry of Education.

COOPERATIVES

185. GAMBIA The first Gambia Volunteers arrived in the fall of 1967. Volunteers in co-ops will assist farmers to use fair and equitable marketing practices and to use profits to reinvest in useful equipment.

186. NIGERIA Working on community plantations in the east and on farm settlements in the west, Volunteers will assist in the establishment and efficient running of these community-based cooperatives. They will serve as liaison men, information officers and grass-roots organizers for a specific cooperative or settlement. Training will be given in two Nigerian vernaculars—Igbo and Yoruba—enabling the Volunteers to participate more fully in co-op affairs. No degree is required. *Training begins summer 1968 and 1969.*

SOCIAL WELFARE

190. SENEGAL Working out of Social Centers throughout the country, Volunteers promote social well-being by helping Senegalese families meet needs in the areas of family and child care, healthy living conditions, and social relationships and adjustments. Volunteers working from Maternal and Infant Protection Centers supplement medical services with health and nutritional education programs. They also make health surveys and home visits.

LAW

195. ETHIOPIA Volunteers are presently working as legal advisers to various ministries in the Ethiopian capital of Addis Ababa.

LATIN AMERICA

COMMUNITY DEVELOPMENT

201. BOLIVIA Volunteers with Bolivia counterparts will serve as village-level workers in a National Community Development program. They will assist in the organization of community groups which undertake projects decided upon by the villagers.

Technically skilled Volunteers—with backgrounds in engineering, home economics, agriculture, construction and other fields—will serve as technical and project support personnel while training Bolivian counterparts in particular skill specialties. *Training will begin summer of 1968 and 1969.*

202. BRAZIL Volunteers, using the health post or school as a focal point, will organize community groups to undertake projects based on the villagers' felt needs. Volunteers with teaching experience or with paramedical skills, as well as liberal arts majors, will promote community development projects. *Training sessions are scheduled for summer 1968, and spring, summer and fall 1969.*

203. BRITISH HONDURAS A small group of Volunteers have begun local action programs in the rural sector of British Honduras. More are planned to continue and to expand this self-help effort. Volunteers will help organize village groups, assist in community definition of problems and participate in activities to improve rural living conditions. Projects may involve construction of rural public works, co-op formation, home arts and nutrition. *Training is scheduled for summer 1968.*

204. CHILE Working within the framework of the Chilean Agrarian Reform Corporation, Volunteers will help develop community action groups, help formulate community projects and assist in the social service and home and agricultural extension programs of the institution in its newly organized "colonies." Volunteers should have some skill in one of the following fields: economics, business administration, practical nursing, construction, surveying, home economics, agricultural mechanics or extension.

Other Volunteers will take part in a major national reforestation program aimed at restocking some one million acres in the next five years. Volunteers will live in rural communities and assist in local reforestation efforts, development of tree nurseries and related community projects. Volunteer foresters will work with Chilean counterparts in supervision and technical support of this program. They will also be called upon to conduct research studies. *Training, summers of 1968 and 1969.*

205. COLOMBIA Teams of trained Colombian and Volunteer community development personnel are to promote higher standards of living in rural areas by stimulating community action.

Each training group of Volunteers will focus on one particular province of Colombia and on area development projects within that province. This is part of the Colombian government plan to regionalize its planning and operations. Technically skilled Volunteers—engineers, agriculturalists, home economists, teachers—will provide support to Colombian and Volunteer field workers in particular community projects and development programs. *Training programs will begin spring, summer and fall—1968 and 1969.*

206. COSTA RICA Volunteers in Costa Rica are working actively with the newly created Office of Community Development. While projects, such as community construction work, water systems and so on, are a major secondary result of this agency's activities, the focus of its efforts is on the creating of autonomous local and regional groups capable of working to resolve local problems.

Volunteers are teaching leadership techniques, organizational skills, achievement motivation and coordination, and planning at the local and regional level. Most Volunteers are working in the relatively less-developed coastal areas of the country in an effort to incorporate these neglected sectors into the national society. *Groups will begin training summer, 1968 and 1969.*

207. DOMINICAN REPUBLIC Volunteers will work in rural areas assisting the Dominican Office of Community Development and the Forestry Service. Volunteers in these programs will serve as rural community action workers.

Volunteers will work in the organization and planning of community projects, most of which will be agriculture-related or rural public works construction. Foresters assist in on-the-job training of Dominican Forestry Service personnel, forest mapping, wood products research, and other activities as part of an important Dominican government program. *This program will train in the summers of 1968 and 1969.*

208. EL SALVADOR Volunteers will assist in community improvement and youth work in rural areas. They will work in conjunction with Salvadorean agencies in health, social work, credit unions and other community action projects. *Training is scheduled for the summers of 1968 and 1969.*

209. GUATEMALA Assigned to work with individuals and communities, Volunteers will aid in self-help projects in agriculture, health, small industries, home economics, cooperatives and credit unions. They will work in rural Guatemala, mostly in Indian-populated regions. *Training programs are for spring and summer, 1968 and 1969.*

210. HONDURAS Volunteers will work in rural development programs throughout Honduras. Some will work with Honduran field workers in a newly established community development agency. Others will teach literacy classes and establish credit unions. Depending on their abilities, Volunteers will also work in such areas as agriculture, construction, carpentry and nutrition. *Groups will train in the spring, 1968 and 1969.*

211. PANAMA Volunteers are needed to work in agricultural improvement, education in and formation of cooperatives, teaching of home arts, recreation, vocational education and general rural community organization.

Volunteers will work with the Panamanian Ministry of Agriculture in the priority rural development program. Activities center around the local community and self-help problem solving. The emphasis of the program is increased rural productivity by working through cooperative structures. *Training is for the summers of 1968 and 1969.*

212. URUGUAY Volunteers are needed to work in rural community organization. They will work with self-help community projects under Uruguayan agencies involved in the field of rural development. Their goals will be to strengthen grass-roots organizations attempting to solve local problems through concerted community action. Since the basic felt needs of the rural population are for improved knowledge of agriculture and home economics, many of the community projects will be related to these fields. *Training programs will begin in summer 1968 and summer 1969.*

COOPERATIVES

220. BOLIVIA Working with the fastest growing cooperative movement in Latin America, Volunteers will assist the National Federation of Credit and Savings Cooperatives to expand its efforts in the formation and supervision of credit cooperatives in Bolivia. Volunteers will also be involved in the creation and supervision of production and marketing cooperatives in the field of agriculture. *Training is scheduled for summer 1968.*

221. COLOMBIA Volunteers are to encourage and develop marketing, producing, consumption and credit/savings cooperatives in rural areas. They will hold instructional and organizational meetings of prospective members, help draft charter documents and process them through government offices, help secure assistance from local and regional offices, assist in establishing financial controls and records, and participate at all stages of cooperative operations. *Programs will train summers 1968 and 1969.*

222. ECUADOR Through the National Federation of Cooperatives, Volunteers in Ecuador are involved in one of the largest and most diversified country programs the Peace Corps has undertaken (146 operating credit unions and 700 other co-ops of various types). They are assisting middle and low-income groups to obtain credit at low cost in order to improve farms, build homes or start businesses. Volunteers become involved in management, financing, membership relations as well as principles and problems of cooperatives, all in an attempt to sufficiently train local officers and members to operate without outside help. In addition, these assignments involve community projects chosen by the Volunteer according to his skills and initiative.

223. DOMINICAN REPUBLIC As in many other areas, the cooperative movement in the Dominican Republic is split between the lofty expectations of the national leadership and the operational necessities of the local cooperatives. The Peace Corps is trying to knit these two tendencies together.

Volunteers provide needed technical assistance in terms of basic training in organizational and promotional programs. At the same time, Volunteers provide a channel whereby the local groups can make their demands for support and services heard directly on the national level. *Groups will train in the summers of 1968 and 1969.*

224. PERU Volunteers are to assist in the education, organization and administration of cooperatives which were hastily formed and now require guidance to prevent collapse. Volunteers will attend meetings of cooperative members and directors, working closely with both groups in all phases of cooperative activity and administration. At the national level, Volunteers will work with counterparts to update records, to survey needs and priorities and generally help establish continuity of service and resources from national agencies to individual cooperatives. *Summer 1968 training is planned.*

225. VENEZUELA Volunteers will help develop efficient and applicable methods of accounting and administrative control while preparing community members to assume administration of their own cooperatives.

In a nation where cooperatives have been of real value to overall community development, Volunteers will also develop new cooperatives and support existing credit, consumer, production or electrical cooperatives. Some Volunteers will open new sites and will concentrate their efforts in the first stages of community development while also investigating and, when feasible, developing cooperatives. *Scheduled to train in spring 1969.*

226. LATIN AMERICA REGIONAL Volunteers will work in selected communities in Ecuador and Bolivia, assisting artisans to understand the nature of cooperative organizations. Where conditions seem favorable, Volunteers will develop co-ops, help artisans to estimate production costs and plan expansion of their enterprises.

Volunteers with training or experience in design, fine arts, weaving, or pottery will help identify marketable products, improve design and/or workmanship for marginal products. They will also experiment with new products, using indigenous skills and materials. *Training begins summer 1968.*

AGRICULTURE/HOME ARTS/NUTRITION

230. BOLIVIA Working with counterpart agents of the National Agricultural Extension Service, Volunteers will develop and demonstrate animal and gardening projects in communities and with individual farmers. Volunteers will carry on an active campaign to inform the community of available extension services, will help form youth groups and will develop simple educational materials to aid in teaching home economics and agricultural improvement. *This project will train in summer 1968.*

231. BRAZIL Working with counterparts of the Ministry of Education, Volunteers will develop rural youth activities including agricultural clubs, demonstration gardens, recreation and health programs, and related community development projects.

In addition, Volunteers are to work with the National School Lunch program in primary school nutrition and related community development activities such as home gardens, adult nutrition classes, literacy courses, public health campaigns, and orphanage programs. *Training groups will begin in summer and fall 1968 and in summer 1969.*

232. CHILE Volunteers are to serve with the Agrarian Reform Corporation and the Agricultural Development Institute in agriculture extension projects. Working in "colonies" and rural communities, their efforts will be directed at improved farming and production practices. These projects will be undertaken through cooperative structures with an important emphasis on agriculture credit and introduction of new technology. *Groups will train in summers of 1968 and 1969.*

233. COLOMBIA Volunteers will work to increase the standard of living and agricultural production in rural areas and to establish cooperative organizations through which surpluses can be marketed profitably. They will work in livestock and small animal husbandry, simple farm planning and record keeping, pest and erosion control, fertilizer use, demonstration farming, and community and school gardening.

Female Volunteers will work with the National Institute of Nutrition primarily with mothers' clubs, conducting nutrition classes in schools and assisting in pre- and post-natal classes. *Training sessions will begin in summers of 1968 and 1969.*

234. COSTA RICA Volunteers working with the agricultural extension service have the general function of bringing the services and benefits of the Department of Agriculture to the people. In real terms, this means that Volunteers work as field extension agents and home economists, concentrating their efforts on small landowners and on the people who live off the relatively well-developed central plateau.

Volunteers work in agricultural research centers in the five distinct geographical zones of the country, at the same time encouraging local farmers to utilize the results of their investigations. Volunteers with business experience are providing technical assistance to agricultural cooperatives and marketing associations. *Training will begin the summers of 1968 and 1969.*

235. ECUADOR An agricultural extension program to stimulate rural inhabitants to improve their way of life will employ Volunteers to help the people achieve increased farm productivity, better health, and social and economic stability.

In specialized fields, civil engineers will work in construction of irrigation and storage facilities, and in design of rural public works projects. Veterinarians will teach at the universities and work with the Ministry of Agriculture in preventive medicine and teaching. Agriculturalists will serve as technical backstoppers for community-based Volunteers while assisting in training their Ecuadorian counterparts. *This program will have groups training in summers 1968 and 1969.*

236. EL SALVADOR Volunteers will be assigned to the Agricultural Extension Office to work with counterparts in organizing, reforming, and strengthening 4-H clubs, and to work in home economics and agricultural extension programs. Volunteers may also involve themselves in other community activities. *Groups will train in summers 1968 and 1969.*

237. GUATEMALA Working in rural Guatemala, Volunteers will help the *campesino* employ new techniques in animal raising, crop diversification, corn growing and insect control. The Volunteers will also help Guatemalan farmers organize credit co-ops. These cooperatives can provide the basis for purchasing and marketing at favorable prices, as well as a means for developing broad-based farm credit. *Training begins fall 1968.*

238. PARAGUAY Working with local counterparts, Volunteers will be assigned to agricultural extension and home demonstration projects. They also will work in the development and expansion of 4-C (similar to 4-H) activities. *Groups will train in the falls of 1968 and 1969.*

239. PERU Volunteers with agricultural backgrounds or training will work with government agencies in agricultural extension and home economics to increase food production among families in the sierra and coast. They will also work with 4-H clubs in food production and education projects. Female Volunteers will serve as home demonstration agents with the agriculture extension teams in nutrition, food preservation, health education, and youth activities. *Groups will begin to train summer and fall 1968 and summer 1969.*

240. VENEZUELA Volunteers assist the Venezuela Agricultural Planning Commission (which consists of directors of eight Venezuelan agriculture agencies) by serving as catalysts in the stimulation of socioeconomic development of rural people and the rural community in which they live and work. Volunteers integrate themselves in the life of rural communities, and work with community members and leaders to inspire their initiative and desire for personal, as well as community, development. *Training begins summers 1968 and 1969.*

RURAL ELECTRIFICATION

245. BRAZIL Electrical engineers are needed to work with the Special Service of Rural Electrification in São Paulo and with the Electricity Centers of Mato Grosso in extending the electrical networks of the state. They will set standards for installation, measure substation and branch line capacities, stake and check lines, install and inspect meters, supervise construction and maintain and repair installations. *Training begins summer 1968.*

246. ECUADOR Working with the Ecuadorian Institute of Electrification, Volunteers are to promote and standardize national electrification and help train nationals in the construction, operation and maintenance of systems throughout the country. Engineers will design, supervise and help administer these systems. *Training programs are scheduled to begin summers 1968 and 1969.*

FISHERIES

250. CHILE Volunteers will serve in small fishing villages which dot the long Chilean coast. Their work includes the organization of fishing cooperatives and the development of management, marketing and accounting procedures. Volunteers with skills in marine biology and commercial fishing will assist in the introduction of new technology and approved fishing practices. This cooperative effort is a high-priority program of the Chilean government and represents a major attack on the problems of protein-deficient domestic production and stagnant economic growth. *Groups will begin training in summer 1968 and summer 1969.*

251. CENTRAL AMERICA In 1967, the Food and Agriculture Organization (FAO) of the United Nations began a six-year fisheries research and development program for the Caribbean and Pacific coasts of all the Central American countries and Panama. The Peace Corps has agreed to provide Volunteers who will work directly with each of the national fisheries offices as technicians and surveyors of local market conditions. The goal of Volunteers will be the growth and development of small-scale fishing enterprises by means of cooperatives formed by local independent fishermen.

UNIVERSITY EDUCATION

255. BRAZIL Working with assistant professors at a dozen universities, Volunteers will teach in their field of specialization, hold seminars, assist in research and focus students' attention on community action. *Training begins summer 1968.*

256. CHILE Combining classroom teaching with work in community development projects, Volunteers will serve as assistant professors and laboratory instructors while encouraging student participation in community development projects. *Groups begin training in summers 1968 and 1969.*

257. COLOMBIA Special projects in university education are being arranged in Colombia.

258. ECUADOR At universities and in several normal schools, Volunteers will teach and lecture in their respective fields and prepare laboratories and workshops. *Training begins summer 1969.*

259. VENEZUELA Volunteer professors, instructors, laboratory assistants and librarians will perform dual roles of formal teaching and outside activity such as community action projects and adult literacy English classes. *This program will train summer 1968.*

260. CENTRAL AMERICA Working in the national universities of the Central American countries, Peace Corps Volunteers are contributing to the increased integration of the Central American educational system by their assistance in curriculum planning and development. In addition, Volunteer instructors often substitute for host country professors who are studying abroad for advanced degrees—particularly in sciences and mathematics. *Training begins fall 1968.*

GENERAL EDUCATION/TEACHER TRAINING

265. BOLIVIA Using schools as the focal point for community activities, Volunteers will work in rural areas to improve education and stimulate community action. They will work with teachers in planning, motivation, appreciation of differences among children, discipline and evaluation. Another task will be to shift emphasis from a rote-method to a child-centered teaching technique and to develop parent-teacher associations, sports groups and youth clubs. *This group of Volunteers will train summer 1968.*

266. BRITISH HONDURAS Volunteers will work in elementary education and teacher training. They will introduce modern teaching techniques and methodology. They will use their knowledge to broaden the present curricula—to provide the necessary groundwork in preparing today's young to be the country's leaders of tomorrow. Through teacher/community participation in parent-teacher associations, youth, community-centered. Volunteers will involve hoped that the self-help concept will be recognized and used to meet the pressing needs of this emerging nation. *Groups will train in the summers of 1968 and 1969.*

267. GUYANA Volunteers will serve as secondary school teachers and teacher-trainers at the elementary level. They will work with relatively untrained teachers to relieve the acute shortage of trained teachers, to tailor curriculum to meet the needs of the country, to improve the methodology and content of teaching methods, to introduce the new math—all aimed toward increasing the number of primary school students eligible to enter secondary school and toward increasing the number of secondary school students prepared to take and pass the GCE examination.

All Volunteers will endeavor to organize and unite the efforts of school and community groups toward mutual goals. *Training begins summer 1968 and 1969.*

268. HONDURAS Volunteers with degrees in education or teaching experience will participate in on-the-job teaching programs designed to improve the teaching skills of rural primary teachers. This work will involve mainly teaching methodology and on-the-job supervision of rural primary teachers. *Training begins summer 1968.*

269. JAMAICA Living and working in small villages, Volunteers will assist Jamaica's educational development through a community-centered approach to rural education. They will serve as resident field workers for three ministries, enabling the government to broaden existing educational programs. Volunteers will work with four basic programs; pre-school education, educational television, vocational training and co-operatives. *Training begins in the summer of 1968.*

270. WINDWARD-LEEWARD ISLANDS In an expanding program previously confined to St. Lucia and Barbados, Volunteers will work in vocational and cooperatives education, in physical education and secondary school teaching programs, and with in-service training of primary teachers. All teaching is to be "community-centered." Volunteers will involve themselves in school-related and community action projects. *Training programs begin summer 1968 and spring 1969.*

TEACHER TRAINING

275. BRAZIL Volunteers, including some with degree in education or teaching experience, are needed to improve the quality of primary school education. This program is directed toward training primary school teachers in the use of a new curriculum, providing on-the-job training for these teachers, and helping to cut the student dropout rate by involving students and parents in the educational process and making schools the focus of community action projects. *Groups will begin to train in the spring and summer of 1968 and 1969.*

276. COLOMBIA Secondary school teaching is to be improved with the aid of Volunteers who will introduce new methods and materials in the fields of math, biology, physics and chemistry to teachers and third- and fourth-year students at leading colleges of education. *Programs will train summer 1968 and 1969.*

277. DOMINICAN REPUBLIC Volunteers will work with the Ministry of Education's in-service teacher training program, assisting rural primary school teachers in methods, curriculum planning, use of visual aids and subject content. Volunteers will visit five to eight schools weekly. Vacation and summer training sessions will be included in the assignment. *Groups begin training in the spring of 1968 and 1969.*

278. ECUADOR Volunteers, serving as teacher-trainers, will be assigned to universities to conduct classes in their field of specialization. Their students will be teachers from rural areas who have been enrolled in a special re-training program. Volunteers will also travel to secondary schools to advise on teaching methods. Additional Volunteers will help to establish overall systems of lesson-planning and classes. They will act as liaisons between the Ministry of Education and local schools. The project is aimed at upgrading the quality of rural secondary school education and *will begin training summer 1968.*

279. PERU Volunteers with teaching experience or education degrees in mathematics, physics, chemistry or biology will work in provincial normal schools training primary and secondary teachers. The goal is to provide the future teachers with new and improved methods and with the capacity to teach practical and problem-solving abilities. *Training begins in the fall of 1968.*

EDUCATIONAL TELEVISION (ETV)

285. BRAZIL Volunteers will help in the production and school-utilization phases of educational television programs which are developing in Brasilia and Recife. Volunteers will be stationed primarily in rural areas where they can work with primary school teachers, demonstrating techniques for use of television in primary education. *A group will train in summer 1968.*

286. COLOMBIA Volunteers will be assigned to work with primary schools using educational television to aid in the orientation of teachers to ETV workshops in educational methodology, working at the grassroots level with a short-term goal to improve utilization of television and long-range aim to raise the level of teacher performance. *Groups will train in summer 1968.*

287. URUGUAY Volunteers will help initiate a major Uruguayan program in educational television. This project calls for people with backgrounds in TV production, film, and primary/secondary education. Under the Ministry of Education, they will introduce ETV into selected classrooms in Montevideo and other population centers. Volunteers will cooperate with Uruguayans in programming, production, and working with local teachers for the most effective utilization of programs in daily course work. *Training will begin summer 1969.*

VOCATIONAL AND INDUSTRIAL EDUCATION

290. BOLIVIA Volunteers with carpentry and construction skills will assist in the National Community Development Program by providing technical support to village workers and to Volunteers with non-technical backgrounds.

Volunteers will help Bolivian instructors improve the level of classroom and laboratory presentations by using modern techniques, coordinating inter-shop activities, developing curricula and teaching aids, and re-establishing on-the-job training with shopowners. The following are needed to *train in the spring of 1968:* welders, electricians, auto and diesel mechanics, engineers, bricklayers, plasterers, draftsmen, sheet metal workers, plumbers and surveyors.

291. CHILE and EASTERN CARIBBEAN ISLANDS Special vocational and industrial education programs will soon be under way in these two areas.

292. PERU Auto mechanics, general machinists, welders, automotive and household electricians, draftsmen, shipmetal workers, cabinet makers, and vocational education teachers in automotive theory will work with three vocational schools in the *barriadas* of Lima. Their job will be to oversee the shop activities of the schools and, where possible, to provide classroom teaching. *A group will train in the spring 1968.*

293. VENEZUELA Volunteers are to teach in vocational and technical-training high schools and also to take active roles in directing adult education, community action, sports and social welfare activities. *Training begins summer 1968.*

YOUTH/RECREATION

295. COLOMBIA Volunteers are to assist youth clubs and service organizations, and to implement youth programs in health education. They will conduct varied activities in physical education and recreation, will handle leadership development courses and programs in inter-scholastic athletics, teacher training, and integration of school and community programs. National television network facilities will be used to broaden the program's scope and carry it to schools currently lacking youth development programs. *Training for this project begins spring 1968.*

296. ECUADOR Some Peace Corps Volunteers will be assigned to the National Sports Federation to conduct clinics, organize teams and to backstop any local Volunteers involved in programs that need their expertise. Others will help establish programs of youth development and recreation in small rural communities under the direction of the Ministry of Education. They will meet with school teachers to aid in school recreational activities and will also encourage greater communication and coordination between the province and cantons. A few other Volunteers will be assigned to various universities to develop physical education departments as well as to instigate intramural and inter-collegiate competitions. *Summer 1969 training.*

297. URUGUAY Programming is under way for a youth/recreation program.

298. VENEZUELA A nationwide recreation program will use Volunteers to work in urban and rural YMCA projects, in slum-area schools (to develop both recreation and physical education programs), with various childrens' and scouting organizations, and in small rural towns without recreation programs.

Other Volunteers, assigned to cities of over 12,000 population, will teach physical education in elementary and secondary schools, teacher-training institutes or industrial/technical schools and will coach in state athletic leagues. *Groups will train spring 1968 and 1969.*

HEALTH

300. BOLIVIA Volunteers will work to help eradicate tuberculosis in Bolivia, the leading cause of death in the population over four years of age. The assignment will be as a village health worker representing the Institute of Transmissible Diseases under the Ministry of Health. Activities include determining the incidence of disease, developing data and recording systems, follow-up visits with individuals and families where TB is detected, and general health education. *Training begins in the fall 1968.*

301. BRAZIL Brazil proposes to reinforce the teaching staffs of three nursing education institutions. Volunteers will demonstrate proper nursing techniques to nursing students on an in-service training basis, as well as help upgrade the skills of auxiliaries and paramedical personnel. *Groups will train in the spring 1968 and 1969.*

302. BRAZIL The National Institute of Endemic Diseases of the Ministry of Health has asked the Peace Corps to aid a new effort to control the parasitic disease known as schistosomiasis (also called bilharzia) which is estimated to infect as many as six million Brazilians.

Volunteers will work with census taking, medical histories, making limited physical examinations and skin tests, measuring water flows, and collecting and destroying the snails that serve as carriers of the parasite. In addition, Volunteers will help to instill community awareness of, and support for, the control program. *Training begins spring 1969.*

303. BRAZIL Volunteers will work with local health posts in Pernambuco, Paraiba, Bahia, Mato Grosso, and Segipe. They will function as health educators, sanitarians, nurses and medical technicians while also training co-workers. *Training programs are scheduled for spring and fall 1968 and spring 1969.*

304. CHILE Volunteer nurses and laboratory technicians are assigned to training hospitals to work with student nurses and technicians. They endeavor to improve technical competence and to instill a pride in nursing practices. Public health activities conducted in rural sites as on-the-job training will also be an integral part of their work with the student nurses. *Summer 1968 training.*

305. COSTA RICA Volunteers with backgrounds in public health training or relevant experience will work with the National Water Agency in the development of pure drinking water, inexpensive water systems and general improvement of sanitation facilities. Registered nurses will be assigned to the Ministry of Health to work in outlying regional centers supervising and providing technical support to the sanitation program. *Training is in the fall 1968.*

306. PARAGUAY Volunteers will work with the environmental sanitation program of the Ministry of Health. They will serve as counterparts to Paraguayan sanitary inspectors assigned to health posts in the eastern region of the country.

Their primary function will be to educate the local population— by group teaching methods and by individual visits to rural homes—in the value and use of proper sanitation facilities (e.g., latrines, wells, garbage disposal). Their work will also be directed against the spread of communicable diseases, especially intestinal parasites. Volunteers with liberal arts backgrounds will undergo special *training for this program in the spring 1968.*

307. CENTRAL AMERICA Volunteer nurses will teach in nursing schools and hospitals and medical centers, training nursing candidates and raising the level of nursing practices. Volunteers will be able to work in outside public health programs. Social welfare projects may also absorb Volunteer skills and time in a number of areas. *Training begins in the summer 1969.*

URBAN DEVELOPMENT

310. BOLIVIA The Volunteer will be a community developer in one of the many mining communities located on the Altiplano of Bolivia. He will engage himself in many phases of community life, of which the following are typical: recreation and athletics, social welfare, youth clubs, teaching, credit unions, health and sanitation, and organizing groups of adolescents and adults for special community services and functions. *Training begins in the spring 1969.*

311. BRAZIL Volunteers will work in satellite cities surrounding Brazil's new inland capital, Brasilia. Volunteers work in collaboration with the Social Service foundation, instigating community involvement in the resolution of social and economic problems that affect large urban masses in Brazil. *Groups will train in the spring and summer of 1968.*

312. CHILE Volunteers are to live and work with urban slum dwellers, advising and assisting them in construction of homes. In addition, they promote the formation and self-help development action of local groups, assisting them to receive and effectively manage available aid.

Volunteers with training in city planning will work directly with municipal governments to introduce new and improved methods of long-range planning, budgeting and city development and management. *Groups will train in the spring 1968 and 1969.*

313. COLOMBIA Volunteers work in slums with the urban section of the Division of Community Action. Their primary purpose is to help slum dwellers to improve their environment through community effort. Activities may include literacy classes, house and community improvement, vocational training, credit co-op organization and recreation. *Training begins in the spring 1968 and 1969.*

314. ECUADOR Volunteers will work in the slums of Guayaquil in efforts to create or strengthen *barrio* organizations dedicated to self-help activity. Guayaquil, the financial and commercial capital of Ecuador, is ringed by some of the worst slums in Latin America. To improve the living conditions and to give the slum communities the leverage and capability to accomplish their wants, Volunteers will help initiate activities such as medical dispensaries, co-ops, youth and community centers, and home improvements. *Summer 1968 training.*

315. GUATEMALA and HONDURAS Volunteers will work in rural hamlets introducing improved methods of administration and planning for local government. They will be assigned to the governmental agency for municipal development. Backgrounds in public administration, city planning, sociology or related sciences will be desirable for this program. *Training will begin in the fall 1968.*

316. PANAMA The Panamanian Institute of Urban Housing, Department of Social Welfare, the U.S. Agency for International Development and the Peace Corps are engaged in a coordinated effort to resolve the most acute social problem in Panama, i.e., the dismal life conditions of 85 percent of the inhabitants of the metropolitan areas in and around Panama City and Colón.

Volunteers are needed to bring a new dimension to the social work activities of the Panamanian agencies through their participation with the teams of specialists working with each urban slum area. This program requires Volunteers with exceptional motivation and the capacity to work efficiently under situations of tension and confusion. *Training begins in the fall 1968.*

317. PERU Volunteers will work with parent-groups and the Ministry of Education in the *barriadas* of Lima, Arequipa and Chimbote in organizing community resources for the building and maintenance of schools and provision of an adequate primary education for *barriada* youth. Auxiliary projects in community education and recreation are anticipated. *Programs will train in the summers of 1968 and 1969.*

318. VENEZUELA Volunteers will work with the Venezuela Foundation for Community Development and Municipal Improvement to assist in a program of municipal development. They are to be assigned to cities in the interior, aiding in the improvement of public administration, city planning, government operation, and related activities. *Fall 1968 training.*

WORLDWIDE

SECRETARIES

600. According to professional qualifications, Volunteer secretaries will serve as office managers or secretaries to Peace Corps staff members in overseas headquarters. Work will include typing, shorthand, handling of bills and petty cash, ordering and purchasing of supplies and general office work. They will work closely with Volunteers and will deal with other Americans and host country nationals. The secretaries also will find activities outside their office work—such as teaching business courses in local schools—depending on their skills and interests.

DOCTORS

700. Medical doctors will work in health education and preventive and curative medicine as Volunteer Leaders. Doctors will spend considerable time in preventive medicine and in the teaching of local doctors, medical students and paramedical and unskilled host country personnel.

Unlike other Volunteers, a doctor is permitted to take dependents overseas. His wife will also be a Volunteer with an assignment appropriate to her skills.

NORTH AFRICA, NEAR EAST, SOUTH ASIA

EDUCATION

401. AFGHANISTAN Volunteers teach English in secondary schools and universities in the capital city, Kabul, and in the provinces. Volunteer teacher-trainers work with Afghan counterparts in teacher-training academies in Kabul and the provinces, in such areas as math, science, arts and crafts, and physical education. The graduates of these academies will become teachers at the junior high school level. Volunteer accountants help train ministry counterparts in Kabul, as well as in provincial centers.

BA degrees are required. Trainees will study Farsi or Pushtu.

402. IRAN Volunteers will work with secondary school English teachers in an effort to raise the level of English language instruction. The Volunteers will work with teachers at several schools, visiting classes, holding seminars and conducting model classes. In addition, they will hold adult evening classes in English for other teachers, government officials and townspeople. Volunteers assigned to colleges and universities will teach English classes directly on a full-time basis.

BA degrees required. Trainees will study Farsi.

403. MOROCCO Volunteers will teach English grammar, composition and conversation 15-25 hours per week in secondary schools. *Training will begin in summer 1968.* BA degrees required; previous knowledge of French desirable. Trainees will also study Moroccan Arabic.

404. NEPAL Volunteers will teach vocational subjects, science, home economics, and English in middle and secondary schools. Volunteer-teachers also assist fellow teachers in improved educational methods and participate in community activities.

Training will begin in fall 1968 and 1969. Trainees will study Nepali.

405. TUNISIA Assigned to secondary schools and adult education centers throughout the country, Volunteers will teach English as a foreign language. BA degree and proficiency in French required. Trainees will study Tunisian Arabic.

406. TURKEY While teaching English as a foreign language at junior and senior high schools and university prep schools, Volunteers will start English clubs, conduct adult education courses and generally involve themselves in community activities. Math and science teachers will work at the Middle East Technical University in Ankara where they will teach both formal and laboratory classes.

BA degree required. Trainees will study Turkish.

AGRICULTURE/NUTRITION

410. AFGHANISTAN Volunteers will work with experimental and research farms under the Ministry of Agriculture in basic wheat research and agricultural extension work.

Training program expected in spring or summer 1968. Agricultural background desirable. Trainees will study Farsi or Pushtu.

411. CEYLON Volunteers will work in basic vegetable gardening, construction, home health, nutrition, child care and dairy farming with Ceylonese villagers. Although Ceylon is among world leaders in tea and rubber production, massive importation of food for local consumption is necessary. Volunteers with agricultural backgrounds or with liberal arts degrees will join efforts to enable this fertile island to become self-sufficient in food and to promote better nutrition practices.

412. INDIA In a program to spur nutrition and poultry development, Volunteers will improve the skills of village level workers through training institutes and extension work with schools, cooperatives and individual villagers.

413. INDIA Working, in most cases, with Indian poultry extension officers, Volunteers will continue efforts to improve feed and poultry products by working with individual private producers, state poultry farms and cooperative markets.

414. INDIA Assigned in teams of four or five to one of the Applied Nutrition Blocks, Volunteers will help spread among India's villagers an understanding of the importance of balanced nutritional diets, find and implement ways of assisting villagers to reach a higher economic level, and help provide villagers with foods that will improve their physical and mental health and improve health conditions among needy, expectant and nursing mothers and pre-school children in their village.

415. INDIA Volunteers with agriculture backgrounds will work in extension programs to motivate, educate and help farmers utilize seeds, fertilizers, pesticides and rodent-proof granaries, and will take part in the bi-annual training programs for farmers before the spring and fall crops. Volunteers with liberal arts backgrounds will work closely with schools in the Applied Nutrition Program to increase production, distribution and use of food.

416. INDIA In terms of four or five, Volunteers will conduct a series of intensive three-month health-nutrition education programs. Volunteers will be centered at Basic Training Schools, but will work also with surrounding primary schools. Emphasis will be on health, sanitation, nutrition and gardening. Instruction will be in both English and the local Indian language.

417. IRAN Volunteers serving as co-workers with Iranian extension agents and women home agents will assist in educational programs, identifying problems and devising correctional measures, supplying technical information and producing demonstrations in fields such as basic sanitation and hygiene, food preservation, youth work, poultry raising, pest control and other fields of practical agriculture and homemaking.

Agricultural degree or background desirable. Trainees will study Farsi.

418. MOROCCO Volunteers will work with Moroccan extension agents in introducing modern agricultural methods to farmers in southern Morocco. Farmers will be encouraged to adopt new farming techniques in planting, plowing, crop rotation, and use of fertilizer.

Agricultural degree or background desirable. Trainees will study Moroccan Arabic.

419. NEPAL Volunteers are working as agricultural extension agents. With Nepali co-workers, these Volunteers show farmers how and when to plant improved seed and to utilize fertilizer, crop protection, irrigation and other methods to increase production.

Training will begin in fall 1968 and 1969. Trainees will study Nepali.

420. TURKEY *An agricultural project may begin training in summer 1968.* Working out of county and provincial extension offices, Volunteers will help villagers start poultry projects and experiment with new wheat seeds. Female Volunteers will work on projects in food preservation and canning.

Agricultural degrees or background desirable. Trainees will study Turkish.

COMMUNITY DEVELOPMENT

430. MOROCCO Women are assigned alone or in pairs to work in village centers helping to raise the standard of living of Moroccan families by teaching the village women and children basic health and hygiene, improved domestic skills and child care.

Male Volunteers work in village agriculture and forestry stations, helping Moroccans improve farming techniques by teaching and demonstrating new ways of fertilizing, plowing and planting.

Training is expected in spring or summer 1969. Single men and women and married couples accepted. Trainees will study Moroccan Arabic.

431. NEPAL Volunteers work with village Panchayats (local governing units). They concentrate on making maximum use of local level leadership, initiative, resources and labor to carry out self-help community development work and integrate the village authority structure into the larger fabric of district, zonal and national administration.

Training will begin in summer 1968 and 1969. Trainees will study Nepali.

HEALTH

440. AFGHANISTAN Nurses will serve in provincial pilot nursing schools as instructors and ward teachers to help meet the shortage of trained nurses. Lab technicians and medical technologists will work in hospital laboratories where they will have on-the-job training responsibility in addition to their diagnostic work.

Qualified doctors, nurses, and medical technicians accepted. Trainees will study Farsi or Pushtu.

PUBLIC WORKS/ARCHITECTURE

450. IRAN Volunteers assigned to provincial capitals are working with the Technical Bureaus of the Ministry of Development and Housing or with community development offices on the village level, on such public works projects as town electrification, drinking water systems, road construction, housing projects, schools and other community buildings. Volunteers serve in technical capacities in planning, surveying, and designing projects, supervising construction, inspecting the work of contractors and similar tasks.

Degrees in architecture or engineering desirable, as is experience in construction, surveying or other engineering skills. Trainees will study Farsi.

451. NEPAL Assisting village Panchayats (local governing units), Volunteers will survey trails and footbridges which link villages and aid in the construction of roads and bridges that will not wash out during monsoon rains. Not merely technical advisers, Volunteers will work closely with the people and councils in the planning and execution of other community construction programs.

Training will begin in summer 1968 and 1969. Trainees will study Nepali.

452. TUNISIA Volunteers will work for the Ministry of Public Works on the design and construction of housing, schools, and community and administrative buildings. *Training will begin in June 1968.* Selection will be made from among applicants with a Bachelor of Architecture degree. Trainees will study French and Tunisian Arabic.

CHILD CARE AND SOCIAL WORK

460. TUNISIA Volunteers will work with Tunisian women in planning and conducting pre-school programs for Tunisian children. *Training will begin in June 1968.* Trainees will study Tunisian Arabic. No degree requirement.

461. TURKEY Working with orphanages operated or supervised by the Ministries of Health and Education, Volunteers will help introduce modern child care practices and increase community interest and participation in the work of these institutions. In addition, some Volunteers may be assigned to children's hospitals and day care centers.

Training is scheduled for spring or summer 1968. BA degree required; child psychology background desirable. Trainees will study Turkish.

TOURISM

470. TURKEY Volunteers will work in southern and western areas of Turkey, in communities where tourism is becoming an important economic factor. Working out of local tourist associations, Volunteers will stimulate community interest in creating and upgrading tourist attractions. Typical activities will include festivals, sale of local handicrafts, clean-up campaigns, courses in English and hotel-restaurant techniques.

Training programs are expected in spring or summer 1968 and 1969. BA degree desirable, as is experience in business administration, hotel or restaurant management, advertising and public relations. Trainees will study Turkish.

CONSUMER COOPERATIVES

480. INDIA Volunteers work as assistant managers for retail merchandising in state consumers' cooperative stores in Punjab and Hariana States. The ultimate aim is to improve personal relations among store personnel, shareholders of the cooperatives, and government officials, so that the cooperatives can play an increasing role in making more consumer items (including food) available and at the lowest possible price.

FAMILY PLANNING

485. INDIA An ambitious family planning program will utilize Volunteers in the training, informational and organizational aspects of the campaign. They will work with Indian co-workers in arranging informational activities about family planning, helping to prepare visual aids, providing in-service training for Indian health and community workers, aiding in communication about program education and implementation, organizing district conferences, assisting in setting up record-keeping procedures and arranging for effective continuous referral channels for medical services.

SMALL INDUSTRIES

490. INDIA Volunteers will work with small-scale industrialists and industrial cooperatives to improve the utilization and rate of depreciation of machine tools, raise product quality, reduce production costs and wastage of scarce raw materials, train entrepreneurs in costing and managerial techniques, develop new products and market them and encourage increased industrial investment and output.

EAST ASIA / PACIFIC

EDUCATION

501. FIJI Volunteers will teach English as a second language in the Fijian and Indian elementary and secondary schools. Applicants with liberal arts degrees are qualified for this project. Opportunities to teach math and science on the secondary level are available to Volunteers with appropriate degrees in these subjects. Education Volunteers will reside in Fijian and Indian villages and will take an active part in community activities, i.e., clubs, sports, recreation, adult education. *Training usually begins in mid-September.*

502. KOREA Volunteer teachers in Korea will be assigned to all the teacher colleges to assist in the teaching of English as a foreign language. They will also serve as a means of introducing new teaching techniques and will assist in curriculum development. The Government of Korea has also requested science teachers who will be teaching their subject in secondary schools as well as introducing modern teaching techniques.

Liberal arts graduates are requested for the TEFL teaching program. Applicants interested in science or math teaching should have a major or minor in one of those fields. *Scheduled to train in June.*

503. MALAYSIA Volunteers in the Borneo states of Sabah and Sarawak will teach English to students from vernacular schools and assist in on-the-job training of Malaysian English teachers.

Throughout Malaysia, Volunteers will teach math and science at the high school and teachers' college level, and will also work with projects for revising curricula in these subjects and developing better teaching methods. Volunteers in rural primary schools will combine community development work with their teaching duties. A number of Volunteers in West Malaysia will be assigned to primary and secondary teacher training institutions to teach educational methods courses and direct practice teaching. *Training for these projects usually is done in Hawaii, beginning in mid-September.*

504. MICRONESIA Volunteers teach English as a second language in elementary schools throughout the six districts of Micronesia. They are performing an important role in establishing English as a medium of communication in an island nation where 10 different languages are spoken. Volunteers are also working in recently developed Operation Headstart Programs, teacher training and curriculum development. *Training usually begins in early summer* with arrival in September. The first completely in-country training program was conducted in Micronesia during the summer of 1967.

505. PHILIPPINES Volunteers teach math, science and English and work with Filipino co-teachers in new techniques and curriculum development, in-service training and educational programming in all levels of the public school system throughout the Philippines. Volunteers also work in selected private teacher-training schools assisting to upgrade teacher competency in elementary and secondary education. Education Volunteers also work in community action programs including malaria control, food production and health during holidays and after school.

Programs will train summer, fall and winter 1968 and 1969. Presently, three training sites are being used: Stanford, San Jose State College and the University of Hawaii.

The majority of assignments will go to liberal arts majors. Teacher training and high school teaching assignments require previous teaching experience and special skills in science, math or English teaching. Trainees will study Tagalog, Cebuano, Ilocano or Hiligaynon (Ilongo). Perhaps Waray-Waray, Bicolano, Chevacano, Pargasinan and other relatively important Filipino dialects will also be taught.

506. THAILAND Volunteers teach English in Thai secondary schools and teacher training colleges using the most modern linguistic methods. In addition, they work with in-service training programs to increase proficiency among Thai teachers. Standards are high, but a liberal arts graduate who wants to teach can meet the requirements of the job.

507. TONGA Voluntary English teachers at the elementary and secondary levels have been requested by the Kingdom of Tonga. In addition to teaching English as a second language, Volunteers at the elementary level will teach general science courses. At the secondary level, Volunteers are needed to conduct courses in mathematics and sciences. The Volunteers will reside in Tongan villages and take part in community activities.

508. WESTERN SAMOA Volunteers teach English in Samoan government and mission primary and intermediate schools using modern linguistic methods for teaching English as a second language. Most live and work in rural areas where they also become involved in public health and agricultural activities. A liberal arts graduate who wants to teach can meet the basic requirements for this job.

Volunteers also teach math and the sciences in Samoan government and mission secondary schools. The medium of instruction at this level is English. Volunteers with majors or minors in math or any of the sciences can qualify.

AGRICULTURE

510. FIJI Volunteers will work alongside Fijian co-workers as agriculture extension personnel. They will assist in implementing improved coconut cultivation including new planting and rehabilitation procedures. Forestry graduates have been requested to help initiate and supervise small scale tree planting schemes by individual farmers and non-government organizations. These Volunteers will also participate in research, surveys and training of forestry assistants. Volunteers with business backgrounds will instruct cooperative members in the basics of farm budgeting, business management and marketing procedures.

511. KOREA Korea needs approximately 36 Volunteer agriculturists for summer 1968. Four Volunteer agriculturists will be assigned to each of the nine provinces in a pilot project to assist Korean farmers in definition of local agricultural problems, as well as assisting in the improvement and development of food and cash crops. Volunteers in this program should have either an agricultural degree or extensive farm background.

512. MALAYSIA Volunteers will be assigned to rural agriculture training centers in East Malaysia to give short courses in better farming methods, help develop youth work in rural areas, and carry on extension work in the field. In West Malaysia, Volunteers will work with Farmers' Associations to help provide essential cost information on production and marketing of various crops, help develop production and marketing of various co-ops, encourage the use of modern agricultural techniques, and work with rural youth.

513. MICRONESIA Micronesia has requested Volunteers to work as agricultural extension agents throughout Micronesia. The extension program includes promoting development of specialty cash crops such as cacao, pepper and rice, making desirable planting material available to farmers, and providing technical assistance to farmers in what to grow. The extension program also supervises coconut rehabilitation projects and provides assistance to producers on improving processing techniques.

Volunteers with degrees or backgrounds in agriculture are preferred, but Volunteers with a strong interest in agriculture and a desire to learn can be taught during training to work effectively in the program.

514. TONGA Extension workers in tropical crop production—Volunteers—will assist in replanting and rehabilitating coconut palms. They will also provide technical advice to farmers for obtaining higher productivity and quality. In addition to carrying on development and extension efforts, Volunteers will be teaching and demonstrating modern agriculture techniques and improved extension methods.

515. WESTERN SAMOA Volunteers will work in rural areas of Samoa to assist the government in the introduction of better methods for soil preparation, care and handling of seedlings, planting methods, use of fertilizers and insecticides. Main crops involved are bananas, coconuts, and cocoa. Willingness to live and work in simple village surroundings is essential for this job.

HEALTH

520. KOREA Volunteers have been invited by the Government of Korea to be rural health auxiliaries. These Volunteers will be assigned to the local health clinics to work with Korean counterparts in health services for the rural areas. This project emphasizes maternal and child health, family planning, tuberculosis control, sanitation, and health education. Liberal arts majors are requested. *Training will take place late summer or early fall 1968.*

521. MALAYSIA Volunteers working in the Malaysian tuberculosis control project will be assigned to district chest clinics in rural and semi-urban areas of West Malaysia and Sabah, will develop procedures, organize mass case-finding drives, follow up positive cases with home visits, and plan and execute vaccination campaigns. Technologists will teach and practice medical technology as related to tuberculosis.

Rural health Volunteers in Sarawak and West Malaysia will concentrate on environmental sanitation projects such as pure water supplies, waste disposal and insect and rodent control, will help develop model village health programs, and will assist in the training of Malaysian public health workers. *These programs train in the spring or summer, usually in Hawaii.*

522. MICRONESIA Volunteers assigned to public health have completed the first Micronesia-wide census and are now working on a program designed to control leprosy, tuberculosis and filariasis. They are also involved in environmental sanitation projects aimed toward the reduction of parasitic and gastro-intestinal diseases which affect a large number of the Micronesian people. In addition to the liberal arts majors assigned to these programs, the Peace Corps sends nurses, x-ray technicians, laboratory technologists and pharmacists to work in curative medicine in both operational and teaching roles. *Public health Volunteers usually begin training in late summer.*

523. THAILAND Volunteers trained in principles of public health and special health techniques work with provincial health offices and rural health centers in rural areas of Thailand. Environmental sanitation (safe water supply and safe waste disposal), maternal and child care, and health education are the most important activities. Interest in people, health problems, and willingness to serve in rural areas essential for this job.

524. TONGA Female Volunteers will serve as auxiliaries to maternal child health nurses in the three island districts. They will assist in control and prevention of the prominent diseases by providing technical assistance (immunizations and health education) and by helping to change health habits and attitudes within the home. Male Volunteers will serve as auxiliaries to local health inspectors in environmental sanitation. The men will help provide waterseal latrines and water supply systems.

525. WESTERN SAMOA Volunteers work with Samoan rural health officers to implement disease control and eradication programs on a national level. Much activity concentrates on filariasis, tuberculosis, and childhood diseases. Volunteers also help to improve community and school water systems and sanitary facilities. Interest in people and health problems, plus willingness to live and work in simple village surroundings essential for this job.

VOCATIONAL EDUCATION

530. KOREA Volunteer teachers will be assigned to the vocational schools primarily at the secondary level. The vocational teachers will be expected to stress on-the-job specialized training as well as encourage more students to remain in school for additional training. Applicants for this project should have some technical education or on-the-job skill prior to training.

531. MALAYSIA Volunteers will teach industrial arts (drafting, woodwork, metal work, basic electricity and power mechanics) in lower secondary schools where they may also be called upon to assist in developing teaching aids, demonstration lessons and the curriculum. Others will offer specialized training in carpentry, masonry, electrical installation and machinery, radio and TV repair, auto maintenance, welding and machine shop to students in trade schools.

Basic agriculture science is being added to the curriculum of Malaysian high schools. Volunteers with backgrounds in the natural sciences will teach basic principles of soils, fertilizers, erosion control, principles of simple farm management at the junior high and high school level. Volunteers with degrees in agriculture will be assigned to teacher training institutions.

These programs train from mid-September to December of each year, with industrial arts training in California, agriculture science in Hawaii.

MALARIA ERADICATION

535. PHILIPPINES The Philippine government has requested Peace Corps assistance in its Malaria Control Program. Plans call for an initial effort beginning late 1967 or early 1968. The program requires Volunteers who are liberal arts majors.

536. THAILAND As Assistant Zone Chiefs with the Malaria Eradication Program, Volunteers will provide on-the-job assistance to lower-level workers and oversee the effective carrying out of home checks, blood sampling and spraying. Willingness to travel extensively in remote rural areas essential for this job.

PHYSICAL EDUCATION/RECREATION

540. THAILAND Assigned to regional supervisory units (General Education Development Centers) in provincial capitals, Volunteers will work with a Thai physical education graduate, teaching in local schools and setting up seminars and in-service training programs throughout the region. The community development-related programs will be designed to assist Thai elementary and secondary teachers who have been assigned to teach physical education without prior experience in that field. Volunteers also will help to organize community recreation programs and to work with community teams in basketball and track and field. A physical education degree is *not* required.

COMMUNITY DEVELOPMENT

550. MICRONESIA Community Development activities comprise a significant auxiliary role to every Volunteer assignment. No matter what constitutes a Volunteer's primary job, he is expected to become significantly involved in community development. As a catalyst in his village, the Volunteer will help his neighbors come together, articulate problems and solve them. It is a job requiring skill, patience and training.

551. PHILIPPINES Education Volunteers may choose to undergo special training in rural reconstruction techniques at the Philippine Rural Reconstruction Movement Center in Luzon. PRRM is a non-governmental agency staffed mostly by recent college graduates.

PUBLIC WORKS/ADMINISTRATION

560. MICRONESIA Engineers, architects, surveyors, draftsmen, and construction supervisors are needed to supply engineering and planning support for a wide variety of projects from roads to water catchments and docking facilities.

In the public administration field, lawyers, public administration experts and secretaries are needed to provide on-the-job training for Micronesians who will represent the needed cadre of trained manpower in this Pacific island grouping fast moving toward self-government.

CREDIT UNIONS, CO-OPS, SMALL BUSINESSES

570. MICRONESIA Volunteers are working throughout Micronesia to establish credit unions and cooperatives and to assist in upgrading the management and accounting skills of cooperative/credit union members and Micronesian entrepreneurs. They provide existing and prospective businesses with counseling, orientation, training, and assistance in matters of production, location, supply, markets, accounting, finance and other problems of effective management. Volunteers in this program should have degrees in business administration, accounting, or equivalent experience.

FISHERY DEVELOPMENT

580. MICRONESIA Volunteers with degrees in biology, ecology, statistics, accounting, oceanography and/or experience in commercial fishing are needed to establish an integrated fishing industry which would catch, preserve and market substantial quantities of fish—Micronesia's most obvious and exploitable natural resource. Volunteers will be assigned to three related areas of activity to meet these needs: biological and oceanographic research, compilation of statistics, and conservation.

PART THREE

The Peace Corps Volunteer

9

DOES THE PEACE CORPS NEED YOU?

Tell your future clients that we want fighters, that we want realists. Realism is what the Peace Corps is all about. All the stuff we do, all the problems we solve and confront are the real world's problems. Tell your future candidates that we want realists, we don't want dreamers— at least we don't want full-time dreamers.

—ASSISTANT SECRETARY OF STATE JACK VAUGHN
to the Peace Corps staff, September 1965

IN ITS EARLY DAYS, the emphasis in Peace Corps recruiting was on specific technical skills. However, it soon became apparent that there were simply not enough technically trained young people to meet the demand. Consequently, the Peace Corps threw open its doors to the general liberal arts graduate, and they have been opening wider every year. As one recent Peace Corps recruiting brochure puts it: "Three-quarters of the Peace Corps contingent overseas is, and always has been, made up of 'generalists'—a categroy which, in Peace Corps terms comprises young people from the comfortable campuses of America who possess great curiosity and flexibility and who have pursued a course of study that prepares them intellectually for anything, but prepares them technically for nothing."

This, of course, does not mean that the Peace Corps does not welcome applicants with specific skills. The trained applicant will, in fact, have a greater chance of quick admission and the skills most sought after by the Peace Corps fall into four broad categories:

1. *Teaching.* Slightly over half the Volunteers sent overseas end up teaching. English is the primary language used in the school systems of most African and several Asian countries. Africa alone needs some 300,000 teachers. The primary need is for teachers to teach basic reading and writing, although science and math teachers are also in demand. There will also be some need for teachers of French. Most teaching

assignments will be at the secondary school level. Volunteers do not need to be experienced teachers, but they must demonstrate an aptitude for teaching.

2. *Agriculture.* The need here is for Volunteers with basic knowledge of agricultural techniques, including the ability to conduct demonstration programs in animal husbandry, farm techniques, seed improvement, and irrigation methods.

3. *Health.* Medical school graduates, public-health experts, food and hygiene specialists, sanitation engineers, and registered nurses are in heavy demand.

4. *Urban or Rural Development.* More than one-fourth of all Volunteers are engaged in urban and rural development. The need here is primarily for community-development workers—engineers, surveyors, and workers with a knowledge of public housing and the construction of small buildings. However, liberal arts majors are often utilized in community-development work after an intensive training program.

In addition, the Peace Corps needs Volunteers who are qualified lawyers, engineers, physical education specialists, geologists, language experts, social workers, business administrators, mathematicians, scientists, home economists, and librarians.

However, as I said, the Peace Corps emphasizes the need for students with a general education, and in a recruiting pamphlet directed at the liberal arts graduate, it talks directly to the would-be Volunteer who is wondering whether he or she is qualified:

"But, you say, you have no usable skills," the pamphlet says. "You majored in psychology or art or history. You're not a carpenter or engineer or farmer. How can you help the people of the developing nations help themselves?

"You can teach. You can do community-development work. You can serve as a librarian, a journalist, a recreation leader. Over 300 skills are used by the Peace Corps and you have one of them. More than half of all Peace Corps Volunteers are liberal arts graduates. The developing nations request people like you—people who can think, who have leadership ability, initiative, and resourcefulness; people who have participated in sports, tinkered with mechanical gadgets, grown a garden, started a library, taught a first aid course, organized a committee. These are the skills of contemporary life; they can help the people of emerging nations take their place in the modern world. There is much you can do in the Peace Corps."

Despite the enthusiasm which the Peace Corps has aroused on the nation's campuses, the Peace Corps does not confine its recruiting solely to college graduates. Graduates of vocational and technical schools and skilled workers are also much in demand. As John Gardner, Secretary of Health, Education and Welfare, once said, "We must have respect for both our plumbers and our philosophers, or neither our pipes nor our theories will hold water."

In search of technically trained workers, the Peace Corps has initiated a special "blue-collar" recruiting program for machinists, bricklayers, carpenters, electricians, welders, pipefitters, etc. At the same time, the Peace Corps is continually working with large corporations and labor unions, urging them to make it possible for skilled workers to serve for two years abroad in the Peace Corps without endangering their pension plans or their participation in other industry programs. "Nobody should think he has too much or too little skill to serve in the Peace Corps," says one Peace Corps recruiting officer. "That is something for us to judge."

To be qualified for service as a Peace Corps Volunteer, a person must:

1. Be a citizen of the United States. Proof of citizenship will be required.

2. Be at least eighteen years of age. Parental approval will have to be obtained by persons under twenty-one who live in states where persons under twenty-one are legally regarded as minors.

3. Be single or, if married, both husband and wife must volunteer. Couples with dependent children under eighteen will not be eligible for service. Persons who are legally separated are eligible to serve.

4. Be in excellent physical and mental health, as evidenced by the ability to pass required examinations and attain adequate immunization.

5. Be emotionally mature, as evidenced by information gleaned through references, tests, and interviews.

6. Be exemplary in his personal conduct, as evidenced by information obtained through references and during the selection and training process.

7. Possess a background of education or experience required for successful participation both in the training programs and in subsequent performance on the job. These requirements will relate specifically to the assignment to be undertaken.

8. Demonstrate:

(*a*) A willingness to undertake tasks requiring considerable sustained effort under conditions of discomfort and possibly danger.

(*b*) Interest in and ability to learn the manners, customs, languages, and history of peoples with whom he will work.

(*c*) Sensitivity which will enable him to understand the views, prejudices, and problems of people of different national, religious, cultural, or racial backgrounds.

(*d*) An interest and ability in activities requiring physical stamina.

(*e*) A willingness to perform dull, routine, or even unpleasant tasks necessary for the implementation of the program of the Peace Corps without thought or regard to personal gain.

(*f*) Ability to get along and work with others.

(*g*) A sufficient knowledge of the United States—its history, its economy, its government, and its social structure—to permit applicant to impart an understanding to peoples of other countries.

9. Be willing to serve in a volunteer capacity, without salary, for a tour of duty of at least 24 months, including the training period.

10. Be willing, at the request of the agency administering the project, to transfer from one assignment to another or from one position to another as the needs of the programs may require, taking into account the skills of the individual volunteer.

11. Agree to undertake such language, area, or other training courses as may be determined by the Peace Corps.

12. Agree to accept the discipline of the Peace Corps, subordinating his personal preferences and interests to the requirements of the programs.

It should be obvious that a Peace Corps Volunteer must be in top physical condition. This does not mean that athletes are preferred, or that the volunteer needs to be battle-tough as a commando. But he will assuredly be called upon to withstand physical stress beyond that normally encountered in civilian life in the United States. The Peace Corps specifically urges that anyone requiring special diets or frequent medical or dental treatment not file a questionnaire; the rigors of life in the Peace Corps will prevent his being recruited.

No consideration is given race or religion, and political beliefs or influence play no part in the final selection. To be selected, the Volunteer must qualify on the basis of general requirements for all programs and specific requirements for particular projects. In addition, certain "plus factors" will influence the chances of being selected. Here are the general and specific requirements, as well as the "plus factors," which guide the Peace Corps in selection of volunteers:

GENERAL REQUIREMENTS

1. *Intelligence.* A minimum intelligence level sufficiently high to

meet the job demands of a particular project and to cope with other challenges of Peace Corps work. Above-average intelligence is generally required for rapid learning in a short training program, for adaptability in the face of unexpected demands, and for the ability to communicate concepts to others on the job.

2. *United States history, institutions, and values.* Knowledge of the history and of the social and political institutions of the United States sufficient to profit from instruction and to be prepared to answer questions intelligently. The Volunteer must not be so lacking in background information that his deficiencies cannot be repaired in a brief training program.

3. *Health and stamina.* Physical condition that will permit effective service. Physical stamina sufficient to sustain, after a period of conditioning in training, the stresses of Peace Corps work.

4. *Emotional stability.* A history of effective functioning in periods of stress. Personality integration sufficient to meet the demands of Peace Corps service with a margin of personal strength sufficient to handle periods of heightened stress, such as would be involved in cultural shock, isolation, danger, and physical discomfort.

5. *Personal attributes.* Qualities of personality required for establishing effective relationships with fellow workers in other countries, such as friendliness, gentleness, patience, ability to lead or follow, interpersonal warmth and sensitivity, ability to communicate, dedication to the service of people, a sense of mission in the context of good judgment, and respect for and acceptance of other people regardless of race, social class, religion, or ethnic origin. It is expected that these attributes will be identified through personal references, tests, interviews, peer ratings, and observation of behavior during the training period.

SPECIFIC REQUIREMENTS

1. *Job competence.* A demonstrated level of competence in giving a service or performing a task that exceeds by a clear margin the requirements of the project to which the Volunteer is to be assigned.

2. *Language aptitude.* For projects requiring a language that must be learned during training or on the job, language projects requiring a commonly taught language, such as Spanish or French, aptitude for or demonstrated competence in the language at a level that is or can be made adequate for the job in a short training period. There are, it should be stressed, many projects in which the only language requirement is English.

PLUS FACTORS

1. A successful experience living abroad, or prior intensive area study of a culture similar to that of the host country for a project.

2. Experience in family or geographical environment in the United States that would speed adaptation to the environment to which the Volunteer will be assigned.

3. An apprenticeship or work experience relevant to the job to be done on a particular project.

4. Successful experience in group activities involving close relationship with people of diverse backgrounds.

Of course, it will not be easy for an individual interested in the Peace Corps to determine whether he has the personal qualities the Peace Corps is looking for in its Volunteers. It is extremely important, however, that these personal character traits be present—"fundamental sincerity," Dr. Al Carp, Peace Corps Director of Selection, has defined them, "integrity, emotional stability, the ability to communicate with others, and an interest in people."

The maturity expected of any Peace Corps Volunteer must include understanding of other people and of alien cultures. Any American who goes abroad with a "we'll show 'em" attitude is certain to do more harm than good. But without being arrogant, the Volunteer's initiative and self-reliance must be developed to a much greater extent overseas than is usually the case at home. As one ICA officer was quoted in *The Overseas American* as saying:

> You've got to be able to supervise yourself here. At home a gold-bricker can get on pretty well in an assembly-line type of operation. But here he's forced to do things himself. Over here, no one is going to drive you. You've got to figure out what to do and drive yourself to get it done. I don't know how to measure this quality. A fellow may do pretty well in the States, then get out here where he has to supervise himself and then flop. This is quite apart from having to adjust to living conditions. A guy has to have the desire to do something and get it done and say to himself, "I did it."

It was once believed that women would not be eligible for the Peace Corps. However, women are very much needed in the Peace Corps—as teachers, home economists, and nurses, both in the field of child care and public health. Thus far, women have made up approximately 41 percent of the Peace Corps Volunteers. If married, both husband and wife must volunteer and possess qualifying skills.

Similarly, the Peace Corps has often been thought of as seeking only young people. But men and women over 50, skilled in most of the trades, vocations, and professions sought by the Peace Corps, are also in demand—*if* they possess the additional qualities of physical vitality, emotional maturity, tact, ability to share, to improvise, to lead. As Sargent Shriver said in a television address: "In addition to the expertness that experience brings, age gives a Volunteer a status of authority that is denied a younger person. . . . We now have about 350 people over 50 years of age who are serving successfully in the Peace Corps. I recently visited a 70-year-old Volunteer in Tunisia who is working in a tractor plant, a 76-year-old engineer in Pakistan, and two ladies, one 65 and the other 64, who are teaching in Ethiopia. We are happy that these older citizens have joined the Peace Corps. We want as many of them as we can possibly get."

On the other hand, young people—youngsters of high-school age—are discouraged from applying for the Peace Corps, although the Peace Corps receives a considerable volume of mail from high-school students asking what they can do to help now. The answer given by the Peace Corps is that the best way high-school students can help is by preparing themselves now to become more effective Peace Corps Volunteers. The Peace Corps has some specific suggestions for young people who wish to join the Peace Corps in the years ahead. If you are in high school now, the Peace Corps recommends that you should:

• *Develop one or more skills which will be useful in the world's less-developed areas.* Teachers, agricultural and community-development workers, nurses and medical aides, home economists, engineers and surveyors, physical education instructors and recreation workers, mechanics, carpenters, bricklayers, plumbers, and "do-it-yourself" builders are among those who will be needed. Volunteers with needed skills and maturity can be admitted to the Peace Corps at age eighteen, but in most cases college or vocational training would greatly boost their potential contribution.

Students hoping to serve in the Peace Corps may want to acquire more than one needed skill. Even a mechanic or an English teacher, for instance, is likely to be a more useful Peace Corps Volunteer if he or she has also been active in a 4-H Club or the Future Farmers or Future Homemakers of America, or has had a summer job in a hospital, on a farm, or at a recreation center.

• *Study the language and culture of one of the areas where Peace Corps Volunteers are at work.* Most high-school students in the United States have many such opportunities, if they will but take advantage of them. French is spoken in a score of African and Asian nations, Spanish in most Latin American nations. More and more high schools are making it possible for students to learn about all the world, and not just Europe and North America, in social studies, history, literature, and geography courses. Educational radio and television stations, as well as the major networks, sponsor an increasing number of programs dealing with Africa, Asia, and Latin America. Community world affairs organizations in many cities welcome the participation of interested high-school students. Many local libraries offer lists of recommended books on the world's new nations.

• *Become personally acquainted with young Asians, Africans, and Latin Americans.* This is easier than many people think.

The Experiment in International Living (Putney, Vermont) is seeking American host families with whom newly arrived foreign students and visitors may stay, as family members, for a month. State 4-H Club headquarters (c/o the state's land-grant college or university) arrange for foreign participants in the International Farm Youth Exchange to live with American farm families for three-week periods. The American Field Service (313 East 43rd Street, New York City 10016) selects families with whom foreign young people live while attending a year of high school in the United States.

By contacting Foreign Student Advisers at nearby colleges and universities, a family may arrange to offer friendship and hospitality to a foreign student from a particular country or area.

International pen-pal relationships may be arranged by writing to World Pen Pals, World Affairs Center, University of Minnesota, Minneapolis 14, Minnesota.

World Affairs Councils and other community organizations often make arrangements for foreign visitors to stay in local homes, or to be escorted on local tours by volunteer guides. The National Council for Community Services to International Visitors (1630 Crescent Place, N.W., Washington 9, D.C.) can provide names and addresses of such organizations.

• *Build a first-hand knowledge and understanding of the principles, achievements and problems of American democracy.* Peace Corps Volunteers overseas face questions about America by the dozen—from questioners both curious and critical. The broader a Volunteer's background, the greater his personal experience with Americans of all social-economic and ethnic groups, the more successful he can be in interpreting American democracy to others.

Courses in civics, history, and social studies and the reading of magazines and newspapers offering good national and world affairs coverage can be a start. They may be supplemented by extracurricular and summer participation in student volunteer work camps, social service projects, citizenship seminars and political campaigns, and visits to legislative bodies, business, farm, and labor organizations. The achievements of American civic and social welfare organizations are admired throughout the world. Firsthand experience in such groups can be of great value to Peace Corps Volunteers.

• *Take part in athletic, camping, or other outdoor activities that will help assure physical fitness.* A Peace Corps Volunteer is called upon to work hard, sometimes under difficult climatic conditions. Every effort is made to protect his health, but one of the Volunteer's best assurances of the strength and stamina to do his job well will be his previous concern for physical fitness. Summer jobs on farms or in factories are good experience. Athletic skills will be useful, too, for many overseas Volunteers find local youngsters eager to take part in spare-time sport activities.

No matter how old or how young, or whether you are professionally or technically trained, or a liberal arts graduate, there is one qualification which all Peace Corps Volunteers must have. For lack of a better phrase, it can be called *a sense of mission.*

Anyone who thinks a tour of duty in the Peace Corps is going to be a sightseeing trip abroad, or wants to join the Peace Corps just for kicks or because he doesn't have anything better to do, might just as well not waste his time applying. It is extremely unlikely that he would pass the Peace Corps's tests or training courses, and if he did he would be certain to be miserable overseas.

Similarly, anyone who is considering the Peace Corps as a means of escaping his personal problems will find, once he gets overseas, that those problems have not changed one bit. The stresses of foreign service will in fact probably aggravate them.

This is not to say that anyone who wants to join the Peace Corps because he is unhappy should not do so. *It all depends on what he is unhappy about.* As pointed out by the authors of *The Overseas American,* if the Vounteer is unhappy about the lack of challenge in the life he leads here, his desire to "escape" into service overseas may well be based on qualities which would make him eminently successful there: "If an applicant is escaping from being 'average,' or 'hemmed in,' or 'intellectually starved,' then the escape motivation, far from being considered an unfavorable quality in the applicant, should probably be regarded as a clue to just that out-of-the-ordinary American who may face with unusual zest the special adjustments required of overseas personnel. After all, the American pioneer was an escapist too."

However, there must also be a sense of service to one's country, plus a genuine desire to help. That undefinable something which must be present in every Peace Corps Volunteer is related to something William James said in his first proposal for a peace army. James commented that there is nothing to make one indignant about the mere fact that life is hard. But that so many, said James, by mere accidents of birth and opportunity, should have a life of *nothing else* but toil and hardness—"*this* is capable of arousing indignation in reflective minds."

The ideal Volunteer for the Peace Corps should be a reflective man or woman who is genuinely indignant about the fact that while he or she has had an opportunity to achieve the good life, many millions, by the mere accident of birth, have nothing but toil and hardship. But the Volunteer must be more than indignant at this situation; he or she must also possess the desire *and* the skill to make at least a small contribution toward correcting it.

10

JOINING THE PEACE CORPS

Ask not what your country can do for you—ask what you can do for your country.

—PRESIDENT JOHN F. KENNEDY,
in his Inaugural Address,
January 20, 1961.

THE FIRST STEP TOWARD JOINING the Peace Corps is to obtain a Peace Corps questionnaire from your local post office or county agricultural agent, your Congressman, or a college in your area. If a questionnaire is not readily available, one can be obtained by writing to The Peace Corps, Washington, D.C. 20525.

The Peace Corps questionnaire also serves as an application form. It is fourteen pages long and contains twenty-six items. Designed primarily to help the selection officers obtain some idea of the applicant's basic skills and competence, it asks for the following kinds of information:

Education

Job Experience

Proficiency in languages

Technical skills

Availability for Peace Corps
    service

Special foreign-area knowledge

Health

Military service

Hobbies and athletic participation

Organizational activity and
    leadership

Geographic preference for
    assignment

Eight references are also asked for, including at least three faculty members if you are in school now. Actually, the Peace Corps sends out requests for letters of reference to a total of ten or twelve people, including former employers or heads of voluntary agencies for whom you might have worked. A Peace Corps applicant is well advised to give careful consideration to his references, because the Peace Corps selection officers rely heavily on the information they receive from people who have observed the applicant over a number of years. Be sure to list names of people who know you well and who will write when requested.

Although Peace Corps Volunteers call it "the monster," applicants should not be frightened by the questionnaire. It is designed to help the Peace Corps find out about your background and skills, but if you are able to fill out only a few of the blanks it does not necessarily mean that you lack qualifications. For instance, if you were raised on a farm and only completed a couple of years of agricultural college, were not very active in sports, and do not know a foreign language, you may not have much to write down on your questionnaire. But you still may be just the person the Peace Corps is looking for—possibly for an agricultural project in a country in which the language is Hindu or Arabic. (The Peace Corps is not expecting to find skilled Volunteers who speak unusual languages; it provides basic training courses in these languages.) Similarly, if you are a skilled laborer, there will be many sections of the questionnaire that you will not be able to complete, but at the same time you will be able to fill in many sections that college graduates and professional people cannot.

In other words, a Volunteer does *not* need to possess the whole range of skills listed on the questionnaire—usually one well-grounded skill will be enough to qualify an applicant.

Once the Peace Corps determines whether the applicant possesses the basic qualifications, he is notified by mail when the next Peace Corps entrance exam is to be given. These are held the second Saturday each month and are administered by the Civil Service. They are given in approximately 1,100 towns throughout the United States. They start at 8:30 A.M. and take approximately one and one-half hours to complete. They can be taken at any scheduled time, even though the applicant may not be available for duty until some time in the future.

The general aptitude and language aptitude tests were developed in cooperation with the Educational Testing Service, which is responsible for the College Entrance Board Examinations, the Graduate Record Examination, the Foreign Service Officer Examination, and the examinations for the military academies. They are designed primarily to measure general aptitude and the specific aptitude for acquiring another language. They take thirty minutes to complete and since they are primarily placement tests, they are noncompetitive and there are no passing and failing grades.

The tests are helpful, however, in determining whether the Volunteer has acquired and currently possesses some of the basic abilities needed to profit from the Peace Corps's rugged academic course work, and also whether he or she has the basic general aptitude for success in the various projects to which Volunteers will be assigned. It is not expected that the test scores alone will tell the whole story, or by themselves indicate future success in training or in projects. A great many other facts about the applicant are considered by selection personnel in making a judgment or hazarding a guess as to his or her probable chances for success in training and in the field.

The General Aptitude Test is composed of three different types of problems: mathematical, verbal, and spatial.

• The mathematical process in the arithmetic questions calls for the applicant to solve a problem, stated in a sentence or two, using processes generally taught in the elementary grades and high schools.

• The verbal questions require the applicant to select from fivt alternatives the synonym for a given word. The questions become progressively more difficult.

• The spatial problems consist of pictures of piles of byocks and require the applicant to judge the number of blocks needed to make up the pile. Many of the piles include blocks which cannot be seen in the picture but whose presence can be inferred from the position of the other blocks. For example, here is a sample block-counting question shown to applicants prior to taking the test proper. The items become more difficult as the test progresses.

Example:

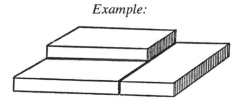

How many blocks? Every block in a pile is the same size and shape as all the other blocks in that pile, but the size and shapes of blocks may change from one problem to another.

(A) 3   (B) 4   (C) 5   (D) 6   (E) 7

(*The answer is* "B")

The *Modern Language Aptitude Test* is designed to provide an indication of the applicant's probable degree of success in learning to speak and to understand a foreign language. The score on this test will depend to some extent on the applicant's English vocabulary, but the test also measures sound-symbol association ability, sensitivity to grammar structure, and the rote memory aspect of the learning of foreign languages.

Section I of the language aptitude test consists of two samples and fifty items, each with a disguised word followed by five English words. The task is to recognize the equivalent English word from the pronunciation of the disguised word.

Example:

MRLD

(A) Marmalade
(B) Precious gem
(C) World
(D) Mister
(E) Miserably

("B" *is the correct answer since "a precious gem" (emerald) is "disguised" in the letters* MRLD.)

Section II is called "Words in Sentences." It consists of forty-five key sentences, including one word which is capitalized and underlined, followed by a second sentence which has five words or phrases underlined. The task here is to select the underlined word or phrase in the second sentence which does the same thing in its sentence as the underlined word in the key sentence.

Example:

GOVERNMENTAL

The Peace Corps is a ——————————— agency.

$\frac{\text{Dr.}}{(A)}$ Smith, who teaches at $\frac{\text{our}}{(B)}$ University, is noted as an $\frac{\text{industrial}}{(C)}$ economist $\frac{\text{as well as}}{(D)}$ a $\frac{\text{fine}}{(E)}$ musician.

("C" *is the correct answer.*)

The examinee is given several sample items and is told that the test measures the ability to understand the functions of words and phrases in sentences. It does this without using grammatical terminology, although the score may be to some extent dependent upon training in grammar. It is designed to separate those who will do well from those who will do poorly in studying the grammar of a new language.

Section III, "Paired Associates," consists of twenty-four "Kurdish" words, each followed by five English words. The examinee is first allowed four minutes to study and memorize the twenty-four Kurdish words and their English equivalents and to try some samples. He then is asked to select the English equivalent for each of the twenty-four foreign words, without referring to the Kurdish-English vocabulary list in the booklet. This is not a memory test; the list of words shows the general relationship of English to Kurdish words, and the test determines if you can grasp relationships.

Example:
    SONJE

(A) Sons
(B) Table
(C) Student
(D) Sun
(E) Hammer

If the applicant thinks that "Sons" is the correct meaning for SONJE, he would mark "A" in the appropriate space on his answer sheet.

The results of the language aptitude test help Peace Corps officers predict the ability of an applicant to acquire a foreign language at the pace demanded in intensive language training. In view of the rapid and intensive learning of foreign languages required of some Peace Corps trainees, the test helps in selecting trainees who are best able to survive this training. The critical importance of the foreign language training in many Peace Corps projects makes it imperative that only applicants with a reasonable probability of surviving this training be put into such training. A poor showing in the language aptitude test will very likely result in an otherwise qualified applicant being placed in a project in which only English is required.

The decision of the Peace Corps to accept or reject an applicant is based on the applicant's questionnaire and letters of reference. If an applicant is chosen, he or she is notified to report for training. Approximately one in four of those who apply are invited for training and about 50 percent of those invited accept.

Transportation to the training site is paid by the Peace Corps, and the moment the Volunteer leaves home he is covered by a group medical and life-insurance plan.

The location of the training site depends on the project to which a Volunteer is assigned; different universities are selected as training sites for different projects. It is recommended that the Volunteer bring with him only as many clothes as will be needed during this stage of training, which usually will be three months: at least one good suit would be handy for the training period. Volunteers are also encouraged to bring recreational equipment such as musical instruments, tennis racquets, portable radios, and so forth.

In addition, it is recommended that the Volunteer bring the following:

1. A birth certificate and/or naturalization certificate.

2. His latest passport, if he has one.

3. A record of all immunizations, showing types of immunization and dates administered, preferably prepared by the Volunteer's physician.

4. The Volunteer's Selective Service registration card or armed-service discharge record.

Room and board during the training period is paid for by the Peace Corps; in addition, each Volunteer receives two dollars a day spending money. The training period counts toward all benefits which the Peace Corps Volunteer receives at the time he retires from active duty.

After arriving for training, the Volunteer is first given a careful medical examination. The results of this examination are reviewed according to physical standards similar to those used by the Medical Department of the Army for enlistment and induction. Adherence to these standards assures the Volunteer who does not meet the necessary requirements that he will not be permitted to work in situations too demanding for his physical capacity.

The Volunteer also undergoes numerous assessments of his personal qualifications and some Volunteers are interviewed by a psychiatrist. During training the Volunteer also undergoes a background investigation conducted by the Civil Service Commission. Once you have received an invitation to a Peace Corps training camp you are well on your way—*but you are still not a Peace Corps Volunteer!* Your invitation to training is just that—an invitation to become a Peace Corps trainee. While odds favor your successful completion of training, you should not tell your hometown paper, friends, etc., that you are a Volunteer until you complete training and definitely have been selected for overseas service.

Do not sell your home, furniture, or car, or cut your ties completely when you accept an invitation for training. Before reporting and during training make arrangements for these things, but try to postpone final action until you are sure you are going overseas. Most programs allow Volunteers about ten days at home between the end of training and overseas departure.

Once training begins, the Peace Corps no longer has to rely solely on an applicant's written record. The potential Volunteer is tested and observed throughout training to see if he or she is the kind of person the Peace Corps needs for the project. The people who judge the trainees want them to succeed and try to help them in every way they can. Here are some tips, extracted from a Peace Corps guide book which will help give you some idea of what the Peace Corps expects of you during training:

"Keep in mind the country to which you may be sent, and conduct yourself as you would there.

"Don't hesitate to talk frankly to staff members about training or any problems you may encounter.

"Remember that we don't expect you to be perfect. You are judged as much by your reactions and adjustments to your shortcomings as by your attitude toward your successes.

"Your attitude toward the training process and willingness to persevere may indicate better than any other single factor that you have what it takes to succeed overseas. Observed shortcomings usually are pointed out during training so you can work on your weak points and demonstrate ability to improve yourself."

Twice during training, a selection board, which is advisory to the Peace Corps Director, considers the accumulated information about a trainee. A trainee may be separated during training if it is clearly the best thing for him or the program, but the Peace Corps usually tries to postpone such decisions until the end of training, when all information is available.

This board includes Peace Corps staff members concerned with selection, training, and program development and, where appropriate, representatives of the private agencies or universities which sometimes assist in the operation of overseas projects. The board also includes representatives from the training institution: its consulting medical officer, psychiatrist, and Project Director. The Peace Corps Representative and a representative of the host country's embassy may be among the others participating.

A selection board can make one of four recommendations—acceptance as a Volunteer, outright disqualification, service in another training program, or disqualification pending correction of some deficiency. This last recommendation usually is reserved for medical cases where improvement seems likely.

If a trainee is not selected as a Volunteer, he can discuss the board's recommendation with the selection officer. While the officer will explain the general basis for the decision, he may not be able to give a disqualified trainee any one specific reason. No single area of performance may be poor, but if a pattern of inadequate adjustment shows up in various situations the board is likely to recommend against overseas service.

According to the Peace Corps, experienced Volunteers list the selection process as one of the clues to Peace Corps success overseas. While some Volunteers initially were upset over the failure of certain trainees to make the grade, they now, after field experience, are among the strongest advocates of a thorough selection process. Experience has shown that one unsuitable Volunteer can jeopardize an entire project and the effectiveness of all his colleagues.

11

TRAINING

The Peace Corps trembles so close on the verge of greatness that the very forces it has generated demand that it go all the way over; that it become, in effect, the model of a new education appropriate to the opportunities and problems of this age.

—JOHN R. SEELEY, Brandeis University.

THERE HAVE BEEN MANY CHANGES in the Peace Corps since its creation in 1961, but the phase of its operation that has undergone the most drastic revisions is the training program. One of the earliest decisions of the Peace Corps was to utilize the training facilities of existing colleges and universities in the United States rather than create training centers of its own. Although there have been exceptions—especially recently— the great majority of Peace Corps training programs have been conducted by colleges and universities; to date, more than 125 institutions have participated in this program.

Thus, it is not surprising that the first Peace Corps training courses were modeled on the academic programs of our colleges and universities. This tendency to stick with the familiar educational methods was understandable considering that neither the participating college faculties nor the Peace Corps training staff knew exactly what they were training the Volunteers for. Time was also a factor. The Peace Corps too often could give the universities only a short time to prepare and organize the training course they had agreed to conduct, and the programs themselves were often not long enough.

However, after the first two years, when the Volunteers began returning, the Peace Corps took another look at the training program to determine its effectiveness in relation to the actual life and work abroad. After considerable study there was virtually unanimous agreement that the Peace Corps's training program, as originally conceived, was not as effective as it could have been. The two principal complaints were that it did not include enough practical experience in the field and that there was not enough language instruction.

To determine what directions a new approach to training should take, the Peace Corps set up an Educational Task Force consisting of prominent educators and Peace Corps staff members. In its Report, "On a River Larger than the Mississippi: The Peace Corps's New Education Program," the Task Force set forth a number of "lessons" it had learned from the Peace Corps's early training experiences. The lessons quoted below illustrate not only what the critics of the Peace Corps's training program felt was wrong with it, but the new directions the Task Force felt it should take:

Instead of Peace Corps training stopping at the water's edge when the Volunteers go overseas, it must be seen as just the first step in a continuing education—an education that began in earlier school years, intensified while in full-time training and coming to a climax overseas and thereafter.

• Instead of as much information as possible being crammed into the Volunteers' heads during the initial three months, the training programs must concentrate on starting processes of learning that will continue throughout two years.

• Instead of one lecture piled on top of another, the emphasis must be on seminars with trainees, professors, returned Volunteers, and foreign participants discussing and questioning around a table.

• Instead of schedules that preclude reading, research, or individual field work, more time must be left to individual learning, with the training period lengthened, where necessary.

• Instead of little but on-campus education, training programs must include considerable periods of community action, practice teaching or other work in radically unfamiliar environments: in slum or rural areas of Job Corps camps in mainland United States, in other cultures such as Puerto Rico, the Virgin Islands, the State of Hawaii, Mexico, Quebec, or Israel—or in the host countries themselves—with some programs taking place entirely in those locations.

• Instead of lecturers who come from various departments to speak from standard notes and then depart, there must be a specially welded faculty who help plan the programs, who work together throughout it, who know the Volunteers, who question and are questioned, who teach.

• Instead of returned Peace Corps Volunteers or staff being regarded as interlopers, they must be full members of the training faculty with a part in the planning and with other defined responsibilities, and the latest field information brought by them must be given full attention.

• Instead of foreign students or other participants from the host country being restricted to a narrow technical role as "language informants," they, too, must be integrated as members of the faculty, and their background drawn out to the fullest extent; and they must be chosen with this in mind.

• Instead of a fragmented curriculum, there must be intercultural comparative studies of issues such as race here and caste abroad, poverty in Appalachia and in the Andes, the sources of American or Nigerian thought, considered and compared in the context of the problems a Volunteer will face.

• Instead of huge programs in which 200 or 300 trainees are herded around according to a standardized schedule, training must be in much smaller groups, seldom larger than a hundred, with individual needs and interests respected, and with trainees participating in some of the decision-making and evaluation of the program.

• Instead of the selection of Volunteers casting a pall over the training, there must be emphasis on self-selection, with procedures for faculty participation, full candor with trainees about any concerns that arise, and a recognized appeal system for those who disagree with a selection decision.

• Instead of the planning and organization of [programs] being left to the last minute, arrangements must be made earlier in the year whenever possible, so that University training Project Directors can start work in time to produce an excellent program.

• Instead of the training institutions being treated like a service station, to which the Peace Corps comes, fills up, and drives off, the training program must be only the beginning of the University's role: the faculty must be invited in various ways to participate in the continuing education of the Volunteers overseas, and the Volunteers encouraged to develop continuing relationships with particular faculty members or colleges and universities.

• Instead of all this beginning only with the formal training programs, for many Volunteers preparation for service must begin months or years before—through Peace Corps campus seminars that discuss case studies, films, or other materials; through courses in a foreign language or foreign society or a pertinent job skill; through work with foreign students and returned Peace Corps Volunteers in the area; or through field experience in American community action or teaching.

• And instead of any of this becoming rigid, further ideas for innovation must continue to be welcomed.

"Since the purpose of education is to spur growth," the report goes on to say, "the purpose of Peace Corps training should be to provide the environment and tools for growth to people who, by volunteering, have expressed a desire to grow. To do this, the theme of Peace Corps training should be, in the words of one Volunteer: 'Expose and prod, expose and prod, and come to no answers too soon.'"

This report was prepared at the end of 1965. As the Task Force pointed out, some Peace Corps training programs had already incorporated many of these new concepts. By the end of 1966, the trend away from the old, rigid, academic-type programs was pronounced. "We want to get the trainee out of the classroom," said Deputy Training Director Alexander Shakow, "and into situations comparable to the ones he will be facing overseas. In the old days, we didn't know exactly what we were training for. But we have learned a lot from the returning Volunteers who have been coming back in large numbers." In fact, the returning Volunteers are themselves proving invaluable as instructors. By the summer of 1966, 400 ex-Volunteers were participating in the training programs, and the trend is toward their increased use.

Most of the improvements in the Peace Corps training programs have been in the direction of innovation and variation; because of this, it is difficult to describe the programs because no two are alike. Certain variations, depending on the countries to which the Volunteers are assigned and the nature of the projects on which they will be working, are to be expected. But the new emphasis on innovation in Peace Corps training has even resulted in variations in programs designed to train Volunteers for the same country and similar projects. Thus, it is no longer possible to describe a Peace Corps training program by saying that 48 classroom hours are devoted to world affairs, 96 hours to area studies, 48 hours to American government and institutions, and so forth.

Generally speaking, a Peace Corps training program lasts from 12 to 13 weeks, including three to four weeks of field experience in surroundings that present the same problems the Volunteer is likely to face abroad. The field experience is held at one of the Peace Corps training sites, in Puerto Rico, in the Virgin Islands, in a camp run by the University of Hawaii in the Waipio Valley, on an Indian reservation, or in an American ghetto such as Harlem, Watts, or Vine City (in Atlanta). Sometimes the field experience is obtained in a "third country," for example, a group of trainees headed for French-speaking Africa may be taught for a month in Quebec.

Regardless of how skilled a Volunteer may be, he will be ineffective if he cannot communicate his ideas. This is particularly true in former colonial areas. The ability to speak the local language often opens doors usually closed to the foreigner, and it also helps the Volunteer understand his host country better. Hence, more than half the Peace Corps training period is now devoted to language study.

Language is usually taught in the Peace Corps training camps by host country nationals who also instruct the Volunteers in the mores and customs of their native lands. The so-called "immersion environment" method is used. Approximately 300–350 hours are spent in small classes (about six or seven students) that meet from four to six hours a day. In addition, time is spent in language laboratories, and the language of the host country is spoken at meals and as much as possible in the daily life at the training camp. The emphasis is on learning to communicate verbally; reading and writing is of secondary importance. In the new concept of training, language studies do not end with the training period; they are continued overseas, and often it is imperative that the Volunteer learn a second foreign language after he arrives in the host country. At the end of his first year of service abroad, the Volunteer is given an oral language test to measure his progress and stimulate further study. At the end of his second year, the Volunteer is given another oral proficiency test to determine his final achievement in language studies. The goal is to place the Volunteer on a level with the natives, so that he can say to people once ruled by white colonists, as one Volunteer did, "I come to speak as equals."

So far, more than 82 languages have been taught in Peace Corps training programs. As a result, the Peace Corps has become the nation's largest consumer of language learning tools. Many of the languages such as Douala (Cameroons), Tumbuka (Malawi), Wolof (Ivory Coast), and Susu (Guinea) were taught for the first time in this country by the Peace Corps which had to write its own text and prepare its own language tapes.

Another goal of the training program is to make the Volunteer more proficient in the skill or profession that he will be taking abroad, and to give him experience in practicing that skill under conditions similar to those he will find in the host country. For example, teachers who will teach English in secondary schools actually practice teaching their subjects on nationals of the host country; urban community-development workers practice these skills in slums where conditions are comparable to those they will be encountering abroad; poultry workers bound for India, often with only a liberal arts background, are taught the fundamentals of poultry raising.

The Volunteer must also be prepared for cross-cultural understanding. The development of American culture and values is discussed in informal seminars along with the problem of communism in the developing nations. Nationals from the host countries—often the language instructors—discuss the culture and customs of their countries. Psychiatrists with experience in the host countries discuss possible emotional challenges that may be experienced—anger, depression, culture shock, frustration, a sense of failure, and an inability to tolerate uncertainty.

Often, one of the Volunteer's greatest challenges in his job is to find that he must really shape and model his own job. "We had a structured training program," said one Peace Corps official commenting on the first Peace Corps efforts, "for one of the most unstructured jobs in the world—the job of the Peace Corps Volunteer." Today, training emphasizes self-reliance, decision-making, and confidence-building. The stress on self-reliance in some training programs is carried to the point where the Volunteers participate in planning the training program, even to the extent of deciding what phase of the program to stress, selecting what topics are to be discussed, arranging the schedule, and planning the field experience. Thus the structuring in training are done largely by the trainees themselves, which is what they will have to do in their overseas jobs.

As mentioned in Chapter 10, midway through the training program and again at the end, the personality and performance of each trainee are assessed. About 25 percent of the trainees are not selected to go overseas; more and more of the emphasis is on self-assessment, however, with the Volunteer himself deciding whether he or she will go overseas on a particular project to a particular country. However, the final decision is still up to the Peace Corps's selection board; according to the Peace Corps *Fact Book,* the board's final decision in the matter is based on the following criteria:

1. *Motivation* that will insure commitment to serve in the Peace Corps despite periods of stress and adversity.

2. *Aptitude* sufficient to meet the demands of a particular program and to cope with other challenges of Peace Corps work, including rapid learning in a short training period.

3. *Personal qualities* including initiative, determination, friendliness, patience, ability to communicate, and respect for other people regardless of race, religion, nationality, social standing, or political persuasion.

4. *The physical stamina and emotional stability* to maintain effectiveness under the stresses of Peace Corps work.

5. *Competence in the skills required* for the assignment overseas.

6. *Sufficient progress in the new language* before the end of training.

7. *Adequate knowledge* of both the host country and the United States.

Selection is made without reference to race, creed, or political affiliation.

As mentioned earlier, Peace Corps training programs are as varied as the number of institutions preparing Volunteers for service overseas. In 1966, for example, there were five separate and varied programs simultaneously training teachers for Philippine schools. None was representative of Philippine training programs nor of other Peace Corps training, but it might help to understand Peace Corps training to take a close look at one of them.

During the last week of June, 47 prospective Volunteers arrived at Stanford University where they were greeted by a staff of about 29, including nine Filipinos and nine returned Peace Corps Volunteers who had served in the Philippines. In addition, the staff was complemented by 45 young Filipino children recently arrived from the Philippines whom the training staff had gathered together from the San Francisco area. "The presence of these children," said one Peace Corps training officer, "symbolized the central approach of the program, which was to break away from the standard divisions of academic disciplines and integrate all relevant parts of training towards producing a Volunteer who realized that the components of the teacher's role in the Philippines not only fit together but overlap. The children not only served as pupils for practice teaching but they themselves were language 'teachers' for the trainees in their five hours every day on the Stanford campus. They also taught the trainees Philippine games and were taught American games in Tagalog by the prospective Volunteers. They ate lunch together and shared experiences throughout the day."

The trainees spent several hours a day developing practical skills in the teaching of English as a second language, including the preparation of lesson plans for practice teaching sessions. A Filipino who runs the English Section in the Philippines Bureau of Public Schools was in charge of the program, which drew heavily in seminar meetings upon Volunteers who had taught English in the Philippines. The preparation was immediately applied in an afternoon practice "micro-teaching" session. Here trainees began with simple teaching situations and moved to more complex problems with a handful of pupils; they were aided by instant-replay video-tape films of their teaching.

From the first day of training the trainees had stood before a class. Halfway through the program, they were taken to Stockton, California, where they taught full classes of children from minority groups in depressed areas of that city, thereby gaining experience with large classes. Then they returned to Stanford to work further on their weaknesses in micro-teaching units.

Several hours a day were spent in language classes taught by Filipinos using the latest aural-oral methods. The trainees practiced their Tagalog with the Filipino children as well as with the Filipinos on the staff, many of whom lived with them in the dormitories. The trainees were also able to use the language intensively during their two-week stay with Filipino families in Stockton.

The Stockton experience and the presence of the Filipino children provided intensive learning experiences for the prospective Volunteers in cross-cultural relationships. Through such experiences, as well as a series of seminars, discussions, lectures, and films, trainees compared and contrasted various aspects of behavior and community life in the Philippines and the United States. History, social issues, and international relations (including the problems of communism) were frequently discussed, but the focus was on the community and the individual, and the discussions stressed the role of the teacher in relation to local culture and the Filipino community. Controversial issues were openly discussed in this context. A prominent Filipino psychologist—who was also the chief assessment officer—was the coordinator for integrated studies, thus immediately immersing the trainees in cross-cultural issues.

Health and physical education were also part of the training program for the Philippines. Dances were emphasized—both Filipino and American—since the Volunteers would be expected to do both well in the Philippines. Games popular in the islands were organized, with the trainees taking an active role. First aid and local health problems were discussed by two doctors recently returned from Peace Corps work in the Philippines.

Throughout the program, the trainees were expected to read in the hours not otherwise scheduled with specific activities. The trainees themselves took over most of the responsibility for looking after the children, and in any time left over they were expected to develop and strengthen their own skills.

After completion of the program in California, Volunteers went on to the Philippines, where they spent several weeks doing practice teaching before heading for their individual assignments.

Summing up the program, one Peace Corps official said: "It treated the trainees as integral parts of a learning community, adults among adults, all seeking to find the appropriate resources to better prepare the Volunteer for a teacher's job in a foreign culture. It drew upon resources available locally to support trainees in deciding whether this was the right course for them to be taking for the succeeding two years by jointly searching for the tools to make those two years individually rewarding and successful for the Peace Corps Volunteer."

It should be apparent that the Peace Corps training program is as thorough and intensive as the staff can make it within the time allowed. But, as the Education Task Force Report stated, the emphasis must be on innovation; hence the Peace Corps is continuing to experiment with new training programs, as will be discussed in Chapter 15.

12

LIFE IN THE PEACE CORPS

This is the hardest thing I've ever done. Absolutely nothing is familiar and I often feel totally alone—the physical difficulties actually help, as they take my mind off myself and the feeling of suddenly being cut off from the rest of the world. You cannot imagine the gulf between East and West, and it makes me laugh now to think that I expected to bridge it with a smile and a handshake!

THE ABOVE WAS WRITTEN by Patricia MacDermot, twenty-four, of New York City, early in her Peace Corps assignment as a teacher in a remote Philippines village. It represents her manifestation of "cultural shock"—the reaction to a strange new world. Other Volunteers have reacted with less awe. "The difficulties," says Bob Gelardin, who served in Sierra Leone, "were increasingly ordinary." Volunteer James Shannon, of Washington, D.C., who taught in a university in Thailand, is even more emphatic: "The idea that people have that joining the Peace Corps is a big sacrifice is a myth," he wrote home. "I feel that I'm doing some useful work here, but at the same time I'm enjoying myself thoroughly."

In short, life in the Peace Corps and the Volunteer's reaction to it vary from country to country and from individual to individual. No two Volunteers seem ·to react the same to their overseas experience, even when they are engaged on the same project in the same country. As the *Third Annual Peace Corps Report* puts it: "For one Volunteer, the experience may involve kings and glamor, for another merely flies and ordinaries." Life in the Peace Corps is made up of thousands of highly personalized experiences, not one of which is really typical and no two of which are entirely alike.

At the same time, the realities of Peace Corps life have little in common with the stereotype which persists in the minds of most Americans. "It comes as something of a disappointment," a Peace Corps report to Congress says, "to the highly motivated Volunteer that not *every* Peace Corps assignment involves physical hardship. Attracted in part by sacrifice, some Volunteers have been made uneasy by the luxury of modest comfort. Life overseas is not necessarily a bed of nails, Volunteers find, and glamor is found mostly in picture books."

Much of what has been written about the Peace Corps Volunteer overseas presents an incomplete or even distorted "image." The most accurate picture of life in the Peace Corps is to be found in the Peace Corps file of letters written by the Volunteers themselves. Some of these letters will be reprinted later in this chapter; however, as a general description of life in the Peace Corps, I have seen nothing better than the following passage, reprinted from a *Guidebook* prepared by the Peace Corps:

> Overseas, while some of you will have a definite schedule, most of you won't. You are no longer told what to do—you have to figure it out for yourself. Going from the ordered routine of training to an unstructured job overseas has sometimes been compared to running off the end of a pier. Suddenly there is no solid footing underneath. There is not a staffer or an instructor in sight, and it's up to you to sink or swim.
>
> Our overseas staff will have tried to be sure that you have a good working situation, but the "variables" may have created pitfalls.

A Volunteer who worked hard on his Mende dialect could end up working in an area where everyone speaks Kono. Another who came out prepared to teach science is assigned to teach geography. Still another, who learned how to build with cinder blocks, is asked to erect a school house of mud, wattle, and mortar.

A community development worker has been under watchful, painstaking supervision throughout training. Now he has been deposited in the middle of a Latin American community that seems to be in urgent need of everything, from a cistern to a village council. He has no funds, no friends, no blueprint for action. He has to start from scratch.

A host country supervisor, learning about the nature and role of the Peace Corps, enthusiastically requests one or more Volunteers to work under him, but, by the time the Volunteers arrive the supervisor has been transferred and they find in his place a hostile new supervisor who has heard only vaguely of the Peace Corps, is suspicious of foreigners, and gives them as little as possible to do.

Or perhaps the supervisor is merely confused or uncertain about how to make use of the Volunteers. Or worse, two of his staff teachers have returned from leave, or half his students have dropped out; in either case he doesn't really need the Volunteers.

The catalogue of hazards is endless:

You may arrive on the job and plunge into it with all the zeal and ability you command. Only instead of inspiring the admiration of your co-workers, you seem to be inspiring their resentment. They regard you as an eager-beaver, out to get their jobs. They think you're putting on airs of superiority. Or you arrive in the classroom ready to pass the gift of learning to a bright-eyed, knowledge-hungry group of young-sters; only instead of craving education, they crave passing grades on their exams. Instead of seeking enlightened discussion and stimulation, they seek to have you write notes on the blackboards that they can copy and memorize.

The road you set out to build is canceled at the last minute because the Public Works Department is out of funds, or failed to get its speci-fications approved; the well you were to dig is held up by a quarrel between local groups over who will provide the labor; the outboard motors you were supposed to install and maintain for the village fish-ing co-op have been held up by a dock strike.

A Volunteer arrives in the host country carrying an image of "roughing it" in rustic surroundings, among innocent, appreciative rural people. Some get their rural assignment, but others are sent to the capital city, where there are hordes of expatriates and the local innocents wear shirts and ties, and go to beaches, movie theaters, and night clubs. There is a welcome for your arriving group at the airport and a round of parties and receptions. But after that no one notices you. You're just another "European" face in the crowd.

These things, and others like them, can erode the enthusiasm, the patience, and the idealism which the Volunteer has brought to the job. They may be part of an "underdeveloped" job in a newly developing society—and they form part of the basis of need which caused a host country to request you.

One or more of these things may happen to you—or none of them may happen. By the law of averages alone, you are bound to encounter at least a few such frustrations. As they mount up, your success will depend on your determination, your patience, and your ability to find another road when one is blocked. Part of the Peace Corps challenge is the challenge to remain energetic and hopeful at a time when your circumstances counsel cynicism or indifference. The romance of the Peace Corps may be the romance of sustaining one's interest and enthusiasm in the midst of tedium.

There is an inherent appearance of arrogance in the posture of the stranger from another country who has come to bring "change" and "improvement." And there is a rhythm of movement and response in the host country which may be conspicuously different from your own. When you have begun to understand this—when you realize that many of your students come to school after working all night in a bakery or laundry or after sleeping fitfully on an earthen floor, that the minister is engaged in a political battle to obtain funds for his own department —that even as an unpaid, idealistic, voluntary worker you may be something of an intruder, you will have begun to come to terms with your circumstances. Returning Volunteers tell us even the periods when they were most frustrated "did something" for them. Many of them, looking back on their two years, can detect at least some small signs of change or impact they were able to bring about. For many, the Peace Corps experience will appear richer in retrospect than in its day-to-day aspect.

At the critical point, when frustration has reached a peak, there may be a tendency to seek the easiest way out. The teacher in Africa, unable to make satisfying contact with the community, may decide it is enough that he is teaching in the classroom and preparing lesson plans at home. The community development worker in Latin America, unable to initiate organization or action, may decide it is enough that he is sitting and talking with as many people as he can. In both situations, there is a tendency to lean back against the trees and lose sight of the forest.

That is the time when the Volunteer is least inclined to bear in mind such abstractions as Peace Corps "goals." But it is also the time when it is most important for him to make a renewed effort to serve all the goals, not just the easiest one.

The Volunteer who gives up on his job and settles for being an ambassador of good will is likely to find himself growing increasingly demoralized. Generally, our most unhappy Volunteers have been those who have stopped trying to make an effective working contribution and are just going through the motions of their jobs.

The Volunteer who settles for "just doing a job" will find he could have done the same job, possibly with more enjoyment, in his own country. Getting the most out of Peace Corps service, for both the Volunteer and the Peace Corps itself, usually means an involvement with the host people beyond the usual requirements of the job itself. The Volunteer who goes overseas without a determination to learn as much as he can about his surroundings sets a limited goal for himself.

You may be able to do the whole Peace Corps job by total involvement in your regular assignment. But often you will have to seek out avenues of participation in community life, whether it is an extra-curricular self-help project, sports activity, or an adult literacy class—and this in the face of the difficulties and frustrations already noted. Even in the areas where it is possible to "get by" on English, a knowledge of the local language will ease the path to community involvement, so language study should continue throughout your service. It is possible to find means of study or tutoring in even the most obscure dialects.

In the larger cities, as in large cities anywhere, it will take a special effort to get involved, and a determination to avoid some of the diversions and temptations of city life. Probably the hardest but most necessary thing to avoid in the city is the tendency to develop exclusively expatriate social relationships.

The whole question of attitude is a crucial one. The Volunteer is not wrong in hoping to effect changes. He is often wrong in the terms in which he visualizes change. Most frequently, he anticipates some galvanic response to his efforts, a swift gathering of ardent spirits, a new energy and enthusiasm among his students or co-workers. The fire turns to ashes not long after he encounters the first misunderstanding, the first reluctance to change what has been accepted for generations.

The change in the Volunteer's own attitude at this point is sometimes striking. Some Volunteers, instead of adjusting the time scale of their hopes, surrender them altogether. Instead of attempting to affect the attitudes around them, however slightly, they begin in some respects to adopt them. It is not uncommon by the fourth or fifth month to hear Volunteers arguing that there is no point in maintaining a modest living standard, that after all they are expected to live like their counterparts, and their counterparts have private cars, three-month-long vacations, idle evenings, long weekends, etc. The great burden on the Volunteer who begins to feel this way is the struggle to maintain his original beliefs even though they seem to produce nothing more than indifference, resentment, or even ridicule among the people around him. This is precisely the time when the energy, doggedness, and consistency of his behavior *can* begin to make a mark on those he comes in contact with, when the example he sets can have the slow, lasting effect of a principle adhered to in the face of adversity.

If a Volunteer teacher participates in extra-curricular activities with his students, even though his counterpart doesn't, if a Volunteer nurse manifests a concern for her patients and for sterile techniques that her counterparts don't, if a Volunteer organizes his 4-H Club or community group on a democratic basis where his counterpart is authoritarian, if he displays concern for the substance of his work in contrast to his counterpart's concern for title and status, if he simply shows a willingness to get his hands dirty in a society that looks upon manual labor with contempt, he may have an example effect that will be far more important than his actual job contribution.

These examples will not be effective if they are furnished self-righteously. Self-righteousness and automatic assumption that the American way is alway best deny the spirit of working together as equals that is the basis of the Peace Corps. They also deny the frequent truth that you will learn as much (if not more) from your counterpart as you will teach. What we are trying to say is that you can be true to what is good in yourself while remaining open to what is good in your counterpart—that both of you, as imperfect human beings, will have much to learn from each other.

It is well to bear in mind that whatever you do in the host country is not entirely unnoticed, even in the crowded cities. The consciousness of being a representative of the United States ought to be carried lightly but firmly, whether in personal habits, manner of dress, or table habits. The Volunteer is not on exhibit overseas, but he *is* under scrutiny. You can evidence respect for local customs and taboos without "going native." You can live modestly without living sloppily. You can explain America without propagandizing. You can represent the best in the American tradition with the humbling awareness that the worst in America should make us offer aid to others through compassion, not charity.

In all this concern about job, goals, motives and behavior, it may begin to sound as if Peace Corps service is one little crisis after another. It isn't; but we want to make sure you know the hard realities because so much of the publicity has been concerned with the rosier side. We want you to be able to make a realistic decision about whether the Peace Corps is right for you.

Think, not about being selected for the sake of being selected, but about the unique combination of frustrations and responsibilities that will be your lot as a Peace Corps Volunteer. For the wrong person, the Peace Corps experience can be traumatic. For the right person, it can be a source of life-long satisfaction.

For the most part, the Peace Corps has a high batting average in picking the right person for overseas duty. Most of the letters written home, or reports prepared by Volunteers in the field, suggest that life in the Peace Corps will be a source of life-long satisfaction for the average Volunteer. Tom Clark, from Portsmouth, Oregon, was 22 years old at the time he served in Peru in a community-development project. He was one of 229 Volunteers in Peru, and his particular assignment was in Barrio San Pedro, a slum just outside of Chimbote. This excerpt is from a report entitled *Community Development—Goals and Frustrations:*

I get a lot of letters saying "how exciting your work must be" or "how picturesque," or "how much you must enjoy it." They imagine Volunteers hiking along in the Tanganyikan sunset, or teaching to eager, bright-eyed students . . . glory and rewards heaped upon Volunteers by loving, thankful natives, topped by a naïve conclusion that what the world really needs is less "stuffy old politicians" and more "real folks."

Volunteers call this the Albert Schweitzer complex. These dreams would not be harmful were it not for what happens to the Volunteer overseas and to his co-workers when he joins for these reasons.

I live in a picturesque bamboo mat house I built myself. I buy my water from a picturesque boy with a burro loaded down with water cans. I read and write under a kerosene lantern, sleep on a cot, and cook on a camp stove. There comes a day when all this suddenly becomes no longer picturesque, no longer quaint, but furiously frustrating and you want like crazy to just get out of there, to go home. This is called "cultural shock." It happens to one and all, usually about the third or fourth month. How hard it hits you and for how long depends largely on this problem of false motives.

Let me tell you about what I do down here. I'm involved in a program of "Urban Community Development." I live in a giant slum or *barriada* on the edge of Chimbote, a city of 120,000 people. My neighbors have come down from the mountains, attracted by the money and in hope of a better life. Because of a lack of marketable skills—for generations they have known only farming and grazing—they find it hard to get a job and end up in unbelievable slums, with diseases and starvation rampant. Largely illiterate, and sometimes speaking Spanish only as a second language after their Indian tongue, they get almost no public service, and many of their rights aren't protected. . . .

My job is to get these people, my neighbors, organized, to make them better able to compete in the city for their rights, and to try and get them to raise their standard of living. I teach in the local school during the days and I teach carpentry to adults at night. Both are important jobs, but I consider them only a beginning.

For example, our school has no roof. It would be a ten-dollar project and about one day's labor for two or three Peace Corpsmen to build that roof. Yet we don't do it. If we gave my school a roof it would always be that, a gift, the Gringo's roof. When it needed fixing, no one would fix it. If it takes me a year to talk my neighbors into

putting on that roof it will be worth it. Because it will then be *their*
roof on *their* school. It would be a small start, but in the right direction. Maybe then we'll take on a little harder project, and step by step
build up a powerful organization that is interested in progress and
strong enough to do something about it. It has to be an organization
that doesn't need me, however; otherwise, it would collapse when I
leave.

In another *barriada* in my town, there are two schools. One is a
several thousand dollar complex with classrooms, meeting halls, and a
medical clinic. It was built by Peace Corps Volunteers: architects
labored with social workers pouring cement, laying concrete blocks,
putting in lights and plumbing. It is now completed and in partial use.
Peruvians call it the "Gringo school."

Next door to this complex stands a two-room school, built out of
grass mats, without windows or lights, and a dirt floor. It was built
because the *barriada* grew and because classroom space was needed.
The teacher, a Peace Corps Volunteer, talked the parents of the students into building those two rooms. Though the school was put up
in a day and Volunteers only gave limited aid in construction, I consider the grass-school a success, and ten times more valuable to the
community than the big complex it sits next to. I think it will remain
a symbol to the *barriada* people of what they can do—working together.

A Volunteer has to be careful and not become too much of a leader.
As I have said, if I stir up all the action, what will happen when I
leave? I hint at things and let my neighbors come up with the ideas
and I let them lead the action. A really good Peace Corps program
receives little credit. Keep that in mind when you read Peace Corps
success stories. This, then, in short, is what I try to do in Barrio San
Pedro. I have a lot of failures, few tangible successes, and a great deal
of frustration. (I was a dreamer once, too, and my fall was hard.)
Now, all things considered, I think I'm doing something worthwhile.
I don't think I'll sign up for another stretch but you can't drag me
away from this one.

Mrs. Nancy Scott, 63, of West Chester, Pennsylvania, was an experienced teacher, and a grandmother, before joining the Peace Corps.
Her Peace Corps assignment was a unique approach to adult education in Africa's French-speaking Ivory Coast. Mrs. Scott and six other
female Volunteers worked in various *Foyers Feminins* around the
country, helping the wives of local officials take their place in the
developing middle-class society their husbands inhabit. An account of
her work is presented in the excerpt below:

> The African sun is fierce when you have to pull yourself together
> after the two-hour noontime break to return to work. All the rest of
> the world is still sleeping. You can almost hear the buzz of sleep as
> you walk by the still courtyards and the houses with their shuttered
> windows looking like closed eyes. The midday meal has left faint odors

of wood fires, fish and fried plantain in the air. Chickens and guinea hens have hidden under bushes and the dogs are too drowsy even to scratch their fleas. Perhaps the fleas are having their siesta, too. You pass by the market, where remnants of the morning's activities are strewn about: squashed bananas, spilled tomato sauce, peanut shells. The *Foyer Feminin* is shaded and cool; the big classroom on the second floor usually catches whatever breeze there is.

About 2:30 my women begin to drift in, though late-comers will turn up during the ensuing hour. Most look very fresh. Many have babies on their backs or toddlers tagging after them. There is an air of gaiety as we greet one another like a bevy of college girls reassembling after a holiday. Some of the students are very young, in their early teens. A few are oldsters, but most are in their 20's. Of course, judging their ages is sheer guesswork on my part and on theirs, too, in most cases.

So classes begin. In the large room are the *débutantes,* in the charge of the *directrice* and her helper, both young African women. I have the *avancées* in a little room adjoining. Most of the time we keep the door between the two rooms open until the din becomes too distracting: "b + a = ba, b + i = bi," and so on, the pitch rising, the volume increasing.

There are only the essentials in the classrooms: a large blackboard, box of chalk, slates, pencils, notebooks, and a primer apiece. But I realize more and more in teaching here the truth of the observation that the best school need be nothing more than a good teacher on one end of a log and a pupil on the other. Moreover, if you need visual aids you have only to get some bottle caps for counters, some carbon sheets and stenopads for duplicator work, and so on as far as your imagination can push.

The Ivory Coast government set up these *Foyers* to meet the urgent need for education of women. The men have had a head start in education and have left the women far behind. This has created a real problem: households consisting of a literate father and children and an illiterate mother. Many of the husbands have positions in government, in education, or in business. They are associated with men of similar education. An illiterate wife is incapable of entering into this aspect of her husband's life; thus a chasm exists in the family structure. To bridge this gap, the *Foyers Feminins* have been created. There are at present 30 *Foyers* in the cities and towns of Ivory Coast and more are being planned. Enrollments range into the hundreds in the cities and down to a dozen or so in the villages. . . .

The schoolroom language is, of course, French. My students speak it well, but when they grow excited, they switch to Baoule, the dialect in my village of Yamoussoukro. When they switch to Baoule, I say, *"Très bien, Si vous parlez en baoule, je parlerai en anglais,* and then where will we be?" They roar with delight at the sound of the English and immediately change back to French.

Foyer classrooms are not peaceful and orderly. Babies cry and are nursed, toddlers upset everything possible and wander out of the room so that in the midst of reciting, mothers shout and run off in pursuit. . . .

What progress have we made in the *Foyer?*

First of all, the women, having stepped out of their domestic routines into a disciplined environment in search of something new, have taken a monumental step.

As for academic progress, the beginners have mastered the vowels and several consonants, the simplest formation of letters, and simple addition. They have read, if mostly by rote, about a half-dozen pages of a primer. . . . In sewing they have made layettes, stitching both by machine and by hand. Also, they have learned to mend and to knit. Knitting in the tropics? Yes, indeed. Ivoriennes feel the slightest chill in the air (and we often have it, glory be!) and immediately bundle up their babies in woolen caps and booties until the sun takes over again.

The women are delighted by handicrafts and master them with remarkable speed. We plan to enlarge this field next year. At Christmas time we made rag-dolls for the children. I doubt if the children ever received them because the women themselves loved them so. Since then I have had to make dozens of them for little children who run up to me and say, *"Madame Scotch, donnez-moi un bébé!"*

The advanced students are about two-thirds of the way through the primer, can read more or less phonetically, can write fairly well, and in arithmetic are on about a level with a second-grader in the States.

There is the question we all ask ourselves from time to time: What, if anything, can I really accomplish here?

I tell myself . . . you can at least be a warm, understanding woman among your fellow women, sharing and understanding basic, human things with them. And, since you happen to know how to read and write, you can make every effort to give them these magic keys.

Nothing spectacular—but there you are.

Of course, there are health hazards in many areas where Volunteers serve, but according to the Peace Corps, if they follow the health rules and instructions provided during training, Volunteers are in no more danger than people at home who take camping trips or who travel extensively. Only eleven Volunteers have died overseas, and the incidence of serious disease and injuries among Volunteers, in fact, is not substantially greater abroad than in the United States.

Volunteers are not placed in work sites where health hazards are so great that real dangers are posed. During training they undergo thorough physical examinations, receive proper immunizations and complete orientation in the health problems they will face in their particular area of assignment. In their host country, they are under the care of U.S. Public Health Service doctors assigned by the Peace Corps

with the specific task of providing medical care for the Volunteers. A
Volunteer is rarely more than a few hours away from competent medical service. And they are visited regularly by the medical staff. Nearly
all Volunteers have initial minor bouts with gastro-intestinal reactions
to the abrupt change in climate, food, and water. But these disorders
are generally short-lived as Volunteers quickly adjust to their new
home. Few have returned home as a result of illness.

Living conditions vary from one country to another. But few Volunteers live in the stereotyped "thatched-roof mud hut." More complaints have been received from Volunteers, in fact, because living
conditions are too good rather than too austere. Before Volunteers
arrive at their work sites, a thorough survey is made to determine if
adequate housing is available. Volunteers generally live in modest, but
adequate quarters, often sharing rented houses or apartments with
fellow Volunteers.

Postal services in most areas are reliable and Volunteers are seldom
more than a few hours away from telecommunication services. Should
an emergency arise, official communication channels insure prompt
delivery of messages.

Peace Corps Volunteers serve at the request of their host governments and are not placed in any country where a record of instability
poses a clear danger. At work, they serve at a true person-to-person
level and are not usually affected by internal political or civil power
struggles. In at least four countries where there have been changes of
government, Peace Corps Volunteers have remained effectively at their
work. Should the need arise, however, an emergency evacuation plan
is available in every country.

Living allowances vary from country to country and sometimes
within a country, depending on local conditions. The allowance is designed to permit a modest but adequate standard of living. The Volunteer is expected to live within his allowance. Any kind of ostentation
setting the Volunteer apart from those with whom he lives and works
is to be avoided.

The Peace Corps has neither a uniform nor a prescribed manner of
dress. Nevertheless, a Volunteer's personal appearance can reflect credit
or discredit on the Peace Corps. Overseas, great importance usually is
attached to neatness and proper dress, particularly in professional fields.
Peace Corps Volunteers are urged to dress suitably for the needs of
their job and to respect host country attitudes toward personal appearance.

One example is beards. There seems little reason why a man who normally wears a neat, regular beard should shave it off. But the Peace Corps feels that a group of Volunteers who suddenly decide to grow shaggy beards as a lark, or as evidence of "roughing it," may hurt the Peace Corps and make it harder for themselves and other Volunteers to do the job. Also, in some countries beards flout local customs about being clean-shaven.

Other examples are short skirts, sleeveless or backless dresses, or shorts or slacks worn by female Volunteers. PCV's are urged to find out what is, and is not, appropriate for the country of their assignment.

The Peace Corps expects exemplary behavior from all Volunteers. This expectation includes every aspect of behavior because the Volunteer is in a twenty-four-hour-a-day job. The use of leisure time has an important effect on how well that job is done. For this reason, every Volunteer's social behavior should be adult and discreet at all times, even in the most private of his social relations with host country persons or other Volunteers.

The Peace Corps does not expect a Volunteer to exchange personal moral convictions for the sake of a particular cultural setting or any other reason, and a Volunteer should not abandon his social and moral behavior because he is away from his own cultural setting. The integrity of his own values should be retained at all times.

The Volunteer is "in view" constantly. Almost everything he does, and how he does it, is observed by many citizens of the host country. Thus the impressions made by day-to-day activities, not just work, play a major part in the Volunteer's effectiveness and in the success of the Peace Corps's work.

This means a PCV not only must avoid doing many things, but must be sure his actions do not appear to be something he wishes to avoid. It may seem strange for the Peace Corps to set standards of conduct for Volunteers who serve their country in the cause of peace. But the Volunteer who violates acceptable standards of conduct—in fact or in appearance—is judged even more harshly than other Americans. Just following the letter of the law does not suffice.

Since many people overseas regard the Peace Corps Volunteer as an American "ambassador," he must be beyond reproach. While he may look like "just another American," the fact that he is in the Peace Corps magnifies any difficulty he may get into. *"Especially make sure to keep out of host country politics,"* the Peace Corps urges all Volunteers.

Basically, the Volunteer is a guest in the host country. He must learn and respect the local customs, manners, taboos, religions, and traditions, remembering that the slightest "goof" probably will be seen and discussed by many persons.

The best way to avoid difficulties is by being courteous, even under trying circumstances. Ordinary politeness can create good will which will do as much to increase the Volunteer's effectiveness, and the Peace Corps's reputation, as hours of work.

Certain areas call for special effort to avoid mistakes. One is public contacts with members of the opposite sex, both host country citizens and Americans. In some countries unmarried men and women never are seen together in public unchaperoned. In others, men hold hands walking down the streets, while men and women stay a discreet distance apart. These and other customs seem strange to a Volunteer; nevertheless they must be respected and understood.

Eating and drinking habits are also important. Here, too, many local customs and taboos apply. While tact and good taste are fundamental, what may be accepted behavior in the United States can be a monumental *faux pas* elsewhere. Lack of ostentation is vital in all behavior, particularly in entertaining, which should include co-workers and others from the host country, and be of the sort that invites such hospitality from them.

The Peace Corps urges that Volunteers look at anything they write for publication not only from their viewpoint, but also from the point of view of co-workers and officials of the host country, who probably will read it later.

The Peace Corps encourages Volunteers to write articles for publication, but asks only that the PCV discuss such plans with the Peace Corps Representative or staff member so they can advise him about possible problems. *The Volunteer may not accept payment for anything he writes or any photographs he takes while a Volunteer.*

There are many practical matters concerning life in the Peace Corps that every prospective Volunteer will want to know. To answer such questions as "How much allowance do I get?" and "How about voting?" etc., the following items of basic information, extracted from the *Peace Corps Handbook,* have been included. Of course, such regulations are always subject to change and anyone wanting the latest policy on any item included below should write The Peace Corps, Washington, D.C. 20525.

1. *Passports:* At the time you accept an invitation to training, you will receive special "no fee" passport application forms. You will have to pay $2.00 to file the application. You must apply for this passport even if you already have a regular passport.

This "no fee" passport may be used for authorized travel while you are in the Peace Corps. And it may be used for travel for not more than 90 days after you complete your Peace Corps service. If you plan to travel more than 90 days, you must apply for and purchase a regular passport from an American Embassy or Consulate. The cost is $10.

2. Social Security: Volunteers must be enrolled in the Social Security system. If you do not have a Social Security card, apply immediately to the nearest Social Security Administration office. Social Security taxes are deducted from your readjustment allowance each month.

3. Life Insurance: When you register for training, your life will be insured for $10,000 unless you waive coverage. The premium of $1.20 per month is deducted from your readjustment allowance. If you waive or cancel coverage, it cannot be reinstated. The policy cannot be converted to any other form of insurance when you leave the Peace Corps.

You must designate a beneficiary or beneficiaries. You may change them at any time by filing the proper form with the Division of Volunteer Support.

Coverage ends 60 days after the end of your Peace Corps service if you terminate overseas, and 15 days after the end of your Peace Corps service if you terminate in the United States. This allows you time to get other life insurance if you want it.

4. Firearms: Trainees and Volunteers will not be permitted to use, carry, or possess any firearms.

Those who wish to hunt while on leave may request the representative's permission to rent or borrow rifles or shotguns for that purpose.

5. Transportation: The Peace Corps will provide transportation from your home to training sites, from there to your overseas assignment, and from there back to your home in the United States.

If you resign overseas, or must be terminated early, the cost of your return transportation will, in most cases, be deducted from your readjustment allowance.

6. Training and Travel Allowances: When you arrive at the training site, you will receive a $16 travel allowance to reimburse you for expenses during the trip from home and other incidental pre-training expenses. When training ends Volunteers will usually have seven to ten days "leave in transit" to prepare for overseas departure.

If you are authorized to travel home at this time, transportation is provided along with an allowance for incidental travel expenses and a small daily allowance. For travel to the port of embarkation or to further training, transportation and a travel allowance are again provided. A small additional allowance is paid for each day of international travel.

During training a small amount of "pocket money" is provided.

7. *Clothing Allowance:* Upon completion of training, you will get an allowance to enable you to buy in the United States any special clothing required for your overseas assignment which will not be available in the host country. If you go to a Peace Corps training camp, you may be given an additional clothing allowance. You will be given lists of suggested clothing for both the host country and the camp.

8. *Settling-in and Living Allowances:* Overseas allowances will be paid to you in the currency of the host country. When you first arrive overseas, you may receive a settling-in payment to purchase in local markets the things you will need to set up housekeeping. Purchases should be consistent with the modest living standards expected of Volunteers. The Peace Corps will not provide any household items except those necessary for your health which cost $50 or more.

Each month overseas you will receive a living allowance. This allowance is not a salary. It is designed to cover the costs of adequate food, clothing, housing, utilities, and incidentals such as laundry, tobacco, film, and postage.

Allowances are based on local living costs and differ from country to country or even within a country. They are subject to change depending on experience or changes in host country living costs. Married couples usually receive allowances equal to those paid two single Volunteers living in the same household.

You are expected to live within your allowance. You cannot receive payment for any work you do while you are in the Peace Corps. Other sources of income to pay your expenses overseas are prohibited, as are investments in the host country or any other activity for financial gain.

9. *Customs Regulations:* During training, be sure to ask about host country customs regulations. They may prohibit the entry of certain items.

Generally, you will not have to pay customs duties on the personal belongings which you carry with you when you arrive in the host country or which were shipped by the Peace Corps as unaccompanied baggage. This privilege applies only to your personal belongings and must never be used to import anything else even as an accommodation for a family member or friend. After initial entry you will have to pay customs duties on goods you import or which are sent to you.

Before you leave the United States you should register with United States customs any valuable articles you are carrying with you to avoid their being subject to duty when you return to the United States. Articles purchased abroad may be subject to United States customs duties.

10. Baggage: On domestic flights enroute to training, and if you return home after training, you may take the amount of free baggage permitted by the airline.

When you fly overseas, your free baggage allowance will be 44 pounds of accompanied baggage and 100 pounds of unaccompanied air freight baggage. As unaccompanied baggage will arrive late, make sure the 44 pounds you take with you includes all necessities—especially your language and work materials—for the first few weeks.

The Peace Corps will not pay any excess baggage charges.

Do not put flammable liquids or explosive items, such as pressurized cans of shaving cream or hair spray, in your baggage.

11. Property Loss: If any of your personal property, including accompanied and unaccompanied baggage, is lost, damaged, destroyed, or stolen at any time while you are in the Peace Corps, *you will not be reimbursed by the Peace Corps* unless extreme hardship would otherwise result—if all your property is destroyed in a fire, for instance. Even then you would only receive the reasonable replacement cost of essential items.

Before you depart for overseas you will have an opportunity to insure your personal property at a low premium, paying the premiums through an allotment.

You should not take expensive personal items overseas with you. They are inconsistent with the modest standard of living expected of Volunteers and are especially attractive to thieves.

12. Mail: Letters and packages will go through the regular international mail, not via diplomatic pouch or APO. Remember that many mail systems overseas are not fully developed and mail may be opened, delayed, or lost.

Many countries have complicated rules limiting the number and value of packages that can be received. Before going overseas, or as soon as possible after you arrive, you should learn about these regulations and inform your family and friends.

Because of these regulations, and because you are expected to get along on your living allowance, you should discourage the sending of packages or money. Also, remember you will have to pay shipping costs or customs duties.

Be sure to tell your family and friends that packages and letters sent to the Peace Corps in Washington or to the Department of State for forwarding will be returned to the sender.

13. Local Transportation: Volunteers may not have their own motor vehicles of any kind, including rented vehicles, during training or while overseas. Motor vehicles may be provided by the Peace Corps but *only* for transportation to and from work locations where public transportation or bicycles are *clearly* inadequate, or when essential for emergency evacuations, or for securing essential food supplies which are not locally available. A Peace Corps vehicle may not be used on leave or for any other personal travel. If you make unauthorized use of the vehicle, your service may be terminated and in case of an accident you may be personally liable. These restrictions are severely applied. If there is any doubt about the need, a vehicle will not be provided.

No Volunteer may drive overseas until he is familiar with the country's traffic laws. Always use host country driver's licenses rather than International driver's licenses which may not be familiar to local officials.

Familiarize yourself with what the host country will expect you to do in case you are involved in an accident or other emergency, especially one involving personal injury or death. The Representative will brief you on your arrival as to host country practices.

Should you be in an accident or any other emergency promptly notify the Project Director in Training, or the Peace Corps Representative or nearest American Embassy or Consulate overseas.

14. Family Emergencies: Before leaving the United States, tell your family that if an emergency arises while you are overseas, they should telephone the Special Services Branch of the Division of Volunteer Support, Peace Corps, Washington, D.C. (**Area Code 202**-393-3111). You will be immediately informed of any emergencies reported to Washington.

If you hear of an emergency in your family, contact your Representative, who will arrange for whatever help or information you need. When necessary and possible, telephone calls will be arranged to or from the United States.

Should a parent, brother, or sister die or become critically ill, emergency leave may be authorized and transportation home provided at Peace Corps expense. If the Volunteer is married to another Volunteer, the Representative may permit both to return home if circumstances require. Normally, emergency leave will be granted only once during a Volunteer's service. This leave is limited to two weeks, including travel time, and no travel or leave allowances will be paid. However, in an emergency you may be permitted to withdraw a single lump sum from your accumulated readjustment allowance. This must be approved in Washington and will rarely be approved beyond one half of the amount in your account.

Illnesses and injuries to Volunteers are reported to Washington. If they are serious, Washington will notify your family unless requested not to do so. If there is some general emergency in your area overseas, the Peace Corps will not initiate contact with your family unless you so request, or unless it has specific information that your health or welfare is affected. Experience shows that unsolicited calls from Washington to report that Volunteers are well and safe usually create more anxiety than they allay.

If members of your family decide to visit you, the Peace Corps will *not* pay for their transportation or travel expenses.

15. Health Care: With some important exceptions, the Peace Corps assumes full responsibility for your health care throughout your service. Medical care will be provided by a Peace Corps physician, by approved medical personnel at approved medical facilities in your host country or region, or, if necessary, by evacuation to a United States medical facility.

The exceptions to bear in mind are that the Peace Corps will not necessarily assume responsibility for:

1. Injury or illness incurred prior to training.

2. Injury or illness incurred in the United States while you are engaged in activities not related to your Peace Corps service.

3. Injury or illness incurred at any time as a result of your misconduct, such as an act intended to injure yourself or other persons.

If a disability due to illness or injury suffered during service persists or becomes manifest after your Peace Corps service is ended, you may be entitled to benefits under the Federal Employees Compensation Act (FECA). In order to qualify, you must complete a Bureau of Employees Compensation form CA-1 as soon as possible after you become ill or injured. During training you can obtain this form from the Project Director and while overseas from the Peace Corps Representative or doctor. You should be sure that they prepare another form, CA-2. After your service is ended, you can obtain form CA-1 and other information by writing the Medical Program Division, Peace Corps, Washington, D.C. 20525.

These benefits may be very important to you in the future. It takes only a few minutes to complete the proper forms for all illnesses or injuries.

FECA benefits are available for injuries or illnesses incurred in the United States during training, or during emergency or special leave, only if related to your Peace Corps duties. Any injury or illness incurred during service overseas is deemed to have been incurred in the performance of your Peace Corps duties.

You are not eligible to receive post-service FECA benefits for conditions which existed before your Peace Corps service or for illnesses or injuries due to your misconduct. Nor will you receive such benefits for illness or injury incurred after your Peace Corps service ends unless, possibly, you are injured or become ill while on the direct route from your assignment in the host country to your home in the United States.

Because neither the Peace Corps nor FECA covers all injuries or illnesses which you may suffer during your Peace Corps service, you may wish to retain any health insurance you have throughout the entire period of Peace Corps service. All Volunteers are strongly advised to retain it at least until they depart for overseas.

You will receive a thorough health examination before your Peace Corps service is terminated. At that time be sure that every illness or injury has been reported by you on a Form CA-1.

16. *International Vaccination Certificate (WHO Card):* The World Health Organization card shows the immunizations you have received. If you lose it, ask your Representative about it, as you may have to take your "shots" again and perhaps be delayed in travel.

17. *"Exposure," or Disease Identity, Card:* You also will receive a card showing the length of time you have been in places where certain diseases are known to exist. This card indicates your "exposure" and will be important in rapid diagnosis if you become ill.

18. *Legal Status:* As Volunteers are not officers or employees of the United States Government, and do not have diplomatic immunity, their legal liability usually does not change as a result of registration as Trainees or enrollment as Volunteers.

Thus, they generally are subject to State and Federal laws in the United States and to host country laws overseas. An agreement between the Peace Corps and each host country usually provides that Volunteers are to receive equitable treatment, the same as is accorded private citizens of the United States residing in those countries.

19. *Leave Overseas:* It is important that each Volunteer gain as thorough an understanding as possible of the area of the world in which he serves. Leave provides not only an opportunity for rest and relaxation but for travel in the country or region of your assignment. Therefore each Volunteer is normally expected to spend the first year's leave in his country or area of assignment.

When visiting other Volunteers or staff members, be considerate. They may have been hosts to many others besides yourself. In some places having even one guest can strain meager finances and the most ample good will. In short, don't freeload.

Volunteers enrolled before 1 August 1966 are credited with 45 days of leave.

Volunteers enrolled on or after 1 August 1966 are credited, at the beginning of overseas service, with two days of leave for each full calendar month of overseas service scheduled for their program.

This is the total amount of leave which you may take during your term of service overseas. For each day of leave actually taken, you may receive $7.50 to cover the extra expenses of leave. This is in addition to your monthly living allowance.

Unless you obtain the permission of your Representative to do otherwise, you must take 30 days of leave by or at the end of 13 months of service overseas or lose the portion of the 30 days not taken and its leave allowance. All leave not used by the end of service—and its leave allowance—will likewise be forfeited.

You may choose not to draw the leave allowance for some leave and to draw the accrued amount for later leave. But remember that the purpose of this allowance is to provide money for use while actually on leave. Thus, if you draw leave allowance in advance and then do not go on leave, you will have to refund the allowance or it will be deducted from your readjustment allowance.

Host country holidays which your co-workers observe may also be holidays for you without charge to leave, unless you spend the time away from your duty station or the holiday period exceeds one week. In those cases the holidays will be charged to leave unless you use week-long holiday periods for vacation projects. You will be expected to work on United States holidays on which your host country colleagues work. Weekends or holidays occuring during leave periods *are* counted as leave.

All leave taken must be reported to the Representative. Leave of six days or more must have the advance approval of both your host country supervisor and the Representative. To take leave for five days or less, you may only need the prior approval of your host country supervisor, but many Representatives require that *all* leave be approved by them in advance.

To help insure that leave becomes an integral part of your service, your Representative may prohibit the taking of leave during the first and last periods of your overseas service.

If you want to travel outside the country of your assignment, you will have to get advance written approval from your Representative. While on leave, and during your Peace Corps service, you may not travel to Sino-Soviet Bloc countries, to Europe, or to the United States (unless on emergency leave).

There is no specific provision for sick leave, but time off will be granted when you are unable to work because of an illness or injury. If it seems likely that an ill or injured Volunteer will not recover within a reasonable period of time, he will be returned to the United States.

Make sure your Representative knows where you plan to travel on leave so that in case of a family emergency, for example, he can find you promptly. While traveling outside your host country, you should inform the Peace Corps Representative in that country, if there is one, or the American Embassy or nearest American Consulate, of your where-abouts.

20. Readjustment Allowance: For each month of service which the Peace Corps Representative certifies as satisfactory, a Volunteer accrues $75 which accumulates—without interest—from the day he registers for training through the day his service ends. Unless allotments have been made, $1,800 will accumulate during two years of service. After deductions for Federal income tax, Social Security and any in-surance premiums, you will get between $1,400 and $1,500.

As this money is intended to help during the transition from the Peace Corps to a job or school, it is payable when you return to the United States. Only for compelling personal or family reasons may you allot or withdraw part of the money while you are still in the Peace Corps.

When a Volunteer is separated overseas after satisfactory comple-tion of his tour of duty, he may withdraw up to one-third of the accu-mulated readjustment allowance for travel and other expenses. If he can show that he is going to work or study abroad for at least one calendar or school year, respectively, the full readjustment allowance may be paid overseas.

21. Allotments: Under exceptional circumstances you can send home part of your monthly readjustment allowance. Such circumstances include support of parents, payment of health or life insurance premiums, educational loans, educational aid to members of your family, and other genuine personal or family needs or emergencies. Allotments for investment are not permitted except for the purchase of United States Savings Bonds.

All regular monthly allotments must be approved in Washington. Allotments greater than half your monthly allowance will rarely be approved.

Allotments may begin or be discontinued at any time during Peace Corps service, including training, except during the last three months. They must be for a minimum of three consecutive months, may not be retroactive, and each payment must be for at least $10.

Allotments will be paid by the end of the month following the month in which they were approved.

In case of an emergency or other special circumstance, you may apply to withdraw a single lump sum from your accumulated readjustment allowance. Washington approval is required.

22. Income and Social Security Taxes: Federal income tax must be paid on readjustment and leave allowance, on part of your monthly living allowance, and on some other allowances.

Federal income and Social Security taxes are withheld from your readjustment allowance as it accrues. The amount of taxes withheld will be shown on a Form W-2 sent you at the end of each calendar year.

You should keep a record of the amount and purpose of all other allowances received. Since taxes are not withheld on these items, the Peace Corps will have no permanent record of the allowances paid to you. When you arrive in the host country, whenever your living allowance changes, and at the end of the calendar year the Representative will tell you what portion of the living allowance is subject to Federal tax.

Each year the Peace Corps sends each Volunteer a special Federal income tax guide which fully explains the taxation of allowances.

Depending on your state of residence, you may also have to pay state tax. You will have to obtain the necessary information and forms yourself.

Generally, you will not be required to pay income taxes of the country in which you serve.

23. Voting: We urge you to vote in elections in the United States, but whether you will be able to do so will depend on your State's absentee voting laws. Before you leave the United States, ask your local election officials if you may vote while overseas and, if so, when and how you must apply for an absentee ballot. Volunteers overseas may use the Federal Post Card Application (FPCA) for absentee ballots. The post card and instructions for its use will be provided by your Representative in advance of all national elections. But remember that absentee voting is a privilege granted and regulated by individual states. The FPCA may help you obtain an absentee ballot, but it does not guarantee that you will be able to vote in absentia.

24. Military Service: If you are subject to military service, you should ask your draft board, before you enter Peace Corps training, for deferment and for permission to leave the United States.

As deferments last only one year, you must request an extension before the end of each year of Peace Corps service. You should also keep your draft board informed of your whereabouts at all times. It is particularly important that as your Peace Corps service nears its end you notify your draft board of your future plans and where you can be reached, especially if you don't expect to return directly home after service. Also, let the board know your exact termination date and be sure to tell them if you plan to extend your Peace Corps service or re-enroll, go to a college or university, or engage in any other activity which may entitle you to further deferment. The Peace Corps will keep your draft board informed of your Peace Corps status and advise it when your service ends, but you are still legally required to do so yourself.

All of this applies equally to your Reserve Unit if you belong to one.

25. Student Loans: While you are in the Peace Corps, interest does not accrue, and you may request that payments of principal be deferred, on any National Defense Education Act student loan contracted on or after September 23, 1961. Forms to apply for deferment will be available during training and may also be obtained from your Peace Corps Representative overseas. They should be returned to the Peace Corps, where your status as a Trainee or Volunteer will be certified and the forms forwarded to the lender. You must annually renew your request for deferment.

Although the above does not apply to NDEA loans outstanding on September 22, 1961, or to other student loans, a lender may, if asked, be willing to grant Volunteers a partial or complete deferment during Peace Corps service. Volunteers seeking such deferments should contact their lenders directly. The Peace Corps will be glad to certify your status for such a lender.

26. Marriage and Pregnancy: Any Trainee or Volunteer who wishes to marry must obtain in advance the approval of the Peace

Corps. During training, ask the Project Director to contact the appropriate Peace Corps staff person. Overseas, talk to your Representative.

In deciding whether or not Volunteers can remain in service after marriage the Peace Corps will have to consider such questions as whether the couple can continue to maintain a modest standard of living, what job and housing changes will be necessary to accommodate them after marriage, and whether the required changes meet the approval of host country officials. The decision may be that the Volunteers cannot continue effectively in Peace Corps service. If the service of one Volunteer is prematurely ended, a Volunteer spouse will generally be required to leave at the same time.

Approval will not be granted if the future spouse has come to the host country expressly to marry a Volunteer. Nor may a Volunteer return to the United States to marry.

Volunteers considering marriage to non-Volunteers should remember that the Peace Corps cannot provide support of any kind, including health care or transportation, to a non-Volunteer. Before marriage to an alien they should contact the nearest American Embassy or Consulate to make sure what they will have to do before the spouse can enter the United States.

If Volunteers who are scheduled to end their Peace Corps service at different times get married, the Volunteer with the longer remaining period of service is still expected to honor his or her service commitment.

Generally, married Volunteers may not serve separately.

The responsibility for deciding whether the Volunteer couple expecting a child can continue in service falls upon the Representative and the Peace Corps doctor. For this reason, couples expecting a child should notify their Representative as soon as possible. The Representative and physician must consider health hazards to the mother and child, prospects for the continued effectiveness of the Volunteers, and plans for supporting the family. If the outlook is unfavorable from any of these points of view, both will usually be asked to resign.

If a married Volunteer becomes pregnant during training the Project Director should be promptly informed. If a pregnant Volunteer or Trainee is permitted to continue her Peace Corps service, the Peace Corps will provide or pay for her prenatal, delivery, and post-natal health care. The Peace Corps will also provide or pay for the health care of a child born to a Volunteer during overseas service while the child is overseas with the Volunteer. However, other support for the child during the remainder of its parents' service, and travel costs afterward, will be the responsibility of the parents. With the approval of the Peace Corps, Volunteers may withdraw part of their monthly readjustment allowance for these purposes. As the Peace Corps has no authority to provide health care to former Volunteers, Volunteers whose service is terminated before delivery are themselves responsible for post-service maternity expenses. A Volunteer's child is not entitled to any post-service Federal Employees Compensation Act (FECA) benefits.

27. Transfer, Resignation, and Early Termination of Service: A Volunteer can resign at any time. The Peace Corps, however, expects that you volunteered with an honest intention to serve for the duration of the term of service and that you will honor that commitment.

A Volunteer can also request a transfer to other work in the same or a different country.

A Peace Corps Representative can return a Volunteer to the United States with a recommendation that his service be terminated. The Peace Corps can also assign any Volunteer to another job in the same or a different country.

Normally, a Volunteer who wants to resign or whose service a Representative recommends be terminated will be sent to Washington. There, he will have the opportunity to discuss his situation with the Peace Corps staff who are responsible for accepting his resignation or deciding if his service should be terminated.

Before the Volunteer leaves the host country, the Representative will show him a brief written statement of the reasons for the Volunteer's resignation or the Representative's recommendation. If the Representative and the Volunteer do not agree on the reasons, the Volunteer can submit a written statement to be included with the papers sent to Washington by the Representative.

During discussions in Washington consideration may be given to transferring the Volunteer to another country in the same or a different region. A Volunteer interested in transferring, however, should realize that because of the difficulties of adjusting to a new assignment in a new country cases of transfer are rare and often entail extension of service.

In cases of resignation or early termination the decision will be made in Washington as to whether the Peace Corps will pay transportation costs.

Unless termination is for medical or other pressing reasons beyond the Volunteer's control, the cost of return transportation will be deducted from his readjustment allowance.

A Volunteer whose service ends before the completion of his full term will not receive any unused leave or leave allowance.

The Director will personally review any decision adverse to the Volunteer if the Volunteer requests it in writing within 24 hours after being advised of the Peace Corps's decision.

28. Extension of Service or Re-enrollment: The Peace Corps encourages Volunteers who have the capacity to sustain their commitment and to serve effectively for an additional period to consider extending their regular term of service or re-enrolling for a new term of service.

To extend, you should inform your Representative at least two months before the end of your original term, as a request for an extension will require not only his approval but usually the approval of your host country supervisors.

A Volunteer who extends for a year or more may take up to 30 days of special leave in the United States, Western Europe, or any other part of the world outside the Communist Bloc. These days of special leave are not counted as part of your year's extended service. Thus, if you take 30 days of special leave, your extended service must end at least 13 months after your original termination date. Volunteers who take special leave will be given a Government Travel Request for transportation costs so long as they do not exceed the costs of round trip direct economy air transportation from the country of assignment to the United States. You will continue to receive your living allowance plus $5.00 per day special leave allowance.

Rather than extend, you may want to re-enroll for another full term of service in the same country or in another country. To re-enroll, tell your Representative at least three months in advance. If you wish to re-enroll in another country you should address your request to the Director of Selection, Peace Corps, Washington, D.C. 20525, and send it through the Representative if you are still overseas.

Re-enrollment for service in the *same country* to begin *within a year* after the end of the first term will generally *not* require the Volunteer to participate in a new training program and go through the regular selection process. Training and selection probably *will* be required if re-enrollment is for service in a different country or is to begin after a break in service of over a year.

29. Completion of Service: Some of the points mentioned earlier in this Handbook are so important to you as you approach the end of your service that they are worth repeating:

Several weeks before your service ends, a completion of service conference for your project will be held in the host country. This conference, usually led by a Washington staff member and a staff member from another country, will give you an opportunity to discuss with your fellow Volunteers your Peace Corps experience and will provide the Peace Corps with information to improve training, programming, and administration of future groups of Volunteers.

You will get a complete health examination just before leaving the Peace Corps. This examination is important. After your service ends it may be difficult for you to establish that you are entitled to FECA benefits for illness or injury not revealed by this examination. If this health examination reveals a serious illness or injury, the Peace Corps may require you to return to the United States for treatment.

Also remember that your life insurance coverage ends 60 days after the end of your service if your service is terminated overseas, or 15 days after the end of your service if your service is terminated in the United States.

If at the end of your Peace Corps service you owe money to the Peace Corps, such as for leave allowance advanced for which leave was not taken or for Peace Corps property not returned, the Peace Corps may deduct these amounts from your readjustment allowance. At the end of your service you will be required to sign a certificate that you have paid all your debts to host country nationals, Volunteers, and others. If you have not, and the Peace Corps has to pay them to avoid embarrassment to its program, it may deduct such payments from your readjustment allowance.

You may want to return to the United States immediately or to travel, study, or work, abroad. You may request up to one-third of your accrued readjustment allowance in the host country at the end of your service. The remainder will be payable upon return to the United States. If you want to travel extensively, you may choose to receive the approximate cash equivalent of the lowest direct fare to your home in the United States. Otherwise, the Peace Corps will provide transportation to your home in the United States. You may send home 100 pounds of baggage by air freight.

If you have not previously done so, you should insure your personal property for the trip back to the United States. The Peace Corps is not responsible if it is lost, damaged, or destroyed. If you wish to take out health and accident insurance to cover you on your return trip, especially if you are not going directly home, inexpensive policies are available.

You will be generally subject to United States customs regulations, which limit the duty free imports of items purchased overseas by United States residents. An explanatory booklet can be obtained from your Peace Corps Representative or at any American Embassy or Consulate. You will be given special customs declaration forms before you complete your service.

13

THE RETURNING VOLUNTEER

*When I got back to my hometown in Ohio and went to work, I fell
back into hanging out evenings in the neighborhood tavern with my
old buddies. After about two weeks of that I gave up the tavern. They
didn't care about the problems of the Indians in Peru, and I didn't
give a damn what happened to the Indians in Cleveland.*

—AN EX-PEACE CORPS VOLUNTEER
who spent eighteen months
in the Andes doing community-development work.

THE PEACE CORPS feels that the young people who volunteer to serve
overseas should *not* look upon this as two years out of their lives, but
as the beginning of an important and rewarding career. And judging
from the studies which have been made of the returning Volunteers,
this is the case; most ex-Volunteers seem to be finding that the direction their lives take after Peace Corps service is strongly influenced
by their experiences abroad. For instance, of the first 1,000 Volunteers to go overseas, 13 percent had had some teaching experience;
when they returned, 26 percent said they planned to follow a teaching
career. "The thing about the Peace Corps," said one ex-Volunteer who
served in Sierra Leone, "is that it doesn't end for you in two years."

Of equal importance is the fact that the individual Volunteer's
Peace Corps experience does not end for America in two years.

Of the first 6,582 Volunteers completing service, 35.8 percent
elected to continue their education (25.4 percent in graduate school);
11.8 percent were employed by the federal government; and 16.9 percent went into teaching at all levels of education. The results of a
study made of this first group of returning Volunteers might be interesting to anyone wondering where a tour of duty in the Peace Corps
might lead:

CONTINUING EDUCATION 35.8%	2,358
Graduate School—25.4%	1,673
Agriculture and business	66
Education	276
Engineering, mathematics, and science	219
Health fields	48
Law	93
Social science and area studies	668
Other	82
All overseas graduate students	32
Undergraduate and Other—10.4%	685
Agriculture and business	74
Education	64
Engineering, mathematics, and science	119
Social science and area studies	226
Other	78
All overseas undergraduate students	5
EMPLOYED 52.2%	3,435
Federal Government—11.8%	775
Peace Corps	292
Department of State	14
USIA	14
AID	115
War on Poverty	39
All other domestic agencies	295
Elective or appointed official or assistant	6
State and Local Government—4.1%	272
State governments	94
County governments	89
Municipal governments	66
War on Poverty	23
Job Corps Centers—1.1%	71
VISTA—.2%	14
International Organizations and	
Foreign Governments—.7%	45
United Nations	22
Foreign governments	35

EMPLOYED (Cont'd.)

Teaching—16.9%	1,113
Elementary teacher or administrator	178
High-school teacher or administrator	479
College teacher or administrator	165
All overseas teachers and administrators, including Peace Corps	106
Not specified	136
Non-Profit Organizations—6.9%	454
Labor union worker	6
Health worker	155
Social service worker	196
All non-profit employees overseas	67
War on Poverty contractor	14
Educational organizations	16
Profit-Making Organizations—10.5%	691
Agriculture and related	33
Business and industrial	252
Skilled and unskilled	289
Self-employed professional	20
Communications	38
All profit-organization employees overseas	41
OTHER 12%	789
Extended Peace Corps service	334
Housewife, not employed	288
Military service	115
Retired	26
Traveling, not yet returned to U.S.	26

Aware of the valuable pool of young, highly motivated people with overseas experience represented by ex-Peace Corps Volunteers, the Peace Corps has made every effort to encourage the returning Volunteers to consider public service—and to encourage others to provide the Volunteers with opportunities for stimulating and rewarding careers. "I hope that when you get back," President John F. Kennedy once told a group of Volunteers about to embark on their missions, "we can persuade you to come and serve in the United States Government in other areas, particularly in the Foreign Service. . . . I hope you will regard this as the first installment in a long line of service in the most exciting career in the most exciting time."

Edward R. Murrow, former Director of the United States Information Agency, made a similar statement pointing out that if the Volunteers "return to conventional civilian pursuits with their overseas experience cast aside merely as a pleasant recollection, they themselves, this agency, and this country will have wasted a valuable asset."

The Peace Corps someday hopes to see its staff made up almost entirely of ex-Volunteers. "We have had from the beginning," said former Peace Corps Director Sargent Shriver, "an unusual government policy known as 'in-up-and-out.' We are proposing a limit of five years on the staff for any one employee, including the director. In a few years we expect the Peace Corps to be manned largely by those who have had overseas experience in its service."

A Presidential Executive Order (11103) was also issued in 1963 stating that ex-Peace Corps Volunteers should have preference in Civil Service appointments. Many Volunteers, some while still in service, have taken the State Department and USIA examinations. If they eventually join the State Department or the USIA after completing their Peace Corps service, they will start at grades FSO 7 and FSR 7, instead of the customary 8 level (which is lower, not higher, than a 7 in the foreign service scale). The U.S. Civil Service also plans to offer the Federal Service Entrance Examination at overseas points to Volunteers interested in eventually joining the government. President Johnson, calling the Volunteers "a new major national resource," instructed Vice-President Humphrey to convene a special conference of returned Volunteers in the Spring of 1965. The purpose: To consider opportunities for further service to their country.

Private industry has also shown a definite interest in returning Volunteers. "It seems clear to me," said Thomas Watson, President of International Business Machines, "that members of the Peace Corps will be particularly employable when they complete their tours of duty. They will have demonstrated their ability to take on tough jobs under extremely difficult circumstances and to follow them through to their completion. There are never enough people of this kind available for any enterprise."

Similarly, Peter Grace, President of W. R. Grace & Co., said, "American business firms operating abroad require men and women who are intimately familiar with the people, the language, the customs, and the conditions in which they work. The Peace Corps offers young Americans an excellent opportunity to acquire this kind of knowledge, to gain experience in adjusting themselves to a different environment and in adapting American techniques and methods of operation to local conditions."

Having spent two years abroad, discovering himself and the world, then returning to find so many opportunities awaiting him, it is not surprising that the first months back home are often a painful period of indecision for the ex-Volunteer. "Two years in the Peace Corps," said one Volunteer at a post-service conference, "showed me how many different opportunities there are in this life. It's an embarrassment of riches. The trouble is, I just can't decide what line to take."

The many different lines which the returning Peace Corps Volunteers take is illustrated by a single group of Volunteers who returned from Sierra Leone in late 1963. A year later, they had gone off in a dozen different directions: teaching school in Africa, working with the Corps in Washington or overseas, taking doctorates in the United States and overseas, teaching in Alaska, working in various sections of the State Department, working in rural communities in the United States, and a multitude of other interesting variations of school and employment.

To help Volunteers decide what line their career should take and, incidentally, to make certain the valuable national asset represented by the returning Volunteers is put to its maximum use, the Peace Corps has established a Career Information Service. First suggested by Thomas Watson of IBM, CIS was established in July, 1964. The Peace Corps emphasizes that CIS is a "clearinghouse" and counseling service, *not* a placement office, an employment agency, or a scholarship committee. In its first year, the CIS informed Volunteers of more than 500 opportunities including over 250 scholarships, fellowships, and assistantships as well as opportunities offered by CARE, the President's Committee on Juvenile Delinquency and Poverty, the Eleanor Roosevelt Memorial Foundation's Internship Program in Human Rights, the Ford Foundation's Study Fellowship Program, various business concerns, the Department of State, the Agency for International Development, and the staff of the Peace Corps itself.

However, before the returning Volunteer reaches the Career Information Service, he must participate in another Peace Corps innovation, not only to help himself but also future Volunteers. This is the so-called Completion of Service Conference held for all Volunteers approximately six weeks before they are terminated from service. The focal point of these conferences is an extensive questionnaire which each Volunteer fills out, evaluating his successes and failures, changes in his attitudes, working conditions, host country attitudes, relationships with Peace Corps staff and co-workers, and many other aspects of his Peace Corps experience. Senior staff members tabulate the questionnaires and discuss the results in sessions with the Volunteers —each session being limited to thirty or fewer participants—over a two-day period. This final meeting of the Volunteers as a group gives them an opportunity to make a balanced judgment of their total Peace Corps experience and to think of it in terms of their future. Although these conferences have provided some blunt and stinging criticism of the Peace Corps, officials maintain that the vast majority of returning Volunteers believe in the Peace Corps just as strongly on their return as they did when they first went overseas. More than 75 percent of the first 1,000 Volunteers to return felt that their work had definitely made a contribution to the economic or social development of the host country; 94 percent felt that they had done at least "moderately well" as Volunteers.

The returning Volunteer's attitude toward physical hardship is also significant: only 1 percent found it a serious problem; 13 percent found it a minor problem. Housing, food, health, and isolation were serious problems to less than 6 percent and minor problems to less than 20 percent. Actually, the greatest challenge overseas is the psychological frustration, not the physical hardship, but according to two former Peace Corps officials, Dr. Joseph T. English, chief psychiatrist, and Dr. Joseph G. Colmen, deputy director of the Division of Planning and Evaluation, overcoming these frustrations led to increased maturity —the distinguishing characteristic of the returning Volunteer.

According to English and Colmen, the average Volunteer overseas faces three distinct psychological crises, and as he masters each one the Volunteer moves a step closer to intellectual and emotional maturity. The first is a Crisis of Engagement. This might begin with the Volunteer's arrival at his worksite. There is a good chance that no one knew he was coming and people wonder why he is there. When he explains that he did not come to hand out money and supplies but that he was just there to help them help themselves, nobody believes him. They smile and wait for the Volunteer to act like other Americans who have been there before.

Meanwhile, the Volunteer sees many things that can be done, but trying to arouse the people to take an interest in doing them is virtually impossible. So he begins to slow down a little, his "messianic complex" subsides and he decides just to make friends with the people. The people are usually agreeable to this and pretty soon he finds he has a lot to learn about them and that he's listening more than he is lecturing. He gradually learns that they have been aroused many times before and bitterly disappointed when nothing happened and he begins to understand why their resistance to him is so strong. He slows down to their pace and tries harder to win their confidence. This will take a long time, he decides, but it must be done. Then, gradually, there are tangible results.

Just before the end of the first year there is a second period of adjustment: the Crisis of Acceptance. By now the Volunteer has become a part of the community, but the pace is agonizingly slow and there is very little intellectual stimulation. He reads avidly and for the first time experiences real solitude. There is no television, and radio reception is poor. He becomes more and more introspective. One Volunteer in East Africa says that one morning he literally looked in the mirror and asked sarcastically: "Mr. Peace Corps's Mr. American. Who do you think you are kidding? . . . What do you really stand for?"

According to English and Colmen, nearly every Volunteer experiences this moment of awakening. He begins to ask himself the eternal questions: Who am I? What am I doing here? What does it all mean? Out of this crisis of self-doubt comes a re-examination of the Volunteer's own expectations—and increased maturity. He becomes more patient, more thoughtful and less irritated by continuing frustration. He realizes how close he has come to the people he is living with and although aware of how hard he has worked and how much he has given, he is also aware of how much he has gained.

Having mastered two psychological crises, there is still a third one to be faced: the Crisis of Re-entry. As the Volunteer prepares to come home, he begins to wonder whether he will find anything in our society as challenging as he has been facing overseas. This leads to a period of indecision about the future. However, in facing this third crisis, certain trends have been noted. In a *Saturday Review* article, "The Peace Corps Volunteer Returns," David Pearson, a former Peace Corps official, has written,

> [Returning] Volunteers are interested in working more with people than with things; more for public service than for private pursuits; more for creativity and satisfaction in their work than for security. Their choice of graduate studies indicates a growing interest in the social sciences and international affairs. Almost 25 percent of them say they will return to the country of their assignment one day, to live and work.
>
> They also express a striking sense of restlessness about some of our own problems. The racial situation in the States is commonly cited.

Having spent two years abroad where for the most part there were no racial barriers—and certainly none between American whites and American Negroes—the volunteers of both races were disturbed to return to a society where "invisible barriers" are ever present. The Negro volunteers have found that they are not accepted by the whites as they were abroad, nor are the white volunteers as readily accepted by Negroes.

They report that whereas they had an intellectual commitment to racial equality before they joined the Peace Corps, their commitment now is an emotional one. This leads them to take a much firmer and more active position in the field of civil rights than ever before.

It is not too surprising that most of the young Volunteers return a little closer to maturity than when they went overseas—a young person's maturity generally progresses rapidly in the years after college. But it is probably not overstating the case to say that as a result of their two years overseas, most returning Volunteers are a little more mature than their friends from college who did not go overseas. They seem to be more aware of the issues of the day, more alert to what's going on in the world, in the nation, and in their own communities. "I found myself wanting to know things about Minneapolis," said one Volunteer who worked in a Latin American community-development program and returned to take his master's degree at the University of Minnesota. "Who lives in what part of town, what are the different groups and interests, the problems, who runs the city. . . . Wanting to know everything I didn't care about before and thwarted because things were so complex. I wanted the same sort of overview of society I got working in a small Latin American village. I felt responsible for things, frustrated because I couldn't get at them, but at the same time not being able to sit back and accept it. . . ."

The returning Volunteers, in general, seem to react sharply to what they consider shortcomings in American society—"commercialism," "racism," "provincialism," "conformity," and the "immaturity" of their own generation. But this does not mean they look on America with contempt; they are genuinely glad to get back: "To rediscover privacy and anonymity after two years in a goldfish bowl is a pleasure," says a 54-year-old ex-Volunteer. "It's great to return to the theater, the supermarket, a good daily newspaper, and a sense of order you have to leave the U.S. to appreciate—and everything works!"

They are glad to be back, but there is one thing on which most returning Volunteers are in complete agreement: Their service in the Peace Corps was a rewarding, instructive two years. As Peace Corps nurse Ruth Dygert put it near the end of her tour of duty in a Tanganyikan hospital: "Would I do it again? Yes. The good and happy things have far out-shadowed the discouragements. Granted, there are days when I feel that I'm knocking my head against a stone wall. 'Is this sterilizer properly filled?' Pointing out such a mistake to the same student nurse for the twentieth time sends my blood pressure to the ceiling, or brings another shrug of resignation.

"But sometimes I hear a new patient being told by one of our long-termers, 'That nurse is not just a *mzungu,* a European. She's an American.' The trust in his voice suggests how much good we shall leave behind."

Peace Corps Volunteer John Murphy, who served in Africa, put it even more simply: "We know that the schools we are building will help raise the level of education. We like being known as *'les blancs qui travaillent.'* It is good to feel that we are part of Gabon's future."

PART FOUR

Conclusion

14

CHALLENGE AND RESPONSE

Thomas Hardy said war makes rattling good history but that peace is poor reading . . . [but] the Peace Corps [has] made the pursuit of peace rattling good history.

—PRESIDENT LYNDON B. JOHNSON.

SARGENT SHRIVER reported that on his first trip around the world to discuss the Peace Corps with leaders of potential host countries, more than one voiced the concern of the African leader who told him, "The Peace Corps is a wonderful idea—if only your people could do it." This skepticism concerning America's ability to respond to challenge had come not only from abroad. Many responsible Americans with practical experience in the underdeveloped nations had also expressed doubts.

The reasons for these doubts were many and varied, and in some cases well founded. Admittedly there had been enough evidence of American "flabbiness" to justify skepticism about America's ability to send out pioneers to work on the frontiers of the world. The television documentary "The Flabby American"; Eugene Kinkead's book *In Every War but One,* in which he analyzed the weaknesses of American prisoners of war in Korea; *The Golden Mile* by Herb Elliott, in which the Australian long-distance runner criticized American youth for its lack of physical stamina; the President's concern over the nation's physical fitness—had all reflected widespread concern that softness was a distinguishing characteristic of our affluent society. "It's a fact," wrote Elliott, "that the warm, soft synthetic existence Americans lead poses a real doubt about their future. . . . The fact that Americans have not produced many outstanding distance runners is attributable to their way of life. They are not a hardy race of people; whereas the Norwegians, Russians, and English are."

Doubts about the Peace Corps Volunteers' physical stamina, however, were not the only reason for skepticism. "We are sure that there are large numbers of Americans," said the English-language *Hong Kong Tiger Standard,* "who are sincerely eager to help the underdeveloped nations. . . . We are not sure, however, how many of these persons will be prepared to have their living standards reduced to the level of the people among whom they will be working. Since these people will comprise the poorer rather than the wealthier portion of the population, this means that the Peace Corps workers will have to accept a mode of life not only more uncomfortable than they enjoy at home, but more uncomfortable also than that enjoyed by the better off in the country concerned."

Could young Americans be transplanted, with less than four months' preparation and training, from a soft, overcivilized way of life to conditions in many cases more rugged than those faced by American frontiersmen a hundred years ago? And could young Americans, brought up on television, the movies, ball games, junior proms, weekends at the beach, fast cars, jazz concerts, cocktail lounges, and fraternity parties face the challenge of living for two years the kind of life suggested by a young IVS volunteer who wrote home from Vietnam:

> The rainy season is starting now, and the refugee farmers and tribes of people in the area are beginning to plant upland rice and a few vegetables. At the college I have just recently harvested some small observation plots of grain sorghum, wheat, and barley. The grain sorghum could well become a commercially important crop in the area, but wheat and barley I planted just for curiosity to see if they would grow at all. They were some varieties we had got from California. The barley did not form much seed, but a Club wheat variety produced many plump heads. Neither crop grew above 18 inches high.
>
> The most important work we are doing is testing many varieties of peanuts, soybeans, cowpeas, field beans and garden vegetables. Since very few of the crops are grown by the farmers near the college, we do not know what their full potentialities are for the highlands.

Boredom and physical hardship were not the only challenges. "The young American idealists," wrote commentator Eric Sevareid about Africa, "are going to be shocked to find a high percentage of their black counterparts in African colleges totally inured and indifferent to the suffering of their own countrymen and interested in freedom, not as individual freedom, but as the political reshuffle that will give them jobs, big houses, cars and servants, their true goals in life."

The attitude of the Volunteer's counterpart abroad admittedly could have been difficult to cope with—a challenge which was beautifully stated by Thomas Loeber in *Foreign Aid, Our Tragic Experiment:*

On the one hand is the American, a child of centuries of progress in Western science and government, who can claim to be the end product of the mainstream of civilization and technical innovation. On the other hand, we have his foreign counterpart, often the end product of thousands of years of stagnation and perhaps centuries of colonialism and oppression. Frequently, he may be the first one in the entire history of his family who has learned to read or write, or perhaps even to wear shoes.

For at least two years, and usually more (with a break for home leave), our American technician must spend more time with this person, from day to day and week to week, than he has with anyone else in his entire adult life, probably including his own wife.

They will work long hours together in the office, travel jammed together in jeeps for thousands of miles, share the same room, eat out of the same dish on occasion, spend days and weeks together in the field twenty-four hours a day under all kinds of circumstances. And through all this, the American, if he is doing his job, must be friend, teacher, leader, critic, and above all, student. At the same time he must, in some way, retain humility, good humor, and dignity. His companion in these ventures may be trying, stubborn, arbitrary, or stupid. But the American is on the spot. He is on trial. The burden of proof is on his individual shoulders. He is being judged wherever he goes. He is the makeweight that can tip the scales of a small segment of foreign opinion in the endless balance of the cold war.

Whether the Peace Corps Volunteer is going to be the makeweight that tips the scale in the cold war remains to be seen, but one thing is certain: There is no more skepticism concerning the ability of American youth to respond to the challenge of life and work in the underdeveloped nations of the world. They have proven their mettle. They have demonstrated their ability to meet the whole gamut of challenges presented to anyone living abroad—from strange food and impossible climates to misunderstanding and occasional hostility on the part of the local inhabitants.

Of course, you still hear some caustic comments. A former career diplomat, Ambassador Elliot O. Briggs, said after his retirement that the Peace Corps is a movement "wrapped in a pinafore of publicity, whose team cry is: 'Yoo-hoo, yoo-hoo. Let's go out and wreak some good on some natives' " and that it is based on the "somewhat irrational idea that anybody who can fix a carburetor can fix anything."

However, this kind of criticism is heard only occasionally now. But there is another kind of criticism based on the Peace Corps's greatest challenge—the magnitude of the job to be done.

"There is nothing like our villages in America," one representative of the Indian government told a Peace Corps official before the first

Volunteer had gone overseas. "Here it can have up to ten thousand people and still be called a village. The houses are clustered together in a clumsy manner. . . . It takes a month or two for the threshing here. We must find a way to do this more quickly. We have a real struggle with nature. We have to put a great deal in the soil. We have dry land; we have waterlogging. We have the mind and heart to do things, but it takes time to move the people."

There is also the challenge of people themselves—the exploding population. "To travel through the vast areas of the world inhabited by the majority of its people," wrote William Vogt in his book, *People: Challenge to Survival,* "is to encounter misery so nearly universal and so harrowing as to be almost intolerable to overstuffed Americans who shrink from a challenge to our complacency and optimism." One member of a United States agricultural mission in India gave "people" as the main reason he was quitting after only five months on the job. "It's no use," he told the editor of the *Saturday Review;* "you can help one man only to discover fifty men standing behind him. Then you help fifty men and five thousand suddenly appear. You help the five thousand but what do you do about the five million behind them and the fifty million to follow? At some point along the line you decide it's hopeless."

Peace Corps officials were well aware of the magnitude of the job to be done, and from the start warned against expecting too much too soon from the Volunteers. "Any idealist," wrote Sargent Shriver in *Life* while the Peace Corps was still a promising idea on the New Frontier, "must realize that he is going to make only a little dent in the problems of underdeveloped areas. His contribution, measured in the whole spectrum of the world's difficulties, will probably cast only a sliver of light—and that sliver may go unseen. After his years of hard work the Volunteer may change a few attitudes, but he probably won't be around to see the results. In the Peace Corps the potential for frustration is great."

Despite Peace Corps officials' efforts to discourage people from thinking that the Peace Corps would change the world overnight, or even over fifteen years, comments about the overwhelming nature of the challenge are still heard occasionally. Columnist Eric Sevareid, for instance, has written: "While the Corps has something to do with spot benefits in a few isolated places, whether in sanitizing drinking water or building culverts, its work has, and can have, very little to do with the fundamental investments, reorganizations and reforms upon which the true and long-term economic development of backward countries depend." Mr. Sevareid did acknowledge that "giving frustrated American youth a sense of mission and adding to our supply of comprehension of other societies fatten the credit side of the ledger," and added, "If fringe benefits were all the Corps originally had in mind, then this should be made clear to the country."

When a *Time* reporter asked Shriver about Sevareid's criticism, he replied, "Hell, I've said many times we could send 500 Volunteers into Borneo and do a good job and the gross national product might still go down." Even more candidly, he once said in a report to Congress that "Some of our projects have been distinguished more by good intentions than by good works."

In his book, *Point of the Lance,* Shriver gives a more thoughtful response to Sevareid's remarks: "I do not agree with him," he writes, "that the second and third purposes of the Peace Corps Act—representing America abroad in the best sense and giving Americans an opportunity to learn about other societies—are 'fringe benefits.' Fulton Freeman, the United States Ambassador in Colombia, believes the whole Peace Corps program could be justified by its creation of a new American resource in the Volunteers who are acquiring language skills and intensive understanding of a foreign society. Former Volunteers will be entering government service, United Nations agencies, academic life, international business concerns, and a host of other institutions which carry on the business of the United States throughout the world. Others will return to their homes, capable of exerting an enlightened influence in the communities where they settle. Many trite euphemisms of the ignorant and ready panaceas of the uninformed will clash immediately with the harsh facts that Volunteers have learned to live with abroad."

That the Peace Corps is having a beneficial impact on American society in a variety of ways not anticipated when it was first created is beyond dispute. For instance, most of the Peace Corps Volunteers' United States training has been contracted to private and state universities; in fact to date, 125 United States institutions of higher learning have helped train volunteers for their overseas assignments. As Shriver said, "No one who has visited one of these training programs in operation can fail to see the impact it has upon the faculty and student body. School official after school official has written us to this effect."

The Peace Corps has had a similar impact on such private organizations as the National Farmers' Union, the Cooperative League of the USA, CARE, the American Friends Service Committee, Heifer Project, Inc., the Experiment in International Living, the 4-H Foundation, the YMCA, etc. While these organizations have also been of immense help to the Peace Corps by providing experienced personnel overseas and cooperating on recruitment, the Peace Corps has also broadened the scope of their activities abroad. For instance, the Peace Corps's work in Latin America has helped quadruple the 4-H Club membership there, and in Chile, YWCA membership has increased fivefold as a result of the Peace Corps.

Also, it is becoming increasingly apparent that the Peace Corps is having a beneficial effect on general education in America. Rather, as some have implied, than stealing teachers from the American school system, the Peace Corps is proving a new source of supply for teachers. At the same time, the Peace Corps has found that many teachers in mid-career are expressing a desire to broaden their experience without losing their professional tenure. They see a way to do this through Peace Corps experience, and school boards are cooperating with them, partly because they realize that granting a teacher leave to serve in the Peace Corps is a way to infuse new knowledge into their own classrooms.

But most important is the impact of the returning Peace Corps Volunteer on American society, which Shriver commented on in his reply to Sevareid. "They will return to the United States," Shriver said, "with the significant and profound experience of having lived among the people of foreign lands not as 'expatriates' but as persons who have eaten their food, lived in their houses, lived under their laws, spoken their languages, and shared their work. More importantly, they will have a new understanding of the aspirations and wants of the people with whom they share this turbulent globe—an understanding gleaned not from books or newspapers or hurried trips to capital cities, but the deep understanding which can only come from being part of the society which you seek to know. Each year, 5,000 of these Americans will come back into government services and private industry, continuing their work in foreign affairs or simply entering the mainstream of American life. Wherever they go, they will enrich the life of their communities, they will help an America profoundly aware of world problems and world responsibilities. . . ."

Finally, the Peace Corps is not as big a drain on the American dollar as some of the critics of foreign aid might imply: 75 percent of all funds appropriated for the Peace Corps enter the United States economy; of the remaining 25 percent, more than half is spent on the Volunteers, who are American citizens.

Returning to Sevareid's criticism, Shriver asked, "Is the second purpose of the Peace Corps Act—to be a good representative of our society abroad—a 'fringe benefit'? A Peace Corps Volunteer reaches the people of foreign countries on an individual basis. He leaves to the diplomat and the technician the complex tools which are peculiarly their own while he sets out to work in the local environment as he finds it."

But, and here is the heart of the question raised by Sevareid, does he do anything for the local environment? "Although I disagree," wrote Shriver, "with Mr. Sevareid's emphasis in dismissing two of the three purposes of the Peace Corps Act as 'fringe benefits,' he does get to the heart of an important question when he compares direct economic impact of the Peace Corps to fundamental investments, reorganizations, and economic development. The Peace Corps's contribution has been less in direct economic development than in social development— health, education, construction, and community organization. We are convinced that economic development directly depends on social development. In his valedictory report this past April [1964] as head of the Economic Commission for Latin America, Raul Prebisch observed that there are *not* 'grounds for expecting that economic development will take place first and be followed in the natural course of events by social development. . . . There can be no speed-up in economic development without change in the social structure. . . .' "

Although Peace Corps Volunteers have only scratched the surface of worldwide poverty, the Peace Corps has some solid achievements behind it, and they cannot be shrugged off with remarks such as: "What difference does it make if the Peace Corps does help a little here and there?" In Ethiopia Peace Corps Volunteers make up half of the faculty in every high school outside of the capital city. As a result high-school enrollment has nearly doubled. "This," says Harris Wofford, then Peace Corps Representative in Ethiopia, "is what the Peace Corps was born for—to enable a country that really wants to move faster than it otherwise could." In Venezuela, a Peace Corps Volunteer virtually revolutionized the method for catching squid, an important source of income for Venezuelan fishermen; a rusting wheat-grinding machine, supplied by United States foreign aid dollars, which had been sitting idle in Punjab, India, for months, was put into action by a PCV, who became something of a local hero. In the village of Zipacon, Colombia, two Peace Corps Volunteers helped spark villagers into what a reporter for *U.S. News & World Report* described as "the biggest burst of civic improvement that Zipacon has experienced in its 400 years of recorded history." In Ghana, 40 percent of all secondary

school children have at one time or another been taught by Peace
Corps teachers; in the Dominican Republic, a PCV who had been
assigned to a village to teach, decided that what the inhabitants really
needed was food, so he started a chicken co-op which eventually produced 13,000 chickens. Peace Corps Volunteers have revolutionized such
crafts as bricklaying and bamboo construction as practiced abroad for
ages, have saved rice crops from unseasonable floods, have helped keep
the heavy construction equipment of one North African country roll-
ing, worked in hospitals, prevented epidemics, sparked villages to solve
their garbage problem for the first time in centuries, started livestock
programs, organized basketball teams, taught thousands of youngsters
the three R's. In Peru a Cornell University team studying the Peace
Corps found that villages in which Volunteers were serving progressed
almost three times as fast as villages that had not been host to Peace
Corps Volunteers.

These are, it is true, isolated successes and admittedly cause a
barely noticeable splash in the sea of humanity which exists in squalor
and poverty around the world. But this kind of argument falls on dis-
interested ears in the isolated villages where Peace Corps Volunteers
have scored their successes; as far as the inhabitants of *these* villages
are concerned, the Volunteers are helping to eradicate poverty and
squalor in their world, and that is all that matters to them. As for the
Peace Corps Volunteer, he has to be content with doing what he can
to help one isolated area—that's all any one young man with a few skills
and a willingness to help can do. It is the global thinker and the big-
picture critics who are concerned with worldwide poverty, but their
lament at the hopelessness of the job to be done can too easily become
an excuse for shrugging your shoulders, turning your back on the world,
and saying what's the use.

The Peace Corps Volunteers are catalysts. They cannot do the job
alone; their only hope of achieving a measure of success is in arousing
others to help themselves. And in hundreds of isolated villages around
the world the Volunteers have done this. Now there is evidence that the
Peace Corps organization itself has become a catalyst by making the
whole world aware of one of its most valuable resources—middle-level
manpower. "I believe," said Senator John J. Sparkman (D-Alabama),
a former Democratic Vice-Presidential candidate, "that the Peace Corps
has tapped an asset we have always had but never used, except in time
of war. I speak of the drive and dedication of the young men and
women of this nation."

Other nations have not failed to notice the lesson of the Peace

Corps—the first government-sponsored volunteer program of its kind —as indicated by the enthusiastic response when President John F. Kennedy invited the nations of the free world to participate in an international conference to discuss the ways and means of tapping their middle-level manpower. "Is it true, as we are beginning to suspect," the President asked when issuing the invitations, "that our joint economic development efforts have been concentrated too heavily in the wrong place—that we have been placing too much reliance on investment in things when perhaps we should be investing more in people?"

For the forty-two nations that accepted the invitation and sent high-level representatives to the conference, held in October, 1962, in Puerto Rico, the answer appeared to be, yes. Studying the proceedings at the conference, two things were immediately apparent: All delegates agreed that the development of middle-level manpower is essential to the economic growth of a nation. "In the most practical sense," the Summary Report of the conference said, "it can be demonstrated that investment in education and training directly yield at least as high a rate of return as direct investment in industry or agriculture, quite aside from its indirect benefits to the society and enriching value to the individual; and we are learning that virtually anyone can be trained and can benefit himself and society from that training. The lessons which unfold from the statistics of the past are reinforced by the practical experience of developing countries. They have found that one major inhibition on their growth has often proved to be in the field of trained manpower."

The second point apparent from studying the conference proceedings was that all delegates agreed that the experience of the U.S. Peace Corps had demonstrated that the Volunteers, in the words of the Summary Report, "are making a significant contribution, both direct and indirect, to the manpower requirements of the developing nations." The delegate from Pakistan stated it more colorfully when he said, "It is possible to beg, borrow, and steal money. But it is impossible to beg, borrow, or steal qualified people."

One result of the Puerto Rican conference was the establishment of a permanent International Peace Corps Secretariat—now known as the International Secretariat for Volunteer Service. The ISVS has headquarters in Washington, is financed by several nations, and has a membership of forty-four countries. Its main purpose is to encourage, support, and assist the formation of government-supported programs similar to the U.S. Peace Corps designed to recruit volunteers not only for overseas but for domestic service as well.

So what was once an idea designed primarily to provide an outlet for the energies of American youth and their desire to help others less fortunate than themselves has become an international movement. From the basic idea, three types of programs have developed: (1) the overseas volunteer service; (2) domestic volunteer service, and (3) national youth service.

Most of the industrialized countries in the world now have programs that send skilled and educated young volunteers to Africa, Asia, or Latin America to provide the urgently needed middle-level manpower (teachers, nurses, agriculturists, machinists, etc.) and to transmit their skills and knowledge to those with whom they are working. France, Germany, the Netherlands, Norway, Sweden, and Switzerland have established government volunteer programs similar to the Peace Corps, while the governments of Australia, Belgium, Canada, Denmark, New Zealand, and the United Kingdom have channeled funds into existing similar private volunteer agencies enabling them to greatly expand their efforts.

Programs of the second type have been established by Chile, Peru, El Salvador, Philippines, Thailand, Vietnam, Korea, and India. The United States also has a domestic Peace Corps known as VISTA— Volunteers in Service to America. In these programs, skilled and educated young Volunteers work within their own country on projects of social and economic development.

Programs of the third type are now in operation in such countries as Zambia, Kenya, Tanganyika, and the Ivory Coast. The United States' Job Corps camps also fall in this category. In these programs, undereducated, unskilled, and unemployed youth join the organizations on a voluntary basis, receive basic education and citizenship training, learn a basic skill, then go out and engage in public works projects.

The total number of volunteers in all the above programs now exceeds 75,000. True, 75,000 young men and women working in the underdeveloped areas of the world is just a beginning—but it is a beginning. The Peace Corps has only been in existence five years, and ISVS a little over three years. But the number of countries launching either an overseas or a domestic Peace Corps is increasing every day, and the existing programs are expanding at a rapid rate.

This is a movement which should impress even the global thinkers and big-picture pundits. If the Peace Corps could not eliminate worldwide poverty, as its more thoughtful critics are fond of pointing out, the spread of the basic Peace Corps idea among the youth of the world might just succeed. There is, after all, no particular reason why it should take a youth from, say, Gary, Indiana, to go into a village in Brazil and inspire the local citizens to roll up their sleeves and start to work on beneficial community development projects; the local youth should be able to do it just as well. The ability of Peace Corps Volunteers to inspire local citizens to action, where other AID programs have failed, has never been better described than by Jamaica's Edward Seaga, Minister of Development and Welfare, commenting on the Peace Corps: "We have been accustomed to receiving technical help from overseas on an administrative and professional level," he said. "What happened is that our own indigenous population, on whom we could call for voluntary service, have felt that since this is the level at which persons from overseas would operate they themselves would not consider operating at any less level. This attitude is now breaking down. The Peace Corps brought a breath of fresh air."

In other words, local youth *can* do the job just as well, if they can only be inspired and taught how to do it. In hundreds of isolated villages around the world, Peace Corps Volunteers have shown that it can be done. Now it is up to local volunteers—with the support of local governments—to show that it can be done in large enough numbers to have a significant impact on the national economies of the individual developing nations. "If, in each of the developing nations," said William A. Delano, Secretary General of ISVS, "a healthy percentage of the hundreds of thousands of young people bursting into their economy can be inspired to volunteer and train for work in their country's development program, the impact on the total economy would be very significant. Since 1962, this is exactly what has been happening throughout the developing world."

This, perhaps, is why one group at least—the Communists—have never looked on the Peace Corps as just a noble experiment in brotherhood and goodwill. From the beginning, the Communists have leveled vicious attacks at the Peace Corps, making it difficult for the organization to remain detached from the Cold War, although it was not conceived as a Cold-War weapon. As Secretary of State Dean Rusk told the Peace Corps's National Advisory Council, ". . . the Peace Corps is *not* an instrument of foreign policy, because to make it so would rob it of its contribution *to* foreign policy." This policy has had its reward; there can be little doubt that by remaining detached from foreign policy and making every effort to ignore the cold war, Peace Corps Volunteers are making a tremendous contribution in the struggle to win the friendship of the developing nations.

"What if the Russians had teachers in 30 out of 36 high schools in Sierra Leone . . . and four of its six colleges?" asked an editorial writer in the Peoria, Illinois, *Journal-Star*. "What if in the oldest African nation, Ethiopia, we discovered that school attendance has been more than doubled under the impact of hundreds of Russian teachers? What if other hundreds were known to be working in the interior of Brazil at grass roots levels, and were scattered in villages and towns throughout Central America? In Colombia? Peru? Chile? . . . These conditions do exist, but the people there are Americans—Volunteers of the Peace Corps." What the Peoria *Journal-Star* thinks about the Peace Corps and the Cold War is summed up in its headline to the above editorial: THANK GOD WE THOUGHT OF IT FIRST.

The Russians believe that time is on their side in the Cold War; that sooner or later the developing nations will turn Communist without a shot ever being fired; that history, social forces, poverty, and the hatred for the colonial powers which still exists in most underdeveloped nations will tip the scales in their favor. "We dare not fail to realize that this struggle is taking place every day, without fanfare, in thousands of villages and markets—day and night—and in classrooms all over the world," President Kennedy told the nation's newspaper editors in the spring of 1961.

The Peace Corps Volunteers are in the front ranks of this struggle, and the intensity of the Communist attacks against the Corps must be a measure of its success. Here is a not untypical account of the arrival of a Peace Corps contingent in Communist Chile: "Twenty assorted spies, belonging to that intelligence service of Yankee imperialism, the so-called Peace Corps, arrived in Santiago from the United States. They come as representatives of the 'Alliance for Progress' which, instead of the longed-for dollars the official decadent circles dream about, sends its well-trained servants."

The Communists continually scoff at the Peace Corps, but there is little doubt that they are aware of the "message" the Volunteers are carrying around the world, as the following comment, made in *Look* magazine by Tung Chi-ping, a young Red Chinese diplomat who defected to the West, suggests:

" 'A political vacuum exists in Africa,' they said," wrote Chi-ping, pointing out that his Chinese Communist superiors felt that Russians had no influence in Africa. " 'And we intend to fill it. Our enemy in Africa is not Russia, but the United States. American agents under the name of the Peace Corps are the most dangerous opposition we have.'

"(This was the first time I had ever heard the expression 'Peace Corps.' When I arrived in the United States, I was anxious to learn more about this organization. I asked Lu Tseng-yu, a former Shanghai University professor who had escaped from Red China in 1957. He soon told me all about the Peace Corps. Not only Lu Tseng, but some government officials were surprised at the fear Red China has of the Corps. . . .)"

The Communists' reaction to the Peace Corps is perhaps best seen in their decision to launch their own Peace Corps—the International Service for Solidarity and Friendship of Youth. The ISSFY has put more than one hundred volunteers in the field, recruited from Russia, East Germany, Poland, Yugoslavia, Czechoslovakia, Hungary, Mongolia, and Cyprus. However, the volunteers only serve abroad for three months, and as Jack Vaughn says: "We find that most of our volunteers really do not begin to do things until about six or eight months after they have arrived."

How well the Communists' Peace Corps will do remains to be seen. But of one thing we are now certain: our Peace Corps Volunteers have met the challenge of life in the nonaffluent societies of the world. They have gone abroad in an "army of peace" with more enthusiasm than William James ever dreamed of. And they are returning with a maturity and an understanding of the world which will make them the natural leaders in a generation soon to inherit the complex problems of an overcrowded planet.

At least two generations of Americans marched off to war in their youth, and twenty, thirty, even forty years later many of the surviving members of these war generations could not resist returning to the scenes of their military service, nostalgic about the places that contributed so much to their maturity, and curious to see how ruined towns and villages had been rebuilt over the years. Similarly, it is not hard to imagine members of this generation twenty, thirty, forty years from now returning to the scenes of their Peace Corps service—but how much more rewarding it will be to see places where their maturity was molded from friendship and goodwill rather than hatred and war; to see how people have continued to build on the things they had helped to start, rather than how they rebuilt what they had helped to destroy.

15

THE FUTURE

In 28 languages, the word for "stranger" and "enemy" is the same. By communication on a person-to-person level, the peoples of the world may one day eliminate the word and its negative meanings from their vocabularies. Communication after all can breed understanding. And understanding can breed peace. We like to think that's what the Peace Corps is all about.

—JACK VAUGHN, in a speech
to the National Press Club,
April 13, 1966.

IN KEEPING WITH the five-year limitation on staff service, a policy which he initiated, Sargent Shriver resigned on March 1, 1966, the fifth anniversary of the Peace Corps. He was replaced by Jack H. Vaughn, Assistant Secretary of State for Inter-American Affairs and a former member of the Peace Corps staff.

Vaughn is slight of build, has auburn hair and a small neatly cropped, auburn mustache. He speaks quietly and his manner is shy and unassuming, but he has a way of fixing his soft blue eyes on you which commands complete attention to what he is saying. He was born in Columbus, Montana, but grew up in Albion, Michigan, near Battle Creek. He was not very large for his age—but he knew how to take care of himself. In his teens he became a Golden Gloves featherweight champion, and later fought professionally. Vaughn graduated from Albion High School at the age of 19 after "three of the happiest years of my life," he says, "all in the eleventh grade. Because of my boxing I was always traveling, so they didn't pass me."

Vaughn entered the University of Michigan, and, as a 21-year-old undergraduate, took a summer trip to Mexico where he developed a strong affinity for Latin America. He also fought 26 professional boxing matches that summer; during his entire professional and amateur career, Vaughn entered the ring more than 100 times. Vaughn also developed a proficiency in foreign languages, and in his senior year he studied Spanish, French, German, Russian, and Thai. In 1943, he graduated with a B.A. in Latin American studies and immediately went on active duty with the Marines (he had also been in the Marine Reserve in his senior year).

After receiving his commission as a Second Lieutenant at Quantico, Virginia, Vaughn was assigned to the 22nd Regiment in the South Pacific, where he saw action at Guam and Okinawa. On Okinawa he won a Navy Commendation Ribbon for scouting enemy forces and his questioning of prisoners of war (he learned Japanese by listening to POWs talk among themselves in the stockades).

After the war he married the former Joanne Cordes of New York (the Vaughns have two daughters: Kathryn and Carol) and returned to the University of Michigan to teach Spanish and French and work on his M.A., which he received in 1947. He taught another year at the University of Pennsylvania before joining the U.S. Information Service as director of its Bi-National Center in La Paz, Bolivia. After serving at a similar post in San José, Costa Rica, he accepted a position with the International Cooperation Administration (which later became the Agency for International Development). With ICA, he spent four years in Panama and two years in Bolivia.

In 1958, he returned to the U.S. and joined the faculty of Johns Hopkins University. But a year later, he was back with ICA as program officer for Europe and Africa. In 1960, he was assigned to Dakar, Senegal, where, a year later, he met Sargent Shriver, who was on a globe-circling mission to measure the response in the underdeveloped nations to the Peace Corps idea. Shriver asked Vaughn to join the Peace Corps staff, an invitation that Vaughn accepted because "the idea of the Peace Corps had great appeal to me. And the people I knew who were putting this idea into effect appealed to me even more."

As the Peace Corps's Latin American Director, Vaughn saw the number of Volunteers serving in Latin America grow from little over 100 in three countries to more than 3,000 in 17 countries. He also helped pioneer the community-development concept, which has had such an impact on Latin America. Vaughn says the greatest lesson he learned from the Peace Corps in those early days was that "a lot of what we worry about is myth." The man he learned this from, he maintains, was Sargent Shriver. "Shriver insisted that we could send Volunteers to teach in Latin American universities with good effect for the universities and for the Volunteers," says Vaughn. "Everybody said

'Don't do it. They can't adjust. They don't have the right skills. They don't speak Spanish well enough.' Much the same was said about sending Volunteers to urban slums, and it was said even more forcefully about sending female Volunteers to urban slums. When somebody said it couldn't be done or shouldn't be done, Shriver would say, automatically, 'Why not?' or 'Let's try it.' "

Vaughn prides himself on having visited more Peace Corps Volunteers—3,500 of them in more than 500 villages and towns in Latin America—than any other man alive, including Shriver. As Director of its Latin American program, Vaughn impressed not only Shriver but Bill D. Moyers, who was then an Associate Director of the Peace Corps and is today probably President Lyndon Johnson's closest adviser. It was undoubtedly this impression that resulted in Vaughn's being appointed Ambassador to Panama in 1964, Assistant Secretary of State ten months later, and Director of the Peace Corps in 1966.

Filling the shoes of Sargent Shriver, whose name has become synonymous with the Peace Corps, has not been easy, and Vaughn is the first to admit it. "Following Sarge Shriver around the Peace Corps was bracing," he says. "Following him as its leader was a bit shattering—like being Robin all alone, with Batman gone from Gotham."

In a conversation shortly after his appointment, he told this writer that he had no immediate plans for altering the machinery Shriver had built up over the years.

As for the future, Vaughn has some definite ideas about the direction of the Peace Corps. For instance, he predicts that by 1971 100,000 PCV's will have served overseas (only 18,000 had served at the time Vaughn took over); that a reverse Peace Corps program will have produced volunteers from over 40 nations teaching and working in communities throughout the U.S.; that Foreign Service qualifications will include two years as a Peace Corps Volunteer; that Volunteers will have served in every developing nation, as well as Eastern Europe and Vietnam; and that the Peace Corps concept will have become such a part of the American way of life that all our citizens will be devoting several years of their lives to volunteer service of one kind or another.

As for his own future, Vaughn also puts a five-year limit on his present tour of duty. He already has some definite thoughts about his replacement. "There are more than 320 returned Volunteers on the Peace Corps staff," he said shortly after his appointment. "It is no secret that I want my own successor to be among them."

As Secretary of State for Inter-American Affairs, Vaughn was directly involved in the Dominican Republic crisis of 1965 and he says that he is proud to have had a hand in stopping a bloody massacre among the Dominican people. However, he is much prouder of having sent the first Peace Corps Volunteers to the Dominican Republic when he was the Peace Corps's Latin American Regional Director. "They and they alone," says Vaughn, "went between the lines and among the wounded on both sides, trusted, believed in, respected, and loved by those who came near them during battle, just as they were trusted and respected before the battle ever started."

Vaughn also says that "when the dictator of the Dominican Republic was killed after reigning 31 years and killing 50,000 to 60,000 of his fellow citizens and 10,000 Haitians, the acting Foreign Minister came to Sargent Shriver and said: 'We've got to have 450 Volunteers next week. [This was when we didn't even have 200 Volunteers in all of Latin America.] We don't want professionals and we don't want technicians. We want young mature Americans to come and join hands with us because we've never governed ourselves and we have a terrible deficiency across the board in our institutions. We don't have any tradition or experience of confidence really to set up a parent-teacher association or a municipal council or a forestry service. We have none of that.'

"Last May I went to the Dominican Republic," Vaughn continues. "The first man I ran into was this Acting Foreign Minister who had asked for the 450 Volunteers. He came up to me, threw his arms around me, started to weep, and said, 'You know, Jack, if we had gotten those 450 Volunteers, this might not have happened.' And I think he was right."

Vaughn continually stresses that the cause of the Peace Corps is peace. But to Vaughn peace means more than the mere absence of war. "It is the freedom to be totally unconcerned about war." But peace and freedom are not virtues in themselves. As President Johnson has said, "What does freedom mean—when famine chokes the land, when new millions crowd upon already strained resources, when privilege is entrenched behind law and custom—when all conspire to teach men that they cannot change the conditions of their lives?"

Under such conditions peace is an illusion. It has not served man —only nations, says Vaughn. "Seven million Indians have lived in the mountains and jungles of Peru, hardly moving out of the eighteenth century—almost entirely in times of peace. Millions of human beings of so-called lower caste have starved to death or died of a dread disease in India and Pakistan—in times of peace. Nine hundred million adult men and women alive today will pass through life without ever having read or written a word in their own or any other tongue—almost all in times of peace.

"And how many countless millions will not so much as lift a finger to change their lot, because they have no comprehension of even the gentlest revolution, in times of peace?"

However, the Peace Corps is showing countless millions how to change their lot, but where this will finally lead is hard to say. One man, at least—the novelist Fletcher Knebel—feels it will lead to the Peace Corps's involvement in a local revolution. "Some day, somewhere, a small Peace Corps unit will clash with the ruling powers of the backward country in which it serves," says Knebel, discussing his novel, *The Zinzan Road,* in which a clash occurs. "When it happens, the Volunteers may find themselves in sharp and painful opposition to their own government. . . ."

Peace Corps officials shudder at such a possibility, but it is apparent that they no longer look on the Peace Corps as a novel experiment in education or a new and refreshing form of foreign aid. "Our relevance to the world," said former Deputy Peace Corps Director Warren Wiggins, "is not that we are a nice bunch of people offering low-paying overseas fellowships." Wiggins sees the Peace Corps as a "critical element in the evolution of a society" and feels that the results will bring changes so great that "we might as well talk about revolution."

There is, in truth, no other word for the impact Peace Corps Volunteers are having on some of the environments in which they serve, especially in community-development work, which is becoming an increasingly important part of the Peace Corps mission. Many Volunteers are assigned to small, remote villages which are only connected to the outside world by a road that runs to the next village. People live there who do not know the names of the leaders of their own country, who have never heard of the United Nations, and who have only heard of the United States in a vague, distant way and would not be able to find it on a map because they have never seen a map. Their knowledge of the world is limited to an awareness of the next village, the village beyond that, and perhaps the largest city in the province. The people work on land they do not own and make a subsistence living at the pleasure of the landowner. There are usually a priest, a teacher, and perhaps one or two government officials in the village. In many of these villages the people cannot speak the language of their country. Volunteers may also be assigned to urban areas in Latin America where hundreds of thousands live in slum dwellings because they find that life is a little better there than in the rural areas since, at least, they can earn a few pennies.

"In these environments," writes Frank Mankiewicz, former Peace Corps Latin American Regional Director, now serving on the staff of Senator Robert Kennedy, "people talk about themselves as abandoned or forgotten. After 400 years, they have lost their belief that they can accomplish anything for themselves. They wait dully for someone to do something for them, for the abandoner, the one who 'forgot' them to return, to remember."

He never returns, however, because he never existed. In his place, into a village or urban slum, where there is no one indigenous to the town who has anything to say about how the economic, political or social system is run, come a handful of Peace Corps Volunteers. In the face of centuries of ignorance, poverty, disease, and apathy, the Volunteer tries to provide the spark and incentive—and perhaps some simple technical skill—to arouse the people to help themselves. What the people may need most is a school, or road, or a bridge, or improved methods of raising poultry—or more likely, all of these—and the task of the Volunteers is to help these people build and develop these things themselves. "He or she," says Jack Vaughn of the PCV's essential role, "should be primarily involved in the changing of human attitudes. The schools and the roads and the bridges and the eggs are means, not an end. The end we seek is a human one—of people able to cope successfully with their environments, of people who are not prey to disease, demagoguery, or despair."

However, once the people of these communities learn to act together, there is no limit to—and no predicting—what they might do. The essential mission of the Peace Corps is to help the outsiders learn how to get in and how to make these authorities aware of them. "Our job," says Mankiewicz, "is to give them an awareness of where the tools are to enable them to assert their political power. The only reason that groups take part in the political, social, and economic life of their country is because they are noticed and taken account of. The ultimate aim of community development is nothing less than a complete change—or a revolution if you wish—in the social and economic patterns of the countries to which we are accredited."

However, once the people in power take notice of the work of any community-development organization, its work is virtually done because you can no longer control it. An excellent example of the Peace Corps's inability to control what it had started occurred in the Indian village of Vicos in Peru in 1964, when the villagers, after learning self-government and the power of collective action, got together and voted the Peace Corps out. Some thought this was a defeat for the Peace Corps, but many staffers agreed with the official who said that it was a great triumph for community development. "The fact of the matter is," this official said, "that the Vicosinos had some misinformation; they voted the Peace Corps back in four or five weeks. But to me, that was not nearly as great a triumph as the fact that they felt confident enough to take that vote and throw us out in the first place."

When Knebel speaks of revolution, he is referring to violence, but when Peace Corps officials speak of revolution they mean the social, economic, and political upheaval in which the people of developing nations become directly involved in upsetting the pattern of a thousand years—but by peaceful means! Jack Vaughn tells of an incident in Bolivia that illustrates the point. During the last six months he was in Bolivia in 1958, he says, "I reached the point where I was reluctant to go up on the high plains near Lake Titicaca to hunt and fish because of the menacing attitude of the Indians. They were all armed, they seemed resentful, didn't speak Spanish and didn't change. That was seven or eight years ago.

"I visited five villages in that very same area in 1965. In all five I was carried into town on the backs of the Indians who wanted to show me that they were in the human race. They had all built a new school, the first school in a thousand years. They all had a clinic for child deliveries, the first clinic in a thousand years. They all had potable water piped in, and they had done it themselves. . . . But more important was their attitude, the openness, the willingness to look you in the eye and tell you about who they were and what they had done, and the pride and self-respect of citizenship. This was done by the Peace Corps. What the Spaniards and the Incas and the Western miners and the diplomats and the AID people couldn't do in a thousand years, the Peace Corps had helped to do in about three years. This is real revolution." But not a shot was fired.

The Peace Corps's objective for the future will be to press forward with its peaceful revolution, developing new programs to meet the challenge of a changing world, and attracting Volunteers who are eager to serve and anxious to be a part of the future. As they have in the past, the great majority of Peace Corps Volunteers will probably be young liberal arts majors just out of college. "We are discovering," says Vaughn, "that the special hero of the Peace Corps is the Forgotten Man of the 60's: the generalist—the liberal arts graduate with a decent education and lots of ambition. At best, he resembles the Renaissance Man—round in spirit and judgment rather than versed in science. . . ."

At the same time, however, as the needs of the developing countries change, their leaders will be calling for more Volunteers who have mastered a profession or a technical skill. For instance, Peace Corps officials are now aware that they must devote more attention to training Volunteers to teach at the college level. Already, more than 600 Peace Corps teachers have taught in the universities of more than sixteen countries, and several more university education programs are in the planning stage.

Similarly, the Peace Corps is preparing to send more doctors abroad. The Peace Corps has already had more than 100 doctors in service, either as Volunteers or as staff physicians on assignment from the Public Health Service. Eventually it is hoped to have 500 doctors in service. There are, of course, special problems for any doctor who is thinking of volunteering for the Peace Corps. In the first place, he is probably going to be heavily in debt by the time he finishes his internship, and he is likely to be married. He is also more likely to be drafted, even after the age of 26 and even if he is married and has children. With these special problems in mind, the Peace Corps is experimenting with various plans to enable more doctors to volunteer.

The Peace Corps is also encouraging the recruitment of more lawyers. So far, more than 30 lawyers have served abroad, mostly in the English-speaking countries of Africa: Nigeria, Liberia, Ethiopia, Nyasaland, and Sierra Leone. The response of the legal profession to the Peace Corps's call for lawyers has been excellent; several hundred have applied, and the Peace Corps plans to expand its legal program. The lawyers are usually given assignments such as the following:

• Providing legal and administrative assistance to improve the administration of justice in local magistrates' courts, where many judges have no legal training.

• Teaching law and doing legal research in newly organized law schools.

• Providing legal assistance in tax administration and enforcement, corporation registration, administrative reform, legislative drafting, and labor relations.

• Surveying customary law and rules for the integration of tribal law with statutory law.

• Writing legal reports and articles for professional law journals.

While there is a definite trend toward more professionalization among its Volunteers, the Peace Corps is also seeking Volunteers with more advanced technical skills. It has, for instance, launched an experimental blue-collar program by conducting recruiting drives at some of the nation's leading industrial plants. "This could turn out to be the workingman's 'Rhodes Scholarship,' " said Shriver in announcing the new plan.

The blue-collar program grew out of an increasing demand for workers with manual skills. The AFL-CIO and 20 leading industrial concerns are supporting the program by promoting leaves of absence and working out policies to guarantee that employees who join the Peace Corps can return to their jobs later with no loss of seniority or pension rights.

As the developing nations reach out to grasp the twentieth century, there is no limit to the kind of work Volunteers are likely to be doing overseas in the future. A good example of possible future work is the Colombia educational television program—a project that, according to one Colombian education official, "will accomplish in ten years what couldn't be accomplished in one hundred years by ordinary means." Almost half of Colombia's 14 million people are illiterate, and the average elementary-school teacher has little more than a fifth-grade education. To reach this audience, the Peace Corps and Colombia decided to take advantage of the fact that the Colombian government owns and operates the largest television network in Latin America, *Radiotelevisora Nacional*. This network has the potential for reaching 85 percent of the nation's population and 94 percent of its public schools. Volunteers, it was decided, could make their greatest impact on education by helping to convert the television system into a medium of public instruction.

Before the Peace Corps arrived in Colombia, a start had been made to utilize television for teaching. At that time, however, few schools had television reception, and so the initial programing was limited to Bogotá, the capital city. To support the Peace Corps in this project, the United States Agency for International Development supplied 1,500 23-inch VHF television receivers for use in classrooms around the country.

In 1963, the first group of Peace Corps Volunteers with skills in education and broadcasting were trained for educational television work in Colombia. They were instructed in television programing, production, and direction; in Colombia they devised and implemented programs in mathematics, natural science, geography, and history that now reach more than 125,000 students. The Volunteers are also helping to train a group of Colombian professionals who will eventually operate the facilities on their own. Classroom response is continually evaluated by roving Volunteers who visit classrooms around the country to show teachers how to make the best use of the teleclasses and the accompanying printed materials. Volunteer reports on student and teacher reaction to each 15-minute teleclass are then relayed to the studio staff for their use in evaluating and improving the programs. Usually the 15-minute TV program conducted by a telemaestro (the Colombian TV teacher) is followed by 25 minutes of classroom work conducted by the regular teacher.

The group of Peace Corps Volunteers who initiated this program returned to the United States in the spring of 1965, but the Colombian government considered their work so important that it has asked the Peace Corps to send another group of Volunteers. The Peace Corps has complied with this request, and it is quite likely that when educational television facilities are available in other Latin American countries, the Peace Corps will plan similar programs there when requested. Some Peace Corps Volunteers are working on a pilot ETV program in Malaysia.

In the opinion of Harris Wofford, teaching is the most important of all Peace Corps activities; thus it will not be surprising to see the Peace Corps continue, and perhaps even increase, the emphasis on teaching in the future. Wofford also expects a deepening relationship to develop between the Peace Corps and the academic community in the United States and hopes the time will come when "Peace Corps courses" are available in the undergraduate curriculum. "I look forward to the day," Wofford says, "when the college undergraduate who wants to go to Latin America will start early in his college program to prepare for his tour of duty with the Peace Corps—with area studies and especially languages. I hope the day will come when every Peace Corps Volunteer sent to Latin America, for instance, will be fluent in Spanish."

One pilot project suggesting the direction a deepening relationship between the Peace Corps and the universities might take is the advanced training program for college juniors. The purpose of the program is twofold: first, to expose potential Peace Corps Volunteers to training at an earlier stage, and second, to increase language efficiency and over-all competence by extending the length of the training time. Under the program, selected college juniors enter training during the summer between their junior and senior years. They complete half the required training, and then, during their senior year, they are encouraged to take, as part of their regular academic program, courses related to their Peace Corps work—primarily languages and area studies. Upon graduation, they complete the last of their training, and, if they qualify, go to their assignments overseas.

Another development along the same line that suggests future directions that the Peace Corps training might take is the "Peace Corps B.A." that has been established by both Western Michigan University and Franconia College in New Hampshire. Under this program, a student completes two years of college, serves overseas in the Peace Corps for two years, and then returns home for a final year at the college and his B.A. degree. Similarly, Michigan State University has established a Master of Arts in Teaching degree for Volunteers it trains and supports in Nigeria. And the University of Missouri is offering an M.A. in Community Development for Volunteers it trains for Latin America. Several universities are working toward establishing degrees of one kind or another in the field of public service, for which credit would be given for overseas experience.

The Peace Corps has also experimented with new ways of channeling America's desire to help, by providing outlets for people other than young college graduates and older people who no longer have pressing family responsibilities. For instance, the Peace Corps reports that it is receiving a flood of letters from mayors, presidents of local clubs and organizations, and leading citizens that ask: "What can we do to help? We can't volunteer, but what can we do at home?" More than fifty major communities have already organized Peace Corps Service Councils so that local citizens can assist the Peace Corps by giving talks to recruit Volunteers at trade and technical schools, junior colleges, and nursing schools.

Another example of a Peace Corps program designed to help local organizations participate in the Peace Corps movement is the school-to-school program in which a United States school sponsors the building of a school overseas. Under this program, the U.S. school raises $1,000 which is used to buy the construction materials. Villagers in the host country, working with Peace Corps Volunteers, build the schools. "From the beginning to end, there will be no paid labor," Shriver said in announcing the plan. "This program could be a major breakthrough in solving the lack of classrooms in developing countries." So far, more than 100 schools have been built abroad, and the Peace Corps hopes to build 3,000 around the world during the first three years of the program.

Having sent more than 28,000 Americans of all ages overseas, and with nearly every host country asking for additional Volunteers, it is obvious that the Peace Corps is no longer on trial. Measured against its initial objectives, it must be judged as one of the most conspicuous triumphs of the Kennedy Administration. But it is also obvious that in a fast-changing world the Peace Corps cannot rest on its laurels or take time out to bask in the sweet, warm glow of success. Its leaders still face the challenge of making the Peace Corps function as well in the future as it has in the past and of continuing to come up with new ideas in response to the shifting demands of the developing nations. But, as Harris Wofford said, "The Peace Corps may remain alive, creative, and free, not because the planners try to program for diversity, but because of its unusual nature as an agency of Volunteers. The Peace Corps is perhaps more alive than any other government bureaucracy because it is, in fact, comprised of 10,000 or 15,000 Volunteers, who bring to the Peace Corps the same challenge and independence they bring to host countries. What the Peace Corps becomes will, in the end, be determined by what the Volunteers do in the field and by what they are.

"With the five-year limit on staff tenure now enacted into law, probably the first such rule in the history of any government, and with a policy of priority to former Volunteers in filling staff positions, by 1970 they will practically be running the Peace Corps, from nearly the top to the bottom. The future of the Peace Corps then will depend on whether or not Jack Vaughn is right—right about enough of them—that everything about them, their reason for going, their performance, their personality, what they are after, what they pray for, 'is revolution, is change, is democracy.' "

Blairsville Junior High School
Blairsville, Penna